WHERE
ARE WE?

WHERE ARE WE?

The Inner Life of America's Jews

Leonard Fein

HARPER & ROW, PUBLISHERS, New York
Cambridge, Philadelphia, San Francisco, Washington
London, Mexico City, São Paulo, Singapore, Sydney

"Chorus of Comforters" from *The Seeker and Other Poems* by Nelly Sachs. Copyright © 1970 by Farrar, Straus and Giroux, Inc. Reprinted by permission of Farrar, Straus and Giroux, Inc.

"In the Darkness" by Amir Gilboa and "Written in Pencil in the Sealed Freight Car" by Dan Pagis from *The Penguin Book of Hebrew Verse,* ed. and trans. T. Carmi. Copyright © by T. Carmi, 1981. Reproduced by permission of Penguin Books, Ltd.

Excerpts from *At the Mind's Limits: Contemplations by a Survivor on Auschwitz and Its Realities* by Jean Amery, trans. Sidney Rosenthal and Stella P. Rosenfeld. Copyright © 1979 by Indiana University Press. Reprinted by permission of Indiana University Press.

FIRST EDITION

Designer: Gloria Adelson/Lulu Graphics

Copy editor: Ann Adelman

Indexer: S. W. Cohen Associates

Library of Congress Cataloging-in-Publication Data

Fein, Leonard J.
  Where are we?

  Includes index.
    1. Jews—United States—Identity. 2. Jews—United
States—Psychology. 3. Judaism—United States.
I. Title.
E184.J5F373   1988   305.8'924'073   87-45613
ISBN 0-06-015872-7

88 89 90 91 92 RRD 10 9 8 7 6 5 4 3 2 1

For Rachel, Naomi, and Jessica

Contents

Acknowledgments

PEOPLE SOMETIMES ASK how long it's taken to write a particular book. Of this book, I cannot say. The questions I address have, in one form or another, been part of my life for as long as I can remember. I argue them with my father to this day, and it seems to me the argument has been going on since the nights of my childhood when he'd tuck me in with bedtime stories that were a kind of soap opera on secular messianism. If my father's stories were about a possible future, my mother's were of an experienced past; her gift was a window to a way of Jewish life that could not have existed just a generation back, but did. So my first thanks are to my parents.

Over the years, I've learned both to narrow the questions and to broaden them, and, now and again, how to search for answers. My teachers—faculty members, friends, colleagues, students—all helped. I am indebted, as well, to the many audiences I've addressed during the last twenty years; though there have been days I've felt like Willie Loman, dragging my word-samples from town to town, the opportunity of trying out my ideas on the people they were meant to describe and listening to their reactions has been of enormous value.

Also of enormous value is the work of those who have written of the matters I here consider. I don't name them; there are far too many, and most are cited in the pages that follow. But here are the names of those from whom I received encouragement and helpful criticism along the way: Steven M. Cohen (to whom I am also indebted for making his data available to me), Stephen J. Whitfield, Carol Kur, Harold Schulweis, Edgar Bronfman, Irv Cramer, Theodore R. Mann, Sandra Shapiro, Avi Shafran, Steve Stone, and William Friedman. Many years ago, I received a grant from the Memorial Foundation for Jewish Culture to study Jewish identity. The intended product of that grant was never completed, but the grant got me started on the path that led to this book, and I gratefully, if belatedly, acknowledge my debt to the Foundation, as also to its president, Philip Klutznick, who has been a valued friend and counselor through the years. The Samuel M. Bronfman Foundation provided timely help, enabling me to continue writing while still fulfilling my responsibilities at *Moment.*

Two people deserve very special mention. My friend Pam Bernstein persuaded me to stop talking about writing this book and to start writing it, and my agent, the same Pam Bernstein, then nurtured the unfolding product and, as necessary, its author. Ted Solotaroff, my editor, offered praise and criticism in deft combination, and his questions and observations forced me to clarify not only my language but also my thinking at a number of key points. He became a good voice in my head.

All in all, a cup that runneth over. But it was full, and then some, even before I started, thanks to my daughters, Rachel, Naomi, and Jessica. My own inner life has been enriched by them in countless ways; this book is for them, with gratitude, love, and hope.

As your answers have become my questions,
perhaps my questions may become your answers.
(after R. Nachman of Bratslav)

Introduction

It was 1860, or maybe 1861, in Minsk, or possibly in Pinsk. Wherever, whenever, there were a dozen Jews who used to get together every Tuesday evening for some good talk.

What did Jews talk about? Why, about what it would be like one day—what, that is, Jerusalem would be like. In exquisite detail, they would imagine Jerusalem—its climate and its curriculum, its cuisine and its culture. Their elaborate continuing conversation had long since developed a near-ritual character—including its periodic interruption by the one skeptic in the group, a fellow named Berl.

Every few months, Berl would say, "Can't we please, just this once, change the topic of conversation? Really, it's quite tedious by now. I mean, if we're really that interested in what it's like in Jerusalem, why don't we pack up and go? If we like it, we'll stay. And if we don't like it, we'll also stay, and make it into something we like."

To which the others would inevitably respond, "Berl, Berl—don't be so naive. Don't you realize how much easier, and how very much safer, it is to sit in Minsk [or Pinsk] and talk about what it might be like than to go and confront the reality?"

And Berl, because he was a sociable fellow, would again drop his complaint and join in the talk.

This was, for those times and places, a rather sophisticated group; indeed, they had some non-Jewish friends. Once upon a Tuesday, they invited one of their non-Jewish friends to join with them, and together they talked until the small hours of the morning, until, in fact, their guest stood and said, "Fellows, I've enjoyed the evening enormously, but I really must get going. Thanks so much for inviting me, and good night."

"Thank you for coming," they replied. "But before you go, we have just one question we'd like to ask."

"Please, anything at all," said their guest.

"Our question is"—here there was an awkward pause, and much clearing of throats—"what we'd like to know is, what do—oh, dear, how shall we ask it?—what do people like *you*—if you know what we mean—think of people like *us*—if you know what we mean?"

"Oh," said their guest, "you want to know how we feel about Jews."

"Yes, that's right, you have it. You see, we are usually so isolated, and we have so little opportunity for feedback. You don't mind telling us?"

"No, not at all. I think you're a wonderful people—passionate, generous, literate. I have only one problem with you."

"A problem? What kind of problem?"

"Well," replied the guest, "there is one aspect of Jewish behavior that really annoys me. You people seem to believe—why, I can't imagine—that you're morally superior to everyone else. Don't get me wrong—I don't think you're any worse than average. But I can't understand your moral conceit, and I find it frightfully annoying."

To their credit—for they knew it was so—his hosts did not deny the accusation, but sought instead to explain their "conceit."

"As you yourself observed, it's very late, so we can't give you the whole etiology of our sense of moral superiority. We'll explain it instead by way of an example. We do indeed think we are your moral betters, and the reason we do is that we don't hunt. You people hunt, and we don't hunt, and that makes us better than you."

Their guest guffawed, and then stormed at them: "You silly, trivial people; of course you don't hunt! We don't permit you to own guns!"

Whereupon the eleven turned to Berl, the skeptic, and said, "Tomorrow we pack, then go up to the land, to Jerusalem, and there we shall prove that even with guns we will not become hunters."

Narrowly viewed, my story of Berl and his friends is a story about how an American lover of Zion, in the fourth decade of Israel's stormy reborn independence, chooses to reconstruct a chunk of Zion's recent history. More broadly viewed, the story is about how, in our generation, the Jews have come to power, in Israel and in America, and about our response to that transforming change in the historic Jewish condition. And the story is, therefore, a path to understanding why the Jews are today a people at risk in an entirely new and more interesting way than the ways in which we have been at risk before.

For today it is no longer our physical safety that is the principal item on the Jewish agenda (though we can hardly take our physical safety for granted); it is the question of whether, now that we have guns, we are on the way to becoming hunters. It is the question of what this people does once it has a choice about what to do—for "coming to power" means, in the end, nothing more or less than having, and making, choices. It is the question of truth in Jewish advertising—of whether, now that we have won some measure of autonomy, we are who we have said we were and want to be.

What is it about the Jews, about Judaism? Why do we, less than 3 percent of America's population, and far, far less than 1 percent of the world's, seem implicated in so much that happens about us? Or is it that, out of our preoccupation with self, we only imagine ourselves implicated? And why is it that some of us are so absorbed with the Jews and with ourselves as Jews, and others of us are so indifferent? How is it that a people so manifestly successful continues to represent itself—and, in truth, to see itself—as a victim people? Is Jewish survival everywhere and always at stake, as Jews so often announce, or ought a people that has weathered 4,000 years of time, much of it traumatic, take its continuing survival pretty much for granted?

What do the Jews of Cochin, Kiryat Shmoneh, Odessa, and Vancouver have in common—or, for that matter, the Jews of Boro Park and the Jews of Manhattan? Here we have one of the world's great religious civilizations; yet if a child comes home and asks his/her parent, "What does it mean that we are Jews?," odds are the answer will not be about belief, or about ritual, or about shared language or shared culture or even shared history. Odds are the answer will one way or another focus on our shared fate, on the horrid prospect that when "it" happens again, we will all again be lined up together.

A Jewish telegram: One whose text reads, "Start worrying, letter follows." And so Nat Hentoff could write (in 1969) that "if the lead headline in tomorrow's paper were to say, ALL JEWS ARE TO REPORT AT THE NEAREST ARMORY BY SUNSET FOR TRANSPORTATION, would those of us Jews over thirty-five, let us say, be totally surprised?" Do we in fact imagine ourselves—as Jews—naked save as we cover ourselves with a shroud?

Yet in Austin, Texas, young people study Yiddish, and on the Lower East Side of New York, old synagogues are reclaimed; in Los Angeles, secular Jewish lawyers study Talmud in a sunrise class, and in Boston, a new Jewish community center is over-subscribed from nearly the day of its opening. Forty years ago, there were two professors of Jewish studies on American college campuses—today there are many hundreds. In January of 1985, on Super Bowl Sunday, 225 Jewish educators gathered for a day-long workshop on teaching Jewish values; more than a hundred had traveled the 117 miles from their homes in Phoenix to join their colleagues in Tucson. Who, a generation ago, would have supposed that in Arizona, too, such levels of Jewish energy would one day be reached? The economy sours—and philanthropic support for Israel grows; Israel pursues divisive policies—and political support for Israel intensifies. Hardly the activities, these, of shroud-wearers.

In the Senate of the United States in 1987, there sit seven Jewish senators, and in the House of Representatives, 28 Jewish congressmen. The Jews are among the two or three most affluent subgroups in America, and by far the best educated. It is as if centuries of Jewish energies and ambitions, pent-up in a Europe of bigotry and pogrom, found here a sudden and stunning release, the Jews seeking to make up for lost, for stolen time. Hardly the achievements, these, of shroud-wearers.

What is it about the Jews that while a born Jew may be a militant atheist, yet remain and be accepted as a Jew, the only way to become a Jew is to testify to one's theological conviction? Why do we pray, we whose belief in the existence of God is so very uncertain, and who surely do not believe that God is responsive to our prayers? Why do we pray words we do not understand—and which we do not mean when we do understand them? And what do we intend when we say "chosen"—or think when we hear it?

A while back, three rabbis met in a Holiday Inn in Tewksbury, Massachusetts, constituted themselves a "Supreme Rabbinic Court," and proceeded to excommunicate some hundreds of Jews who had endorsed rights for homosexuals or condemned Israel's policies in the West Bank. Who are these rabbis, and what have I to do with them? And not long ago I received in the mail the monthly newsletter of the Lubavitch Hasidim, which includes a calendar of this month's Jewish holidays. Among the holidays listed, along with Hanukkah, is the wedding anniversary of the Lubavitcher Rebbe. Who is the Lubavitcher Rebbe, and what have I to do with him?

How can a people so politically liberal as the Jews have taken Menachem Begin and Ariel Sharon so enthusiastically to their hearts? Ah, they say, we have abandoned liberalism, we are galloping toward conservatism. Very well—but then how is it that in 1984, while America-at-large was voting two-to-one for Ronald Reagan, we were voting two-to-one against him?

The questions tumble in on each other. But it is futile to try to search out the one correct answer. Different Jews will answer in different ways; we are confronted not with a general consensus or an authoritative understanding but with multiple choices. And it is no evasion to assert that "all of the above" is usually the correct response to that multiplicity. There is not—despite the claims to the contrary—any one authentic Jewish way; there are diverse and divergent Jewish traditions, and looking at them from the outside, one is reminded of the Talmud's resolution of the continuing debate between the great Sages, Hillel and Shamai: "These and those are all the words of the living God."

But the Jew looks at the answers not only from the outside; he/she is in search not merely of a way of analyzing Jewish diversity but of living with it, of making choices among the multiple answers the traditions propose, the people present. And not every choice a Jew makes is a Jewish choice. However fuzzy they may be, there are boundaries, and that means that there are choices that fall outside the scope of the acceptable. Who decides what is acceptable? And how? Again, questions. Where are the answers, the certainties, religion comes to provide? Why buy into a system of endless perplexing questions and partial, conflicting, enigmatic answers? Why agonize—especially since the agony has been and might again be physical, not merely intellectual? Why, now that Judaism is no longer a condition but an optional commitment, why be Jewish? What are the motives that move Jews to act as Jews, and sometimes to live as Jews? And what are the ways in which those motives are given expression, the methods of Jewish living?

This book is about such questions, large and small, as they touch on the lives of American Jews. It is about how we have sought to answer such questions, explicitly or implicitly, ingeniously or clumsily. It is about our commitments and our evasions. And it is about some ways we might search out more satisfying answers. It is about the pride so many of us feel in being Jewish, and the paralysis we suffer when we try to explain what being Jewish, here in America, and now, means.

It is also about the largest question there is, the one question that has only one correct answer, Judaism's one certainty. The largest question was also the first question. It was God's question to Adam, back in Eden. And it is, simply, "Where are you?"

Why such a question? Obviously, the Bible does not mean to imply that God does not know the answer. What it means, therefore, to teach is that we, too, must know the answer—but that our knowledge of it cannot, as can God's, be taken for granted. (Indeed, Adam gives the "wrong" answer—a kind of denial—just as only twenty-four verses later, Cain will give the wrong answer to the related question, "Where is your brother?")

To that question, "Where are you?," the Bible offers, implicitly and often explicitly, only one proper answer: *hineini*—Here I am. That is the answer Abraham gives when God calls him to tell him to take Isaac to the top of the mountain to be sacrificed, and that is the answer Abraham gives Isaac the next day when Isaac calls to him on their way up the mountain. Isaac and Joseph and Moses all give that answer, sometimes to God, sometimes to other human beings. And finally, in Chapter 58 of the Book of Isaiah, it is God who gives that answer, who promises that on "that day," on the day, that is, when time stops, at the end of days, after we have "loosed the fetters of wickedness" and "undone the bands of the yoke," when we have "let the oppressed go free" and "broken every yoke," when we have "dealt our bread to the hungry" and "brought the poor that are cast out into our house," when, therefore, our "light breaks forth as the morning" and "our righteousness goes before us"—then when we cry out, God will answer us, "Here I am."

These days, these deafening days of bombs and of babble, of roulette wheels and refugees, are very far from the day of God's "Here I am." In fact, it is hard, very hard, even to hear the question, to know that we are asked, relentlessly, "Where are you?"

Judaism—the Judaism that rivets, that obsesses me—is an elaborate attempt to ensure that none who is Jewish will ever not hear the question, no matter the noise level, the Babel. We are first a people that is commanded to listen. The central enjoinder of our faith begins with the command, *Shma!*—simply, "Hear!"

And Judaism is also a set of exploratory answers. "I'm sorry, I've been busy" is not an acceptable answer. Nor is "In Las Vegas," nor, "Can I put you on hold while I finish another call?" The only right answer is, "Here I am." But "here" covers much territory, and it is plain from looking at the Jewish experience that it embraces many different "heres," all the way from studying Talmud to marching with the lettuce workers, from being Isaac Stern to being Barbara Myerhoff.

This book is about the "heres" of American Jews. For reasons I will explain much later, the American Jewish experience is among the most intriguing—and, I believe, exhilarating—in all the chronicles of Jewish wandering. Specifically, there has here emerged a new chapter in the history of Jewish understanding, a chapter properly entitled "the American Jewish Way." It is the product of the intersection of two complementary traditions that have been immeasurably enriched each by the other. So if I write of the choices we have here made, of the American Jewish experience, I do so not only because it is the experience I know most intimately but also because it is an experience of genuine significance, of historic consequence.

My own generation, and my children's, come to the multiple choices of Judaism with a wary eye. Old certainties have been rendered tentative by recent events. How could we not feel uncertain? In all of Jewish history, there have been no more than a dozen dates that will be remembered as long as there are Jews to remember things. Two of those dates took place within the living memory of any Jew older than forty-five or so. Where most generations of Jews have come and have gone without ever witnessing Jewish history except through the clouds of memory, those clouds have parted in our lifetime not once, but twice. Is it, then, a surprise that on the morrow of the Holocaust and Israel's rebirth our ways of saying "Here I am" have become somewhat confused? Is it any wonder that we have lost our balance, we who have trembled in the ravine and exulted at the mountain's top? And if it takes another hundred years or more before we settle on three, four persuasive and compelling ways of life—for a way of life is a way of saying "Here is where I am, where we are," is a response—wherefore is that unreasonable? Indeed, why even expect of this generation that it will understand life as response rather than, say, life as revenge—or as resignation? Why insist that it hear a holy question when its eardrums have been punctured, again and again, by the rattle of death?

Because there is no time to waste. The normal rituals of mourning, which might plausibly occupy us for the next seven-to-the-seventh-power days, are an unacceptable indulgence, the celebrations of achievement an impermissible diversion. For the challenge of power, of the uses to which we in America and our kinfolk in Israel put our power, awaits. We are the children of Berl and his friends: use our power foolishly, meanly, huntingly, and a generation of Jews will vanish in boredom or anger, disillusioned with all the pretty words about clothing the naked and feeding the hungry; use it well, use it wisely, use it generously, and the stories live; a generation and more will be inspired by them to refresh the Jewish commitment, and thereby help mend the world.

For this generation of Jews, in short, the more urgent question is not how to defend the Jews against their external enemies, but how to defend Judaism from its internal erosion and corruption. For the threat to Jewish survival in our time is less that the Jews who bear Judaism's meaning and message will be destroyed, more that the meaning and message will be forgotten or distorted.

And yes, for Jews such amnesia would surely be fatal. Hence Jewish survival is, after all, at stake.

A book about the choices Jews make is also about the choices Jews are called upon to make, the choices they might make. Those choices are never too far from the Jewish consciousness, with its pervasive superego orientation. Prescription becomes an ingredient of description, for the possible—call it our dreams, call it the end of days, call it the promise—has always been a part of our reality. Indeed, there have been long periods when, for better or for worse, we were more alive to the future, to the promise and the possibility, than to the present. Our vision of the end of days has often been clearer than our vision of this day.

It was the great Yiddish writer Y. L. Peretz who, hired to conduct a demographic study of Jews in outlying Polish towns, soon came to understand that there was often more instant, more comprehensive truth in the stories the Jews invented than in the statistical "facts" of Jewish life. So a book about the Jews is not only about our numbers, and our opinions, and our education and income; it is also a book about our stories, our imaginings, the tomorrows that inform our todays. Our "here," in short, was never defined in space or in time; it was, it is, a location in another dimension entirely, in a moral dimension. Accordingly, this book, which is about the things we wrestle with, or might, or should and sometimes don't, and about the attendant joys and benefits—and, yes, the pain and hazards, too.

PART I

1

Starting Over

JUST A GENERATION or so ago, it was generally assumed that American Jewry was rapidly approaching its end. Not that there would soon be no more Jews, but that the vast majority of us would fade away, whether through active assimilation or, more likely, through indifference and apathy, leaving behind only a small band of cultists. By now, however, it is apparent that though all may not be well with America's Jews, we are hardly at death's door. The Jews endure—and more: beyond the unpredicted persistence of Jewish commitment, there has been a dramatic resurgence of interest in matters—ideas, interests, ways—Jewish.

What happened to transform a community that so recently suffered from acute atrophy into a community of Judaic energy and ambition?

In 1880, there were 230,000 Jews in the United States; by 1930, just fifty years later, there were 4,400,000—a twenty-fold increase. Natural increase aside, nearly all the growth—almost 3 million of it—came from the mass migration of Jews from Russia, Poland, Rumania, and other East European countries. (Note, however, that Jews were hardly the only newcomers. During the fifteen years of heaviest Jewish immigration, from 1899 to 1914, there were some 2 million Jewish immigrants—and 18 million others.)

America, in the heyday of the immigrant, was truly the preferred destination of Europe's "huddled masses yearning to breathe free," as the poet Emma Lazarus put it. But her poem, written in 1883 and inscribed on the base of the Statue of Liberty, also spoke of "the wretched refuse of [Europe's] teeming shore." Whether the immigrants themselves understood the implication we do not know, but there is no doubt that their offspring, for all the pride they felt that it was a Jewish poet's words that had been chosen to express America's welcome, sensed that their parents were more or less officially viewed as wretched refuse.

The remarkable thing about America, this self-proclaimed "new Zion," is that it did not reject the people it defined as wretched refuse. Indeed, it offered them full partnership and—virtually incomprehensible to Jews—safety. It was hardly conceivable that such an offer, even if sincerely intended, was meant to go unreciprocated. For Jews especially, the great promises of life were traditionally viewed as conditional: "*If* you will be My people, I will be your God." The Jews would be safe in America? America actually promises not to treat the Jews as Jews—that is, as the Jews have historically been treated in the lands of their dispersion? Surely, unless the whole thing is a tragic mistake, there must at least be a very large "if."

Try this one: "If you do not behave as Jews, you will not be treated as Jews. True, you've come here as wretched refuse—but in America, 'only in America,' your yesterday does not matter, there is only tomorrow. We won't impose your yesterday upon you—on condition that you not drag it with you. Here, we do not inherit tomorrow, we invent it."

And, truth to tell, the Jews most likely to come to this land were in any case those least tied to yesterday, to the traditional ways. Whether it was freedom or fortune they sought here—or both—they came the awesome distance they did in pursuit of change, in order to invent their future. Their mobility was not merely geographic; it was in at least equal measure psychic.

What awaited them was an America that announced itself as the new promised land. Hence its people must be the new chosen people. Why not trade in the old and tangled Jewish promise for the new American promise, to bigotry no sanction (George Washington's pledge to the Jews), a new deal, a new frontier, a great society, the promise of progress unending?

Historically, being Jewish had generally been a fixed condition. The "outside world" defined the location (separate) and status (unequal) of the Jew, and the inside world, the world of the formal Jewish community, further circumscribed his choices. But during the century between the French Revolution and the beginning of the mass migration, Europe—home in 1800 to 1.5 million of the world's then 2.5 million Jews—was transformed. Old social, political, and economic structures crumbled; new possibilities emerged, enticed. Educational and economic opportunities, new places and new ideologies beckoned. (In 1813, there were some 8,000 Jews in Warsaw; by 1900, there were 219,128. In 1789, there were 114 Jews in Budapest; by 1900, there were 166,198; in 1816, there were 3,373 Jews in Berlin; by 1900, there were 92,206.) Mobility in virtually every sphere was now the norm; by century's end many of Europe's now nearly 9 million Jews dwelt in the largest cities, and though there were still diverse barriers to their full equality, they were vigorous participants in virtually every sector.

Yet Yiddish remained the language of the overwhelming majority, and for most—especially those in the small towns and villages of Central and East Europe—their Jewishness remained the principal element in determining both their identities and their prospects. America offered more than new options for its growing number of Jews; here, Judaism itself became an option. One could choose to be Jewish, after whatever fashion, without thereby separating oneself from the rest of society—or one could choose to abandon Judaism without thereby "joining the enemy." No act of conversion was demanded, no pledge of disallegiance. The nation was so vast, its energies so raw, its opportunities so abundant, that one could simply slip into the flow of things, be carried by that flow to who knows what fresh shore of new possibility.

Israel Zangwill, the Jewish playwright, contributed the image of the "melting pot" to our language. Here is what he wrote in his 1908 play by that name:

America is God's crucible, the great Melting Pot where all the races of Europe are melting and reforming! Here you stand, good folk, think I, when I see them at Ellis Island, here you stand in your fifty groups with your fifty languages and histories, and your fifty blood hatreds and rivalries, but you won't be long like that, brothers, for these are the fires of God you've come to—these are the fires of God. A fig for your feuds and vendettas! German and Frenchman, Irishman and Englishman, Jews and Russians—into the crucible with you all! God is making the American!

Come to a new land, to the quintessential new land, why not become new? (Around the same time, the pioneering rebuilders of Zion were trickling into Palestine, singing: "We have come to the land to build it and be rebuilt by it." The words would have been as appropriate if engraved in the large hall of Ellis Island.)

Freedom's promise was not merely political; true freedom meant freedom from class, from group, perhaps, above all, from the past. It meant, therefore, the freedom to stop being Jewish.

There were, from the beginning, more steadfast Jews—some for whom America was merely a way station on the road to the authentic Zion, others who took the American blessing of freedom as it was meant to be taken, for granted, and saw this place, therefore, as a place to be and to do Jewish without impediment. (To these last, stubborn defenders of one version or another of Jewish continuity, much is owed by our generation. It was largely their fight against the odds that created the institutional and intellectual infrastructure we inherited. They kept Judaism "available," and their gift to us has not been adequately acknowledged in our histories.)

To be and to do Jewish without impediment—one did not really have to develop amnesia in order to become fully American. So much was plain even from Zangwill's language: this is not merely any old melting pot, this is God's own melting pot, it is God Himself who is making the American. What a very large statement!

Elsewhere, the revolutions of interest to the Jews had not been in God's name at all. To join those revolutions meant to profess heresy. Here, however, the revolution was ongoing—and required no renunciation.

Quite the contrary, in fact. The startling promise of America was that you could keep your god while you were having your revolution. In fact, America went beyond permission; it expected of its citizens that they keep their gods. Mean by "God" whatever you choose to mean when you sing "God Bless America," when you say, "in God we trust" or, "so help me God," this one nation, this nation that is about making one out of many, this nation lives under God, God sheds His light on it.

The temptations to assimilation were great; Judaism was actively abandoned by some, allowed to wither away by significant numbers of others. But in the end, why bother? Unless you had a pressing need to join, say, the New York Athletic Club, or to vacation where neither Jews nor dogs were allowed, you could be a complete American *as* a Jew. It took a generation and more for that awesome proposition to sink in, but there it is: incredible, dazzling.

Oh, Thanksgiving. Imagine that the Pilgrims had found a wild boar instead of a turkey, that they had chosen to offer their thanks not *en famille,* but in church. But no, the most religious of America's new holidays was perfectly, exquisitely in tune with the Jewish experience and the Jewish sensibility. Bless this house, O Lord (not O Christ), we pray, for we gather here together, our family, at home, to eat turkey and ask the Lord's blessing. A new nation invents a new holiday and that holiday is entirely accessible to the Jew, as Jew. And not because the nation sets out to make an inclusive holiday, nor, on the other hand, by accident; instead, because the central metaphors of the nation and of the Jew are so kindred.

No need, then, to defect; enough to adapt, to amend the forms of Judaism so they might be more in keeping with American ways and tastes. Drop the Yiddish, drop the traditional garb, move from Rochel to Rachel to Rochelle, from Shlomo to Solomon to Sumner, from *davening* to praying to worshipping to attending services, perhaps even substitute "Hebrew" for "Jewish," it sounds more elegant, more American, shift from passion to decorum, focus on the "Judeo-Christian tradition," emphasize the brotherhood of man, don't be "too" Jewish.

At one end, the assimilators; at the other, the defenders of the faith; in the vast and disjointed and sometimes disoriented middle, the adapters, a dash of this, a pinch of that, Judaism seasoned to taste. Not a bad way to get started in a new land: test, probe, experiment, nothing in America is ever final, no decision is irrevocable.

But hardly a way to reflect the vigor and passions of a people that insisted, withal, on its uniqueness. So improvised a Judaism, a Judaism of tentative dipping rather than of total immersion, could hardly sustain the interest of its adherents. If there was no compelling reason to abandon Judaism here in America, neither, it turned out, was there any apparent reason to pursue it. If Judaism was no bother, why bother?

So the great scholar Harry Wolfson could say of American Jews early in this century that their Judaism "is no longer an inheritance, it is a set of inherited characteristics. It is no longer a discipline, it is a day-dream. . . . To remain as Jews it is not sufficient for us to continue to be what we are, for we are not what we should be. Jewish life of today is indeed peculiar, but it is not peculiarly Jewish."

The competing possibilities the Jews discovered in America, and the ways in which they maneuvered, balanced, stumbled through those choices (and still do), are the stuff of a detailed social history that lies beyond the scope of my concern here (and even farther beyond the scope of my competence). This sketch is not about such details; it is meant as a way into the larger themes of Jewish life. More precisely, it is meant as a way to introduce a tension that has informed Jewish life since almost the very beginning, a tension every Jewish immigrant had already experienced long before he/she set out for this country.

The truth is that the dilemma with which America confronted the Jew—to be "more" Jewish or "less" Jewish, to be more concerned with Jewish continuity or more concerned with American integration, to be more connected to the part or more connected to the whole—was hardly new in the Jewish experience. The Jews are, after all, the tribe that discovered the universal god—but insisted on staying a tribe. Jewish history can easily be read as the story of a people trying (and sometimes succeeding) to keep its balance at the unstable place where the particular and the universal intersect. And if our tradition and ideology had not brought us to that intersection, our circumstances surely would have: the condition of being Jewish in a world where most people are something else required of the Jews that they define their differences from all those others, specify the circumstances in which the boundaries matter and those in which they do not.

The special quality of the Jewish "American dilemma" as it unfolded over time lay in the ease with which one could here move back and forth from part to whole, the permeability of America's social boundaries, the consonance of American symbols and rhetoric with Jewish symbols and rhetoric. In earlier times and places, much of the Jewish concern with boundaries was entirely a theoretical exercise: whatever the Jews might conclude, others would decide just where the boundaries lay and how permeable they would be. In America, the responsibility shifted: the Jews were invited to draw their own boundaries. (Until World War II, the invitation was more often formal than actual; in the years since the war, it has become ever more actual, a fact to be taken nearly for granted. And "nearly" only because Jews take hardly anything fully for granted.)

The fact that there was enough room in America to accommodate virtually any Jewish response did not mean that American doctrine was indifferent to the choices Jews made. From the time of its founding, the bias of America was plainly in the direction of the *unum* rather than the *pluribus*. America was the first nation of, by, and for immigrants, and for quite some time that was a fact to frighten, not to inspire. Zangwill was hardly original when he made the point that given America's unprecedented diversity, it would be best to start over, to build something new, to dehyphenate people. Thomas Jefferson had fretted about immigration, fearing that the immigrants would "infuse into [legislation] their spirit, warp and bias its directions, and render it into a heterogeneous, incoherent, distracted mass." John Quincy Adams had held that new immigrants "must cast off the European skin, never to resume it. They must look forward to their posterity rather than backward to their ancestors." Woodrow Wilson had said that "A man who thinks of himself as belonging to a particular national group has not yet become an American."

So, the melting pot—and no great imposition, after all, given that most of those who came here were eager to leave the lands of their birth, predisposed to permeability.

To get along, then, melt along. The urge to integration, to permeable boundaries, led Jews to cite Shakespeare's words, as given to Shylock to speak: "Hath not a Jew eyes? Hath not a Jew hands, organs, dimensions, senses, affections, passions? Fed with the same food, subject to the same diseases, healed by the same means, warmed and cooled by the same summer and winter as a Christian is? If you prick us, do we not bleed? If you tickle us, do we not laugh? If you poison us, do we not die?" We are, in short, no different from you in the things that matter. Hence there is no reason not to accept us.

So far, so good—even if America could not always and everywhere deliver on its integrationist promise. At least, when offended or excluded, the Jews could appeal to that promise. But the Shylock argument, urgently put before America in a hundred different paraphrasings, was overheard by the children of those who made it. They could not know that their parents were dissembling, that for all they may have thought the words useful, they rarely thought them true. For while some Jews truly wanted the American melting pot, most—for a wide variety of reasons—preferred America as a beef stew. The thing about a beef stew is that the meat and the potatoes and the carrots and the onions all simmer along in a common gravy, bits and pieces occasionally breaking off to get lost somewhere in the general mess, but by and large maintaining their identities. (The more elegant images, whether Horace Kallen's symphony orchestra or Jesse Jackson's rainbow, tend to be too compressed; they exaggerate the harmony, the coherence.) The overwhelming majority of immigrant Jews simply had no intention of melting; they just wanted to change their clothes.

Publicly, then, one Shylock speech; privately, however, another. Shylock politely rejects Bassanio's dinner invitation, saying, "I will walk with you, talk with you, buy with you, sell with you and so following—but I will not eat with you, drink with you, pray with you."

That statement of selective integration is much more complex, and riskier, too, than "Hath not a Jew eyes?" It points to a pluralism that is a direct challenge to the melting pot and the undifferentiated mass the melting pot implies. For it is by no means clear that you can in fact walk and talk and buy and sell with people without, eventually, coming to eat, drink, and, yes, pray with them. Nor is it any more clear that you can refuse to eat, drink, and pray with people and still expect them to want to walk, talk, buy, and sell with you.

Yet that is exactly what the masses of Jews had in mind. The risks, of course, were enormous, precisely because the issues were no longer theoretical. Move too far toward walking and talking, and Jewish continuity might be fractured. Refuse too bluntly to eat and drink, and the promise of integration into America might be withdrawn. How precarious, how delicate a balance was required!

Best, then, to muffle Shylock's second speech with his first. For public purposes, the stuff about passions and diseases and poison was far, far safer, emphasizing as it did our common humanity. Why let on to others that the real agenda was to figure out the nature of Jewish claims and the nature of American claims, to ascertain where the differences between the two might lead to conflict, to determine as well where the similarities between the two might make Jewish separatism seem irrational? Why acknowledge that the very goodness of this place transformed the age-old tension between particularism and universalism from an interesting hypothetical question into an increasingly urgent policy problem?

Instead, swallow hard and insist on essential sameness. And pray that by so doing, you will neither hasten the exit of those of your kinsfolk who don't care a fig for Jewish continuity in any case, nor confuse your children, nor obscure the underlying rationale for Jewish continuity. For sooner or later, someone is bound to ask: If we are not different, why do we stand apart? The question might come from an enemy, or from an observer—or, most poignantly, from a child.

And it did come. Back in the early 1960s, the Levy's rye bread folks of New York launched an advertising campaign at whose heart was the assertion, "You don't have to be Jewish to love Levy's real Jewish rye."

The campaign was testimony to how far Jews had come in this land, to how much they had made it their own, to the ease they had here attained. It was also, however, a remarkable clue to the continuing Jewish dilemma. For if you do not have to be Jewish to love Levy's real Jewish rye, the implicit follow-up question cannot long be repressed: What *do* you have to be Jewish to be able to do? That is, what can a Jew do and feel and know and think and say and be that another cannot do and feel and know and think and say and be? And if the answer is "Nothing"—then why stay Jewish?

Inertia? Perhaps, in a world where there are no costs attached to being Jewish, one might as well stay as leave. But this is not such a world. Though the costs may have diminished, none will deny that there are still costs. Why suffer the costs if there is no substance behind them, if the only thing that sets the Jews apart is that they call themselves Jews? If you eat the same rye bread—or junk food— and drink the same wine and, for all practical purposes, pray the same prayers (or worship the same idols)—why not share the same table, the same bed, the same dreams?

A distinctive culture? But a living culture is based on actual, not merely remembered, experience. How long can Isaiah significantly connect Jew to Jew, significantly separate Jew from other, in a world where Johnny Carson's presence is more immediately compelling to Jew and non-Jew alike—or, for that matter, in a land where Isaiah's language is part of the common rhetoric?

Religious belief? Try fitting the same suit of theological conviction on the members of Los Angeles's Hillcrest Country Club, Williamsburgh's Satmar Hasidim, and the Central Conference of American Rabbis, the professional association of Reform rabbis. No Jew doubts that (if there is a God) there is only the one God. We agree on God's (unpronounceable) name—but there the agreement ends.

Language? Hebrew school in this country is mainly remembered as the place where Hebrew wasn't learned. The proportion of Israeli Jews who speak English is many times greater than the proportion of American Jews who speak Hebrew—or, for that matter, even read it. And Yiddish, for most, is the language the grandparents spoke when they didn't want the children to understand.

Interests? Defending against anti-Semitism, ensuring Israel's safety and welfare, pressing for freedom for Soviet Jews, insisting on the separation of Church and State in America—all these are ways of protecting the Jews. If the Jews are safe, then they may practice their Judaism. But if they do not know what the Judaism they are safe to practice is, they are unable to make use of the opportunity the successful defense of their interests has earned them. Will that not sooner or later dawn on them? Will it really suffice to mobilize vast numbers of Jews to protect interests that matter only to a tiny few? It may be necessary for the Jews to come together as a political action committee—but that cannot be sufficient, that cannot be the whole of Judaism.

Stiff-neckedness? We are told that we are a stiff-necked people. So long as there are those who would deny the Jews their rights, who would thereby destroy Judaism, the Jews may be depended on to resist. But if that is all there is to it, then Judaism lives only so long as its enemies act. Is that the dreary lesson of 4,000 years of majesty and mayhem?

As I will argue later, there is, indeed, more to it—much more to it—than this listing of inadequate responses suggests. But for very many Jews, as late as the mid-1960s, it was the logic of such listings that drained their Jewish motives. The temptations of America, a land of so many available parts, were immediately at hand; as against them, Judaism appeared to offer only guilt as its motive: Stay Jewish, for if you do not, our people will die.

Before 1963 or so, the threatened demise of the Jews lacked not only aesthetic but also bite. The common (but not universal) response was a yawn. So what? Judaism is about Europe, or about the Lower East Side, or about general and non-distinctive ethical stuff. Judaism was then; this is now. Or Judaism is about God, and God is either dead or (same thing) irrelevant or too confusing.

A digression: Once upon a time—this is a different part of the story—there were Jews who believed that a world could be fashioned in which all boundaries would be dissolved. Come the Revolution, we'd speak Esperanto (a language intended to be universal, invented by Zamenhof, a Polish Jew), we'd unite the nations, the whole world would melt into one pot of universal brotherhood.

Isaac Deutscher was a Jewish Communist, a biographer of distinction (of Leon Trotsky, especially), whose immortal gift to the Jewish vocabulary was the notion of "the non-Jewish Jew." It was himself Deutscher so described, and the logic that led him to the language is worth reviewing.

I am not, Deutscher argued, a believing Jew. In fact religion is, as I see it, a dark superstition, an anachronism, merely an opiate of the masses. Come communism, we'll be done with its divisiveness, its backwardness.

But in the meanwhile, I cannot ignore anti-Semitism. Given anti-Semitism, it would be dishonorable to abandon the Jewish people. ("Religion? I am an atheist. Jewish nationalism? I am an internationalist. In neither sense, therefore, am I a Jew. I am, however, a Jew by force of my unconditional solidarity with the persecuted and the exterminated.") Accordingly, I shall stay a Jew. And I shall labor even harder for communism's victory, for on the day of that victory, I will, at last, be free—free to stop being a Jew.

Communism is hardly this century's only secular messianic movement. Science, too, promised one day to free us from the fatal superstitions that have ravaged human history. And it is, I think, not entirely a coincidence that so very many Jews were drawn to the shining promise, whether the revolution's or the laboratory's. Both offered roads on which to move *away* from the Jewish community without moving *against* the Jewish community. For was it not the end of anti-Semitism your efforts would ultimately bring about?

Labor, then, for the advent of the messianic age. It is less important that you have secularized its definition than that you have retained its fervor. Better, indeed, secular messianism than the bourgeois religious complacency of so many of your "co-religionists." Indeed, be persuaded that you are closer to the true prophetic intention than those so absorbed by the texts that they have forgotten why they pray; you, not they, are heir to the redemptive mission.

Echoes of these views may still be heard in America. Radical universalism remains a siren to Jews in every generation. But by and large, for reasons that will presently come clear, today's non-Jewish Jew is typically no longer an ideological utopian, a searcher for the secular messiah; he/she is, instead, a residual ethnic, filled with Jewish pride but of uncertain Jewish purpose.

And now it is time to say why it is that so many Jews, starting in 1963, accelerating after 1967, stopped shrugging their shoulders, began to care, and to wrestle.

The America the Jews encountered was, as I have tried to suggest, as much a faith as a place. The God who shed His grace on America did not exclude its Jews; they shared the American bounty in full measure. Their ideological confusions hardly impeded their success, and the sweet smell of that success doused their traditional apprehensions, balmed their confusions.

On Friday, November 22, 1963, America-as-faith began to come undone. The killing of John F. Kennedy marks the beginning of America's most traumatic twentieth-century decade, more wrenching still than the Great Depression, a decade of assassinations (Robert Kennedy, Martin Luther King, Jr., Medgar Evers, Malcolm X), burning cities, political corruption—and, above all, Vietnam, where, in the name of democracy, this "last, best hope of mankind" sought to napalm its way to victory.

(No, it was not quite that simple. The Lyndon Johnson of the deceptions was also the Lyndon Johnson of the Great Society, the president who virtually led a joint session of the United States Congress in the singing of "We Shall Overcome"; the Henry Kissinger whose lies, big and little, distorted public debate for eight years was also the Kissinger of the Mideast shuttle, brilliant and indefatigable; the petty and corrupt Richard Nixon, he who dishonored his office, was the Nixon who recognized China and pursued detente. The point is not that the period from 1963 to 1973 was in its entirety a disaster, but that its disastrous components were a direct challenge to the notion of America-as-faith.)

Most starkly, it appeared that God's grace had been withdrawn. We did not, after all, have all the answers, and some of the answers we thought we had were plainly wrong. Nor could we any longer simply assume that the heady progress we had known was our inevitable destiny.

And once the old faith was tarnished, once question marks began replacing exclamation points, other flaws became apparent: Why, indeed, had this country closed its doors to the Jews in the hour of their most urgent need? And not just "this country," but the very president in whom the Jews had most enthusiastically believed, Franklin Roosevelt himself? (Most Jews first became aware of the failure, and of Roosevelt's own inadequacy, through Arthur D. Morse's *When Six Million Died,* first published in 1967.)

More: In 1968, in New York City, the old and comfortable alliance between blacks and Jews was shattered. The context, a battle over community control of the public schools, culminating in a prolonged strike by schoolteachers, accompanied by vicious accusations of racism and bigotry, was doubly disturbing. Not only did the long history of fervent Jewish participation in the civil rights struggles of this century mean—apparently—nothing, but the public schools, long seen as the principal vehicle for Jewish upward mobility, were suddenly endangered.

More still: Even the universities were in trouble. At a time when barely three of every ten Americans of college age were attending college, nearly nine of every ten Jews of college age were enrolled. In the public schools, we had learned English, and manners, and how to take tests; in the universities, we had learned law and medicine and business management, literature and sociology and economics and physics; we had learned success. And now, in these sheltering groves, the galoots were screaming "Fuck you!" and burning our research papers. And to add terrifying insult to painful injury, the galoots were our own children, the first generation (we had imagined) of complex-free Jews, born with no memory of the ghetto, heirs therefore to America.

Spurning their inheritance, they turned their backs on America (hence "Amerika"), turned their backs on the laboratory, turned their backs on success, on mobility, on their parents, on "plastics." They turned to drugs and to communes, they turned to things we did not know and did not want to know. We had understood about moving up the ladder, rung by rung; they, born near the top, could not imagine a life devoted merely to climbing the last few rungs, nor did they appreciate the miracle of our own achievement. Instead, they spoke of "consciousness expansion," toyed with Zen, lectured us on our own narrowness, and demanded that we subsidize their rebellion.

What sort of promised land was this, a land that set its children against their parents? (At the end of the Bible comes the prophet Malachi, and at the end of Malachi, hence at the end of the Bible, these words: "Lo, I send the prophet Elijah to you before the coming of the awesome, fearful day of the Lord. He shall reconcile fathers with sons and sons with their fathers, so that, when I come, I do not strike the whole land with utter destruction.") What sort of faith was this, this America, if our own children had turned against their fathers and mothers, had become heretics? This was to have been the Land of Enlightenment. One could accept an occasional throwback, since no one was so naive as to suppose that all the darkness was already gone. All that was required was a decent trend line. Was it possible, was it even thinkable, that there was no such trend, that the American promise, too, was a chimera, as the Jewish promise mostly seemed to have been, that the promise was merely a form of self-advertisement, a local booster's fantasy? How terribly frightening, disorienting, here, on the verge at last of a permanent mooring, to be cast adrift again.

Call it miracle, call it coincidence. Just when this house came to seem cursed rather than blessed—or, more precisely, just when it came to be seen as a mixed blessing—there transpired an event so awesome, so spectacularly precise in its dimensions, in its structure, even in its timing, as to offer the Jews new hope, new faith.

In May of 1967, President Nasser of Egypt closed the Straits of Tiran to Israeli shipping. In the weeks that followed, the conviction grew that Egypt, as well as Syria, was planning to attack Israel.

So much has happened since those days in May that it is now exceedingly difficult to recapture the sense of how it was back then. But the unexaggerated fact is that around the world the growing crisis had the feel of a medieval morality play, Good against Evil, and back then there was no doubt whatsoever, anywhere in the free world, that Israel was Good. Such an assertion today, in the wake of everything that has since transpired, seems implausible, if not downright absurd. But that is how it was in the days of Leon Uris's *Exodus* and the *fedayeen,* as Arab terrorists were then known. (Nor had it yet occurred to the media to call them "guerrillas," much less "freedom fighters," rather than terrorists.)

In Tel Aviv, new cemeteries were prepared to receive the anticipated victims of the war that loomed; 20,000 graves were dug. In Minneapolis, Jews frenziedly sought to locate the gas masks that Israel had urgently requested to counter the poison gas it was feared Egypt planned to use. In Miami and Wichita and Spokane, people in the hundreds, then thousands, non-Jews as well as Jews, volunteered to go to Israel to help defend the country, gave millions, then tens of millions, ultimately hundreds of millions of dollars to help prevent what everyone feared: another Auschwitz.

The fear was precise, and "another Auschwitz" was its name. Back then, no one yet knew how resourceful and how tough and how skilled at war the Israelis had become. So, when some Arab leaders boasted that the Jews would be driven into the sea, the Jews of America felt terror, as Jews.

Nowadays, people tend to remember the war itself, those remarkable six days in which Egypt's air force was destroyed while still on the ground, and the Golan Heights were scaled in hand-to-hand combat, and Jerusalem, the city with the wall in its heart, was reunited. The swiftness of it all, and the surprise of Israel's victory— a victory that soon enough came to be widely resented, as the world tried and failed to adjust to the notion of the Jew as victor, a victory whose fruits would soon enough turn bitter to the Israelis themselves as they tried and failed to find surcease in its aftermath— would alone have been sufficient to impress themselves upon the American Jewish consciousness. But it was, in the end, less the stunning victory than the weeks of terror that preceded it that made the month from the closing of the Straits to the silencing of the guns so watershed an experience.

Terror as Jews. Perhaps, then, the experience could serve as a reminder to a people newly adrift of the power of ancient moorings? Perhaps, in search of a new faith, one had only to revert to the old?

If, after decades of numbness, Jewish nerve endings were still so alive, the availability for fear and trembling, hence also for awe and wonder, so immediate—perhaps then here was a place to drop anchor? Perhaps God Himself had remembered His ancient promise, had finally remembered the Jews, His people?

I use religious language here because for very many Jews, the experience of the Six Day War had religious significance. Specifically, it was after the Six Day War that Israel came to occupy the center of the Jewish religious consciousness and consensus. In a very precise way, Israel had now become the faith of the American Jew.

I will have considerably more to say about Israel's place in our lives in later chapters. Here it is important only as part of the story of the change in the general response of American Jews to the fact of their Jewishness. Suddenly, that fact had become considerably more salient: just when the faith in America was tarnished, the faith in Israel was enhanced.

And this at a time when America itself was—for some of the very same reasons—undergoing a critical transformation, having to do directly with the notion of the melting pot.

Whether or not the melting pot ever really happened—the scholarly debate is unsettled—the 1960s and 1970s were decisively a time for the celebration of the particularities of America's diverse cultural elements. Congress passed an "Ethnic Heritage" act that would have been unthinkable a generation earlier; ethnic neighborhoods were rediscovered, and praised for the antidote they offered to the faceless urban place; community control was pressed as a way to acknowledge in politics the intractable ethnicity that was manifest in society; Poles and Irish, Italians and Swedes, all became "beautiful." In a massive reaction to the gray-flannel seriousness of the fifties, flower children and urban ethnics, blacks and gays and a dozen (or a hundred) others came to insist on their own distinctiveness.

Social theory began to catch up to social reality; the case of the blacks is especially instructive. For decades, America had preached color blindness—and practiced racism. Initially, the blacks had supposed—much like the Jews—that if only they adjusted their behavior, they'd be accepted. But America, it turned out, could not see beyond the color. Ultimately, stuck, as it were, with their color, black Americans shifted course, chose to assert that what others saw as stigma was to them a badge of pride. Hence "Black is beautiful."

In so saying, the blacks violated the theory of the melting pot that had traditionally informed intergroup relations in America. Yet thoughtful Americans were hardly able to argue against that violation, since it was so painfully obvious that the theory had never worked for blacks. Ironically, the new black strategy pushed back the boundaries of the classic theory, making more room for all who were or would be "different." Even Jews, whose particular kinship with blacks had made them especially sensitive—and vulnerable— to the new black pride, and who therefore often felt themselves the undeserving victims of black assertiveness, came to discover (if not always to acknowledge) that they were instead among its unintended beneficiaries. For if the lesson—better, one lesson—of the times was that America could make room for blackness, could learn to say the word and accept the fact and not insist, vainly, on the individual as the only unit of social and political consequence—if all that was so, then perhaps there was room as well for the Jews . . . as Jews.

In retrospect, it is astonishing to observe how quickly one social understanding was replaced by another. In 1963, for example, on the eve of the saga I have here been sketching, Norman Podhoretz, then the newish editor of *Commentary,* wrote a widely praised article entitled "My Negro Problem—and Ours." In that article, revealing with startling candor a widespread elite sentiment of the day, Podhoretz asks why Negroes should wish to survive as a distinct group:

> I think I know why the Jews once wished to survive (though I am less certain as to why we still do): they not only believed that God had given them no choice, but they were tied to a memory of past glory and a dream of imminent redemption. What does the American Negro have that might correspond to this? His past is a stigma, his color is a stigma, and his vision of the future is hope of erasing the stigma by making color irrelevant. I share this hope, but I cannot see how it will ever be realized unless color does in fact disappear: and that means not integration, it means assimilation, it means—let the brutal word come out—miscegenation.

So: If a group is ideologically connected (memories of glory, dreams of redemption), perhaps it is warranted in its desire to preserve its identity; otherwise, let it dissolve. In 1963, it was not easy to imagine another way. The American experience did not readily allow the formal recognition of the group. In diverse decisions, the Supreme Court had endorsed that denial, insisted that the system could recognize only the individual, not the group. And progressive Americans were nervous in the extreme in the face of claims to ethnic or racial self-determination, having witnessed far too often the dark places where assertions of kinship and blood might lead.

In 1963, the possibility that the group might take its place in the American sun was not plausible, not unless the group was a quaint, exotic outcropping—the Amish, for example—that chose to dwell apart. Or, to be sure, a voluntary association, based on instrumental rather than organic relationships. And in 1963, for some of the same reasons, a leading Jewish editor and intellectual, later to become a fervent advocate of Jewish assertiveness, could put his speculations on why the Jews "once wished to survive" in the past tense. And why not, after all? If the group, as group, had no logic behind it, no theory under it, and if, at the same time, the religion was in disarray, if none could say what it was that connected Jews to one another as they were not connected to all others, why the desire to survive? Time, instead, to move along, to move beyond anachronistic instinct.

Still, whether understanding their reasons or not, most Jews did and do want to remain, somehow, Jews. Traditionally, American Jews had understood that their best shot at group survival was to emphasize their religious—as distinguished from their ethnic— partnership. The nation, after all, at best ambivalent toward ethnicity, was relatively cordial toward religious diversity. The legal system, too, did not acknowledge ethnicity, but offered special protection to religion. Religion was respectable, ethnicity scruffy. So most Jews found it easier to stake their claims on America in religious terms. And as a religion, Jews were accepted as full partners in America's tripartite—Protestant, Catholic, Jew—arrangement, whereas as an ethnic group we were only one among very many.

This emphasis was wholly artificial, even a distortion: Judaism cannot be separated from Jewishness. Unlike other ethnic groups,

Jews are connected not only by their history and interests but also by their ideology; there is, after all, an "ism" in the Jewish experience. Jews may no longer know quite what that "ism" means or where it points, but the fact of it distinguishes the Jews from, say, the Irish: "Irishism" is not part of the language or even the intention of the Irish. But unlike other religions, Judaism has a history that is not merely ecclesiastical. The history of the Jews is not principally the history of their religious doctrine and development—even though one may become a Jew through a formal act of conversion. It is, instead, the history of a people—of, if you will, what Mordecai M. Kaplan called "an evolving religious civilization."

As a child, I'd often listen to Paul Robeson's recording of "Ballad for Americans." The chorus repeatedly asks the soloist, "Who are you, Mister?" Finally, the soloist answers: "I'm just an Irish, Negro, Jewish, Italian, French and English, Spanish, Russian, Chinese, Polish, Scotch, Hungarian, Litvak, Swedish, Finnish, Canadian, Greek and Turk and Czech and double-Czech American! And that ain't all: I was baptized Baptist, Methodist, Congregationalist, Lutheran, atheist, Roman Catholic, Orthodox Jewish, Presbyterian, Seventh Day Adventist, Mormon, Quaker, Christian Scientist, and lots more." It did not escape my proud attention that we Jews were the only ones included on both lists.

But the Jews, sensitive to America's biases, themselves confused regarding the contemporary meaning of peoplehood, sought to emphasize their status as a religion, to downplay their status as an ethnic group. They did this not because of their religious fervor or certainty—in fact, there was little fervor, still less certainty—but because it seemed better to suit the American circumstance. (The discrepancy between what Jews privately perceived and what they publicly proclaimed was somewhat unsettling, but not intolerably so.)

Then came the final installment of the miracle: In 1967, the distinction between faith and ethnicity collapsed. The reunification of Jerusalem could hardly be classified as only a piece of national history; Israel's toughest and most secularized generals approached the Wall as pilgrims, the whole House of Israel—that is, the Jewish people—wept in transcendent gladness. As Jerusalem was reunited, so were (briefly, as it turns out) the ethnic and religious elements of the Jewish understanding. It would no longer be possible for American Jews to deny their ethnic commitment.

And just as it ceased to be possible, it ceased to be necessary. Overnight, prodded by blacks, America had changed its mind about ethnicity. The system that twenty-five years ago was blind to groups today wrestles with affirmative action and quotas, with a growing number of people who seek status, recognition, and protection not as individuals, nor even as partners in religion, but as members of racial and ethnic groups, of age-defined and sex-defined and sexual-preference-defined groups. Ethnicity has become a fact to celebrate, not a condition to escape.

(On the eve of the Six Day War, at the height of the panic, a Jewish community in the Northeast debated how to respond to the Arab threat. One proposal was to delegate the most auspicious leaders of the community to travel to Washington, there to intercede with the authorities on Israel's behalf. A second proposal was to call a mass rally in the city's major public park. The first proposal was easily adopted; the second was debated for some hours, the opposition centering on the "unseemliness" of such an assertive public act. Was it not too divisive an assertion of group interest? In the end, the compromise that was adopted was to hold the rally, but not to publicize it. Today, there'd be no question about holding a rally, except that the park is most likely booked for such rallies months in advance.)

Twenty-five years ago, observing Jewish confusions, one might have wondered, as some did, why the Jews would want to survive. Today, the naive utopian universalism that regarded the Jews as a transient anachronism, that promised a homogeneous America, that taught many Jews (along with others) to deprecate their own heritage, lies by the wayside, victim to a decade of trauma—and to pluralism's maturation.

And so the question has changed. In an America so enthusiastically, almost giddily, of, by, and for groups, it is no longer possible or necessary to speak of the Jewish "subculture." A subculture implies a "superculture," but where in America today is there such a regnant model? Where are the WASPs today? If they persist at all, it is only as yet another of the jostlers for a place in the sun. Indeed, were the Jews disposed to assimilate—what is there left to assimilate to, to be assimilated by?

If a Jew today wrestles with his Jewishness, it is no longer because he/she supposes that it will go better for him, for her, with a different color nametag. Nor is it because America in any discernable way crowds out the Jew. Today, more than ever before, one can move up as Jew.

Yet the wrestling does persist, and it is a more serious wrestling than yesterday's. For as the liabilities traditionally associated with being Jewish have receded, so, for some of the same reasons, has the relevance of being Jewish. But if Jewish is, in the end, merely a nametag, it can scarcely warrant the kind of loyalty and commitment its preachers and its pedagogues exhort. What, then, is the rationale? What is the connection that binds the Jews, across space, across time?

And so we return to the questions. It could scarcely be otherwise in a time so dense with change. Nor could the Jews have remained so vigorous had they not found answers, of sorts—and had answers not happened to them. It is time for us to examine those answers.

2

Jews, God, and Judaisms

THE THOUGHTFUL CHRISTIAN READER—and some Jewish readers too—may well wonder what all this is about. Is it not plain, he/she might ask, that Jews are adherents to something we know as Judaism, which is to say, they are partners in faith? Is it not their religious belief and practice that connects and moves the Jews, their God that is their "answer"?

It is, and it isn't, but before we enter the brambled thicket of Jewish religious understanding, I had best say something about God-talk in general. Talk of God makes many people feel distinctly uncomfortable. Most of us learn what we learn about God when we are small children, and although we come to know, as we grow older, that the God of our childhood is not quite the same God the theologians discuss and describe, we are stuck with our pre-pubescent notions. We do not want to discuss such notions, lest our childishness be exposed. We have neither the vocabulary nor the categories for serious conversation, and, besides, we vaguely fear that our expression of interest in such conversation would be taken as evidence that we lack sophistication, that we are not fully at home in our so definitively secular world. So we avoid the subject, which is not hard to do since our friends and neighbors, for the most part, also prefer to avoid it; they are no less intimidated than we by the thought of it.

Does it help if I begin by suggesting that one does not have to take God literally in order to take God seriously?

There is a teaching that holds that all the Jews—the living, the dead, and the still unborn—were present at the Revelation at Sinai. (A young friend of mine was once wandering in the port area of Haifa, in Israel, when he noticed a hasid, in full hasidic regalia, walking toward him from the opposite direction. My friend, a genial sort, smiled. The hasid stopped, squinted, and asked, "Do I know you?" To which my friend replied, "Yes, of course: we met at Sinai." The hasid slapped his forehead and exclaimed, "Oh dear, you must forgive me. It was so hot and crowded that day. How have you been?")

Now, the question of whether or not there was a Revelation at Sinai seems to me considerably less important than the question of whether or not I was there. The first question requires of me a faith I do not have, cannot invent, and regard (perhaps for that reason) as irrelevant; the second requires of me a faithfulness that is mine to offer.

How can one have been present at an event that did not take place? By willing oneself into the metaphoric system the entire story evokes. "Did it happen?" is either an empirical question, which can be answered only by formal evidence—contemporaneous accounts, archeological discoveries, and such—or it is a "faith question," which is no question at all, since the system of belief in such things does not permit us to ask, "How do we *know?*"

"Were you there?," on the other hand, is an invitation as much as a question. "Were you there?" means, among other things, "Do you choose to associate yourself with the event/story/idea? Do you accept what it implies, whether or not you accept that it actually happened?" It is plain (to me) that when I say, "I was there," I am not speaking an empirical truth; I am offering my consent. I am freely choosing to associate myself with a myth I find uplifting, informative. I am choosing to accept the implications of a legend as if it were no legend at all. (It was Theodor Herzl, the founder of modern political Zionism, who said—in a very different context— "If you will it, it is no legend.") I am never entirely unaware of the "as-ifness" of my choice, but neither am I much impeded by it.

True, I might as easily decide that for me, it is "as if" the Revelation itself happened. But faith, as I understand it, is belief in the actuality, the factness, of a thing or event; faithfulness, as I understand it, is concerned not with the thing's actuality, but with my actualizing of it.

Perhaps my point is better made as my teacher, Rabbi Harold Schulweis, and others have sought to make it. They speak of a "predicate theology," a theology that is more concerned with godliness than with God. Since God is, in any event, unknowable (save as It chooses to reveal Itself), the closest we can come is to try to form ourselves in our image of God—that is, to be godly.

If we start with predicate theology, then we do not begin sentences with "God is . . ." There is little point in trying to fill in those blanks, and it is presumptuous, to boot. Yet we can speak easily of God, of God's expectations and disappointments, for such talk becomes part of an elaborate system of metaphors with which we choose to inform our thoughts and our behavior. We can bypass the sterile debate over God's existence, the tedious discussion of God's attributes, and focus instead on those elements of the system that help us make order out of chaos, that induce awe and wonder, charity, justice, and all the other elements of righteousness. We can enter the text not to find a description of what once was, but a vision of what might yet be.

Later, there will be time to speak of law and of ritual, and of whether these are or can be helpful. For now, my purpose is to reassure the apprehensive reader that my references to God neither presume nor recommend belief; they are simply the way in which Jews, whatever the state of their belief, have found it useful to talk to each other. Religion is, in a way, the *language* of the Jews. One does not "believe" or "disbelieve" in a language; one uses it, or does not. For a Jew, for the Jews, it may well be difficult to speak of God. But it is impossible—or at least unthinkable—for the Jews not to speak of God.

Nor does God-talk offer us just a word list, a vocabulary; it offers that, but it provides also a grammar, a set of rules for putting the words to use. (The giants of Yiddish literature were in the main non-believers. Yet consider Sholom Aleichem's Tevye, engaged in an endless conversation with God, or Peretz's "Bontshe Shweig," which takes place in the Heavenly Court of Justice.) Does a Jew, for example, have to "believe" in order to derive pleasure—and sustenance, and insight—from the following narrative from S. Ansky's *The Dybbuk?* The speaker, a hasidic rabbi, begins by asserting that "God's world is great and holy," and goes on to describe its four "supreme sanctities": the Holy of Holies in the ancient Temple in Jerusalem; the High Priest of the Temple; Yom Kippur, the Day of Atonement; the name of God.

> And once during the year, at a certain hour, these four supreme sanctities of the world were joined with one another. That was on the Day of Atonement, when the High Priest would enter the Holy of Holies and there utter the name of God. And because this hour was beyond measure holy and awesome, it was the time of utmost peril not only for the High Priest, but for the whole of Israel. For if in this hour there had, God forbid, entered the mind of the High Priest a false or sinful thought, the entire world would have been destroyed. (Pause.)
>
> Every spot where a man raises his eyes to heaven, is a Holy of Holies. Every man, having been created by God in His own image and likeness, is a High Priest. Every day of a man's life is a Day of Atonement, and every word that a man speaks with sincerity is the name of the Lord. Therefore it is that every sin and every wrong that a man commits brings the destruction of the world.

Is that language inaccessible to the non-believing Jew? Does it require of us a leap of faith to understand, even to speak that language? Hardly; not faith but fluency in the language of Jewish moral imagination is the measure. And, as to faith, the question seems to me not whether one believes in a God who is, in any event, both faceless and nameless (God's name, according to the tradition, is not pronounceable); the real question is whether we can make a leap of love, not a leap of faith. To make a leap of love means to love God whether or not He (or She, or It) exists. It is in loving God, rather than in only talking God, that we move from metaphor to meaning.

Some readers will think these prefatory words heretical, others will dismiss them as mumbo-jumbo. Perhaps they will seem less idiosyncratic if we examine what I have called the "language of Jewish moral imagination."

There is a way of imagining called *midrash,* and it is at the heart of the Jewish religious endeavor. *Midrash* is a term that refers both to a specific body of literature and to an interpretive method; it is the method in which I am interested here.

Midrash: If the only word we were permitted to speak or to write were the correct word, the finally right word, we would be rendered mute, for we neither know that word nor could we overcome our fear of misnaming it. Happily, *midrash* offers us a more playful vocabulary, a way that allows us to sift through the sand, letting the grains slip through our fingers even though we know that one of the grains we let fall may have been the Word. Indeed, we prefer it that way, for to know the Word at last is also to come to the End. It is God who engraves His words in stone; we merely trace ours, tentatively, in the sand. And then the waves wash up and obliterate even those vague markings.

Which is to say there is no text without a reader. The letters are inert until they are lifted off the page by the reader's eyes and his voice and enter his living struggle. Imagine the text not as a story, but as a score; imagine the reader as its performer. Each reader, bounded loosely by the notes and by our tacit agreement as to what interpretations they do not permit, may then—must then—play the text. And, with regard to the Text, *al achat kamah v'chamah*—all the more so—for the Text does not reveal itself. We know from the Talmud that God Himself studies and interprets the Torah—a bold recognition that the words in and of themselves only provide the occasion for their interpretation, that their interpretation is not only invited but also required. We are not asked to know what *does* the word mean, but what *might,* what *can* the word mean? Because the text is cryptic, we are not asked to reproduce it but to perform it.

To perform the *text.* The fact that we are literate is not sufficient; the texts we are given are not merely collections of familiar notes, words over which our literacy gives us mastery. There is a context to those words, and they cannot quite mean whatever we want them to mean, even if what they do mean is uncertain, even if they may have multiple meanings. To play the text one must know how to read the notes, the score.

Still, our purpose is not to divine the one "literal" meaning; there is none—not, at any rate, which we can safely say we have finally determined. And even were we able to fathom the "original intent" of the redactors—what then? Their intent and ours are separated by many centuries; we are not and cannot be the passive receptacles of their intent. One can perform a Mozart concerto on the authentic instruments of Mozart's time, as has lately become the fashion, and the exercise is interesting. It permits us to go halfway toward hearing the music as Mozart intended it to be heard. But only halfway, for our ears are not the ears Mozart's audiences brought to his recitals. Nor, for that matter, can we know how Mozart would have intended us to hear the music had he had available to him the instruments we now have. Nor is there any compelling reason for us to suppose that we are bound to hear according to Mozart's intentions. We ought, out of a sense of deference to his genius as well as to history, make note of his intentions, perhaps even explore them, but they need not be our own, nor is it reasonable to suppose, 200 and more years later, that they will be.*

Or: " 'Is not My word like a hammer that breaks the rock in pieces?' [Jer. 23:29]—as the hammer causes numerous sparks to flash forth, so is a scriptural verse capable of many interpretations." (Sanh. 34a) And which is the "right" interpretation? As well ask which is the "right" spark. This spark illuminates this corner, that spark another. It is vanity to search for or to proclaim the superiority of this spark or that, this interpretation or that. There is no final interpretation, there never can be, for the Jews live in order that their questions and their writings and yes, their lives, become an interpretation. On the day of the last interpretation, the finally correct interpretation, the Book is sealed, and the Jewish people done.

Anyone who interacts with a text, be it Mozart's or God's, is bound to interpret it, no matter his/her view of its origins and status. The early rabbis, seeking to make their own interpretations

*The continuing debate on the importance of original intent in interpreting the U.S. Constitution is of some interest here.

authoritative, claimed that the original revelation was not only of the Written Law but also of the Oral Law which they themselves were codifying. Those who today accept that claim argue that the Text is not a Mozart concerto; it is Revealed Truth and can be validly interpreted only by those who accept its sacred status.

There is an important difference between those who claim that theirs is the only valid rendering and those whose truths are tentative, between those whose style of interpretation is an ongoing search for "original intent" and those whose purpose is less to hear what Moses heard, more to search for a usable truth. Venerability does not establish authenticity. To say that he or she is most authentic who most precisely does Judaism as it was done in the times of Abraham, or of Moses, or of Yohanan ben Zakai, or of his own father, her own mother, is to discard the whole of the history of the Jewish people as a relevant text. Following Mordecai M. Kaplan, we may say that the Jews are not in the antique business; we needn't suppose that simply because it is old, it is authentic, much less worthy. Every generation of Jews, since the very beginning, has had its interpreting to do, and has made its own mistakes. Authenticity requires not imitation but active interpretation—that, more than anything else, is the authentic mandate. The status of the text, on this reading, does not depend on its source but on what meanings we are able to wrest from it.

The tradition itself endorses this view: The Talmud tells of a certain Rabbi Eliezer who stood alone against his colleagues on a matter of law. After failing to persuade them, he invoked the support of heaven: "If the law agrees with me, let this carob tree prove it!" Whereupon the carob tree "was torn a hundred cubits out of its place—others say four hundred cubits." But Rabbi Joshua observed that "No proof can be brought from a carob tree." So Rabbi Eliezer said, "If the law agrees with me, let the stream of water prove it!" And the stream began to flow backward. But again Rabbi Joshua dismissed the evidence: "No proof can be brought from a stream of water." Rabbi Eliezer did not desist: "If the law agrees with me, let the walls of the schoolhouse prove it!" And the walls of the schoolhouse where the rabbis were meeting began to fall, until Rabbi Joshua rebuked them, saying they had no right to interfere in a legal dispute. ("Hence they did not fall, in honor of Rabbi Joshua, nor did they resume the upright, in honor of Rabbi Eliezer," and that is why they still stand inclined.") Finally, Rabbi Eliezer called on God Himself: "If the law agrees with me, let it be proved from heaven!" Whereupon "a heavenly voice cried out, 'Why do you dispute with Rabbi Eliezer, seeing that in all matters the law agrees with him?' " To which Rabbi Joshua exclaimed, 'It is not in heaven!' "

The story continues, asking what Joshua meant by his exclamation. Rabbi Jeremiah explains: "That the Torah had already been given at Mount Sinai. We pay no attention to a heavenly voice." And the reason we do not, he then adds, is that the Torah itself tells us that the majority must prevail. There is no appeal to heaven, hence (because majorities may change) no final proof. God is surely an expert witness, but it is still for the jury to decide.

Then the story concludes: Rabbi Nathan met Elijah himself, and asked how God reacted when Joshua dismissed the evidence of heaven. "He laughed with joy," Elijah replied, and said, "My sons have defeated me, my sons have defeated me!" (Bab.Met. 59b)

I want to say something more here. I want to say that we, the living Jews of this generation, *are* the text, as our grandparents were in their day and as our grandchildren will be, God willing, in theirs. Unstudied, our books are parchment and ink, no more; learned, they live in us. Our books, our memories, our dreams, and yes, our lives—these are the text.

What does it mean to live within the boundaries of such a text? It means that we live with a consciousness of time, with the awareness that we are neither the first nor the last, that we inherit and we owe. Do such boundaries hem, confine? On the contrary, they liberate. The text offers freedom in two ways: It offers freedom from death, inasmuch as our acceptance and transmission of it are our only assurance of immortality; it offers freedom to invent, for its implicit mandate is to make of our lives a *midrash* on the text.

I mean this last quite literally. *Midrash* is more than a collection of interpretive tales based loosely on a standard text. We not only tell stories, we live them; our lives are stories, whether or not written down, and what the peoplehood of the Jews must mean is that the stories Jews live are, for better or for worse, interpretations of the text.

The purpose of our teachers, therefore, is not to teach us what the text means, but to teach us how to read it, and then to help us see whether our interpretations—our lives—are consonant with the text, or fall outside its boundaries.

One source of the confusion so many Jews experience in trying to think about the relationship between Jews and Judaism comes from the word itself. In Hebrew, there is no ready equivalent for "Judaism," and *yahadut*, which comes closer than any other, is not to be found either in the Torah or in the rabbinic writings. Nor, still more important, does *yahadut* necessarily suggest a coherent dogma. (Yiddish has a different word, *yiddishkeit*, but *yiddishkeit* is a more folksy term, suggesting behavior rather than doctrine, more aptly translated as "Jewishness" than as "Judaism.") It is the "ism" in Judaism that throws us off-track, that leads us to search for what cannot—and need not—be found. (Unless, of course, we are prepared to incorporate the term "Judaists" into our vocabulary, thereby detaching Judaism from Jews-in-general and tying it to some subgroup of Jews. But then to which subgroup does it "belong"?)

Custom is the culprit here. The word "Judaism" is too widely accepted for us to excise it, even if we cannot say precisely what it means. Yet it misdirects us, suggesting as it does that Jews are best defined by their adherence to a system of belief, an "ism." What is that system of belief? We cannot say: even the Talmud, seeking to assert the core beliefs, founders, its authors debating whether to accept all the 613 precepts God gave to Moses, or King David's basic eleven principles, or Isaiah's six (or, later, two), or Micah's three, or Habakkuk's one. Hillel, approached by a heathen seeking to convert to Judaism but only on condition that he be taught the entire Torah while standing on one leg, replies, "That which is hateful unto thee do not do unto thy neighbor." But Ahad Ha'Am, the modern essayist, argues that he would have told the heathen instead, "Thou shalt not make unto thee a graven image, nor any manner of likeness."* Perhaps the best we can do—and it is not so bad, after all—is to recall that Hillel's instruction did not conclude with the negative

---

*Judaism abides skeptics, agnostics, and atheists, but not idolators. The prohibition against idolatry is absolute; it is the subject of the first and second commandments.

prescription I have cited. Before the heathen had lowered his leg, Hillel added, "That is the whole of the Torah. The rest is commentary. Go and study."

Or go and wrestle, knowing that different Jews in all the places we have been have studied and proposed and lived different answers to Micah's question, "What doth the Lord require of thee?," and that the heart of Judaism may lie in taking the question itself as the most urgent question that is asked of us. Ask it in those words, or in its briefer form: "Where are you?"

Some Jews will surely object at this point, claiming—correctly— that you don't have to be Jewish to ask such questions, any more than you have to be Jewish to take Micah's answer—"Do justice, love goodness, and walk modestly with your God"—to heart. The objection reflects a concern that unless Judaism is a unique teaching, it cannot be justified. That is a common and important misunderstanding. Judaism—by which henceforward I mean the ways in which Jews have wrestled with God, have searched after godliness—has no monopoly on either the essential questions or the most compelling answers. Normative Judaism is a mandate: hear the question, and seek its answer, as others, too, must and will. (Else our God is only *our* God, and that is precisely the opposite of Judaism's central theological insight.) Historical and empirical Judaism is a method: these are the (diverse) ways in which *this* people, the Jews, tries to ensure that the question will be heard, its answer sought. The mandate is universal; it is the method that is particular, unique.

In his autobiography, *Morning Star,* Zalman Shazar, Israel's third president, described the library he encountered as a young man in the home of Baron David Ginsburg, aristocratic scion of Russia's leading Jewish family. It was 1907; the place was St. Petersburg. The students at Ginsburg's academy came to the baron to request more course work in the historical study of the social and economic life of the Jews. He responded with fervor:

> Dear ones, I am deeply grieved by this request of yours. I am certain that you have no intention in the world of causing me unhappiness, and it is very difficult for me to say no to you. But how can I hide

my concern from you? You have come here to study the nature and destiny of the Jewish people—and now I hear you asking to be taught what occupations Jews were compelled to engage in to keep alive. It is as if a scholar had been asked to lecture to you on Kant, and then, instead of teaching you the *Critique of Pure Reason,* spent his time describing the restaurant Kant frequented and the kind of cutlets his wife gave him. And it is not Kant you are studying, but that sublime people God chose for His own! . . . If you do research on horses—there is such a science, too—it is obviously very important to investigate what fodder should be put in the horses' crib: oats or barley. But when the subject of your study is the wisdom of the chosen people, do you think their fodder and their crib should concern you?

What I have been saying, of course, is that it is precisely the fodder and the crib that must be studied, and the digestive tract as well. Judaism is not just an idea, nor even just the history of an idea; it has a body, hence a biography.

Imagine, for example, that in Heidelberg there sits and studies a genius of a theologian. He has mastered all the texts there are, speaks a dozen languages of ancient times, knows the whole of the Talmud and all of the codes by heart. But these things are all he knows; he has never laid eyes on a Jew, has not read medieval Hebrew poetry or nineteenth-century Yiddish stories or twentieth-century American Jewish novels. He knows nothing of the context in which Hasidism arose or of Jewish participation in the civil rights movement; he has never heard of refuseniks or of the United Jewish Appeal. Can it be said of him that he is an expert on Judaism?

I think not. He knows a great deal, much more than most Jews, but what he knows cannot properly be called "Judaism." That would be to mistake the part—the texts—for the whole.

Or: Earlier, I suggested that our texts are a score, we its performers. I am told that there are people so profoundly musical that when they sit in a quiet room and read the score, they hear the music. And now and again comes a composer who, far from any instrument that might give voice to his harmonies, wrests them out of his mind and onto the paper before him; there is the composer who is utterly deaf, yet hears the music he has made. But for most of us, a score is not yet music; no more is the text itself Judaism. The score is music potential, not music actual. So, too, the text is a method of notation; it is not Judaism until it is performed.

Some performers will strive to discern the composer's (Composer's?) will; others will take the text as a theme for their own variations; still others will take it as the inspiration for a series of jazz improvisations. (Invariably, they will be criticized for having gone too far, for having abandoned the original or violated its intent. And only in the course of time will we know whether the boundaries are sufficiently elastic to contain the new departure, or whether it must remain outside them.) And very many, of course, will be altogether deaf to the diverse possibilities. Until, perhaps, an overheard performance so captures their need or their yearning that they too become musicians. Until, perhaps, a new conductor or a virtuoso performer reveals new possibilities that had not hitherto been imagined, possibilities that render the text accessible to those who had supposed it closed. It is in the performance—in the performances—that Judaism is defined.

Still, and again, not *only* fodder and crib, nor performance; the history of Judaism is not quite the same as the history of the Jews. Judaism points beyond theology, but it is not wholly sociology. What we eat matters; so do the blessings we chant, reject, or forget. In order to wrestle and to seek and to listen and finally to hear, in order to live our lives as a response not merely to solicitations and emergencies but to God's call, we must be capable of recognizing the call when we hear it. The history of Judaism speaks both to the call and to our capability, to mandate and to method, to God's "Where are you?" and to our response. To study Judaism is to study the history of the interaction between a people and its ideas.

God is one of those ideas. Historically, the idea of God has been widely used as a way of explaining phenomena we otherwise do not understand. But as science, in its precise and powerful way, explains more and more of that which yesterday we did not understand, the value of God-as-explanation diminishes, the scope of religion shrinks. Indeed, insofar as science and religion compete head-to-head, whether in explaining the origin of species or why drought happens or the roots of evil, religion comes out the loser every time;

compared to the precision of the laboratory, it appears as murky superstition.

But explanation of natural phenomena is not the principal business of religion. We are inclined to think it is because it was so central an element in primitive religion, and because so much of primitive religion remains intact in our liturgies and in our yearnings. Still, in our time, religion has a very different and far more urgent purpose: we may turn to science to answer our "how?" questions, but science is entirely useless as a way of answering our "what for?" questions. And these are the questions that religion (in general, and at its best) tries to deal with. Religion is least compelling when it offers us answers about the past; it is most compelling when it offers us questions about the future.

Because so much attention is commonly focused on religion's answers rather than on its questions, and because the fundamental propositions of religion are untestable (hence not disprovable), it is easy—and in some circles fashionable—to dismiss religion as unenlightened, intellectually irrelevant. The Marxist views religion as subversive, the liberal as quaint. And one consequence is that "what for?" questions, the kind of questions in which religion specializes and on which science is silent, are dismissed from public discourse. The loss is grievous and gratuitous. For although the religious way of knowing is not the scientific way of knowing, it is a vital way. Who among us, after all, is wholly satisfied by science, is closed off and sealed up against mystery, indifferent to art?* Religion comes to raise questions science leaves alone, and those questions are as compelling as the questions science asks and tries to answer.

As to religion's answers, they are a mixed bag, a collage of humankind's development from the most primitive to the most sophisticated. If we enter religion, as many of us do, only with questions the child who abides within us asks, we will hear only its least sophisticated answers. It is unfair to religion to ask that it comfort us when things go bump in the night and then, with the

*We are told that when Werner Heisenberg, who discovered the Uncertainty Principle, had finished playing the Beethoven Opus #111 for a group of colleagues—he was a gifted amateur pianist—he observed, "If I had never lived, someone else would have discovered the Uncertainty Principle. But if Beethoven had never lived, no one would have written the Opus #111."

coming of the dawn, to accuse it of triviality. Religion is capable of far richer and more serious meaning, but it cannot offer that meaning to those who do not seek it. To seek that meaning we must know that religion does not come to answer questions that are not otherwise answered; it comes to ask questions that might otherwise be lost.

A particular religion comes as well to provide its adherents questions they can share, hence that are not entirely subjective or idiosyncratic. It comes to offer answers—rituals—that may help us deal with today's tensions and traumas, and answers—visions of the right way—that may help us shape our hopes and make of them a common purpose. Religion proposes not only a sensibility but also a structure for honing and transmitting that sensibility.

Judaism is a religious way; there can be no ambiguity about that, no matter what the proportion of Jews who attend to its precepts. But to say that Judaism is wholly a religion is to mislead, for it is to suggest simply a dogma that can be set down on stone, on parchment, or on paper, that has a life independent of its adherents. There is dogma, to be sure, but there is something other than dogma as well: there is Judaism as a way of life. I cannot specify what part of the whole is dogma, what part culture, what part behavior; the mix is neither stable nor constant. Moreover, as we have seen, even Judaism-as-dogma cannot be neatly rendered; its texts are too cryptic, too dependent on interpretation and reinterpretation to permit immutable and comprehensive doctrinal certainty. Nor, finally, is it my place or my intention to suggest the dogmatic minima to which a Jew "must" subscribe in order to lay legitimate claim to Judaism. That effort is doomed.

Still, it is quite common to encounter articles and symposia on the "Jewish view" of this or that. What shall we make of them? With distressing frequency, one comes away from such encounters with the impression that the writers or the speakers have gone to the sources there to find support for their own prior dispositions. And, virtually no matter what those dispositions are, they will find the support they seek. The same tradition informs us, for example, that on the one hand, "Every man will be held accountable before God for all the permitted things he beheld in life and did not enjoy," and, on the other hand, that "This is the way of Torah: a morsel of bread with salt must thou eat, and water by measure must thou drink, thou must sleep upon the ground and live a life of anguish the while thou toilest in the Torah."

The fact is, as Harold Schulweis observes, that we are confronted by an "absence of structured ethical theory . . . and [by] the casual and unsystematic form of ethics in traditional literature." And the further fact is that the relationship of the values of any generation of Jews to the norms asserted in the traditional literature is necessarily an open question, this for two reasons: First, over and over again we learn from modern scholarship that the nature of the rulings of the rabbis was, as must be obvious, shaped not only by the received tradition but also by the social, political, and economic circumstances of the time. Therefore, if one seeks to extrapolate from the wisdom of eighth-century rabbis principles that will help guide us through, say, the thicket—more likely the jungle—of genetic engineering, one ought not be surprised if the effort proves of little value, or if it produces conflicting principles. (In the standard Orthodox view, *all* knowledge is implicit in the texts; a trained scholar can search out the applicable principle, arguing either directly or through analogy. But most contemporary Jews would say that such a view, quite literally, does not stand to reason. More precisely, to Reason.)

In any event, the "Jewish view" is a term that almost always refers to one or another normative view of Judaism, which may or may not correspond to the actual values of the Jews. As we know from our history, all the way back to the Biblical narrative and the prophetic writings, the norms of the tradition, even where straight-forward, have had only a loose correspondence to the behavior of the people. (One presumes that the fashioning of the golden calf more accurately reflected the dispositions of the Israelites of the time than did the various normative injunctions proscribing such behavior. When Moses and the later prophets chastised the people for their chronic lapses, it was because of the sizable gap between norm and behavior.)

There are, to be sure, some who think the effort to assert dogma is useful. A liberal Orthodox rabbi, Saul Berman, interviewed on the Bill Moyers program, claims that "It would not be consonant with Jewish identity for a Jew not to believe in certain things: for a Jew not to believe in the universality of God, for a Jew not to believe in the unity of God, for a Jew not to believe that God is involved in human affairs, for a Jew not to believe that God's will is expressed through the revealed Torah."

And what if one does not believe in these things? Does that mean that one's "Jewish identity" is somehow attenuated? Or may we take heart from Berman's own immediate postscript, that even when those beliefs are absent, "one remains a Jew. . . . It's the translation into behavior that is much more critical than the underlying beliefs"?

Still, there is no glossing over the beliefs. In Berman's view, "The underlying beliefs, as it were, create the foundation for living a certain kind of life. It's our [read: Orthodox] conviction, of course, that living that kind of life can't for long be sustained without the foundation." Or, in the tougher words of Rabbi J. David Bleich of the Rabbi Isaac Elchanan Theological Seminary and a distinguished Orthodox scholar:

> Acceptance of Torah as the revealed word of God and acknowl-
> edgement of its immutable nature are matters which are both unbe-
> clouded by controversy in traditional Jewish teaching and which are
> also of profound significance with regard to virtually every aspect
> of Jewish life. These principles are fundamental to an axiological
> system which serves to define the intrinsic nature of Judaism.
> . . . The fact that certain contemporary sectarians may reject these
> axioms or reinterpret them in a manner which makes it possible for
> them to claim equal or even exclusive authenticity for their beliefs
> is entirely irrelevant.

My view, as might be expected, is different: It is the living normative culture of those who call themselves Jews that offers the essential foundation. Still, as much as we may disagree regarding the
foundation, Berman and I—and perhaps even Bleich, too—quite
likely do not disagree completely regarding the behavior we think
essential, the behavior the beliefs are meant to promote, the behavior I have called—as would Berman—"a way of life." And that is
because, in the end, Jewish identity is not something one *has*, but
something one *does*.

I write here as a tenaciously non-traditional—by Orthodox standards, surely a non-believing—Jew who will not give up his claim

to Judaism. I take what I need from the tradition, and what I like, and what I can, the parts that make substantive sense and the parts that have stylistic appeal. In the blessing over the wine, I wince a bit when I come to the place where we thank God for having "chosen us from among all the peoples," and I am grateful the words are in Hebrew. When I recite words I do not believe, it is not out of humility, a sense that perhaps I may be wrong in my rejection of their meaning. It is out of deference. The principle of community means more to me than the principle of consistency.

Some people I know—not many—prefer a minor change in the Hebrew, from the original *mikol ha'amim* to *im kol ha'amim*—from "from among all the peoples" to "together with all the peoples." The problem here is that once we insist that none of the words may violate our beliefs, there are very many words that will require change, or, at least, extensive and often tortured interpretation. Better simply to accept that sometimes the structure does not support the sensibility it is intended to promote, and to live with the discrepancy—or, if it is too blatant, if it cannot be reconciled, to modify the structure. So when, in the Grace After Meals, I reach the line where we say, "I was young, and I have become old, and I have never seen the righteous abandoned," I cannot and do not say the words; there are boundaries of belief I cannot bring myself to cross.

I could, I suppose, concede the matter, go glumly or gaily along my Jewish—but not Judaic—way. But I am merely secular, not a secularist; I make no ideological claims for my secularity, it is not an "ism" to me. Which means that though I am closed to the beliefs—those beliefs Saul Berman calls "the foundation"—I am open to the language, to the question, if you will, and, I should like to think, to the life, the life of a Jew—by my lights, a religious life. Fundamentally, I have decided that I will not permit my problems with the tradition to separate me from it, nor will I permit the particular claim the Orthodox lay to the tradition to deter me from entering it as I will, as I can, as I see fit. I will not be intimidated into abandoning that which I find sustaining because others tell me I misconstrue its meaning or that selectivity is not permitted. Nor will I accept that theirs is inherently a superior authenticity, a more rigorous commitment. It is a mistake to think that traditional observance and religion are synonymous.

At the same time, I will enter the tradition, and yes, its ritual elements, without a chip on my shoulder; I will enter with deference. For the methods of the tradition amount to a structure that has sustained very many people in very many places over centuries of time. I cannot pretend to understand thoroughly the mystery of how Judaism's structure has worked so well as it has. I can only be pleased that I am heir to it, and I can allow myself to wonder whether the aspects that make no sense to me—there are many—owe to the tradition's limitations, or to my own.

So I must study. And wrestle. And listen. And err. And rejoice. And listen. And hallow. And listen. And know that if my life is a commentary on the text, then yours is, too.

3

Competence and Meaning

THE SUGGESTION that there are multiple authentic Judaisms may be more easily understood and more readily accepted by American Jews than by Jews elsewhere, for the American Jew dwells in a land that lives with and on competing interpretations. Elsewhere, the competition may well be seen as a threat; here, though there is some of that, we are mostly satisfied to accept the inevitability of differences, not to feel the urgent need to overcome them. The American ethos is conducive to the understanding that Judaism may take multiple forms.

But that is only a starting point. Save as Jews are able to speak Jewish—that is, to share a language that goes beyond slogans and beyond instincts—we may find that what we have is not a creative debate about competing interpretations but an amorphous Judaism, a Judaism not of multiple forms but of no form at all. And it is plain that many of us have grown distant from such a language. Some have never heard it, do not know that it exists. Some suppose that the only authentic language is the one Orthodox Jews speak, and they find the language of Orthodoxy forbidding rather than inviting. Some are simply uncomfortable with a language they know to speak only haltingly.

The question before us, then, is whether there is a vocabulary and a grammar for Jewish life in America that is accessible to those of us who want to talk Jewish but do not yet know how.

Orthodox Jews, of course, claim that there is—it is the language they speak. But to enter the world of the Orthodox, even briefly, is to learn how different it is from the world most Jews inhabit.

Formally, all Orthodox Jews accept that God's will is expressed through the revealed Torah, and that it is the doing of God's will that ought be our organizing purpose.* Until recently, the general assumption about Orthodoxy had been that it would, in due course, peter out, unable to withstand the assault of modernity. By and large, Orthodoxy was thought to be the immigrants' religion (those immigrants, that is, whose religion was not socialism), a religion simply incompatible with American culture and American perspectives. The rapid rise of Conservative and Reform Judaism in the first half of this century appeared to confirm the conventional wisdom.

There have been two great denominational surprises in the American Jewish world these last twenty years or so, and the greater of them is the extraordinary durability of Orthodoxy. Suddenly, it has become evident (perhaps it was evident to the Orthodox all along; surely to no one else) that Orthodox Judaism has learned how to survive—and, at the margins, even to thrive—in America. Some of the Orthodox have managed by becoming what is called "modern Orthodox," integrating entirely conventional American life styles with entirely traditional Jewish behaviors. And some have accomplished their survival by walling themselves off, learning to use the system to enable a self-willed ghetto. (The other great surprise? That Reform Judaism has not proved to be merely a way station on the path to assimilation, the last stop before the border.)

The persistence of Orthodoxy has had a most provocative consequence: it has challenged the bourgeois "religiosity," the sentimental attachment to Jewish religious slogans without Jewish religious substance that has characterized—and still characterizes—most American Jews. It has made explicit that which was comfortably

---

*So stated, Conservative Judaism would not demur. Its difference with the Orthodox is formally a methodological difference; it is about *how* we come to understand God's will. But that is a doctrinal matter: to say what Conservative Judaism holds is not to say what Conservative Jews believe.

ambiguous, it has made manifest that which was only latent. Specifically, it has asserted—it asserts—that there is after all a dogma to this thing called Judaism, and that only Orthodoxy is entitled to offer the authentic articulation of that dogma.

An Orthodox correspondent writes to me, "You are assuredly a Jew, and much of what you do I applaud. But do not delude yourself: what you preach and what you practice is 'Jewishism.' Do not suppose that it is the same thing as Judaism. Judaism is what *I* preach and what *I* practice. It is the authentic tradition, the tradition you have chosen to forfeit."

His is a beguiling formulation, proposed in order to embrace the heretic but not the heresy. To be sure, it skirts the problem that there are competing interpretations within the Orthodox community, that Judaism, because it lacks hierarchical structure, is incapable of producing a single authoritative statement of doctrine. But that is not a fatal flaw; within Orthodoxy, there remains a consensus of sorts, and while the consensus may be too fuzzy to permit perfect agreement in distinguishing between the "Jewishists" and the "Judaists," it will be unanimous most of the time.

This kind of distinction, as may be imagined, sets the teeth of religiously serious non-Orthodox Jews on edge, for they are hardly prepared to concede Judaism to their Orthodox kinfolk. But most non-Orthodox Jews are not religiously serious, and they know that about themselves. In the popular view, the several denominations are hierarchically ordered: Orthodoxy is "most," and Conservatism is "next most," and Reform is "least." And if more is better, than surely most is best—"best" meaning most authentic, most committed, most Jewish. It is the Orthodox standard from which they deviate—and the Orthodox standard is the classical standard, the unmodified standard, finally, *the* Jewish standard.

Had Orthodoxy conformed to the predictions, had it withered away, this admiration from across the divide would not have been a problem. A touch of wistful nostalgia for a way of life now gone is not a direct challenge to the way of life now chosen. But Orthodoxy did not wither away. Instead, the Lubavitch Hasidim tool about in their "mitzvah mobiles" searching for Jews who might be induced to fulfill this commandment or that, and they open centers in such unlikely places as Palm Springs; the lawyers and physicians and scientists of the Young Israel movement enjoy secular success by day and learn Talmud by night; Orthodox practice becomes the norm for the organized community during its formal functions.

If the Orthodox can hack it in America as religious folk, what is wrong with us that we cannot? And for every American Jew who replies to that question by saying, "We could, but we choose not to, for our way is as good, as authentic, as Jewish," there are ten American Jews who are tongue-tied by the question, who are left to feel inadequate; worse yet, inauthentic.

That is what happens when one "branch" says to the others, "We grow closer to the trunk," and when the others have neither the knowledge nor the courage to say "no," much less "NO!"

Nor have they the desire to say, "If that is the case, let me come to where you are." Orthodox Jews in the main do not understand that the rejection of their way, be it the only authentic way or not, is not a consequence (always) of laziness. It is a consequence of a difference in perspective so vast that one is tempted to call it a difference of mentality. It is not that the Orthodox are "most," or even "more." From the non-Orthodox perspective, the continuum ends abruptly just at the border with Orthodoxy. And the reason it does is that the Orthodox are, above all else, *different.* The world they perceive is even more different from our perceived world than the world they create is from the one we seek to fashion.

Our world is a world organized on the principle of fallibility. And because that is so, we say, "This is *our* way, and it works, at least for us." But to be Orthodox means to say, "This is *the* way, and it is the Jewish truth." For us, the text is a homily; for the Orthodox, it is a template. For us, the truth is in the process; for the Orthodox, it is in the Word. For us, there is a sharp distinction between the mandate and the method, and if the method comes to seem fussy or alien we will abandon it; for the Orthodox, mandate and method are the indistinguishable gift of God.

I have set "us" against the Orthodox here, and that is a distasteful thing to do. I say "us" because some 90 percent of America's Jews are not, by their own definition, Orthodox. But I do not mean, not at all, to suggest that the Orthodox are merely a quaint and anachronistic outcropping, still awaiting the Enlightenment. Orthodox Jewry in America includes not only some of American Jewry's most vital and energetic institutions, but also some of its most thoughtful and insightful actors. These are not by any stretch of the informed imagination a primitive cult; these are people who have seen the Enlightenment, and the relativism that is its necessary consequence, and have found them wanting.

So I speak here of the difference between "us" and "them" not to imply dismissal of their claims, but to speak the disconcerting truth: the difference is so very great that we are bound to speak of Judaisms, not of a single Judaism. The Jewish people may, as it repeatedly announces, be one—though even that is doubtful; but the doctrine of the Jewish people is not even approximately unitary. We share some of the same texts, and more of the same rituals, and many of the same concerns and purposes. But we do not share, not even nearly, the way we look at the world. The religious language of Orthodox Jews is a language very few non-Orthodox Jews speak, or care to learn. We know some of its vocabulary; we do not know and do not want to know its grammar.

How, after all, might non-Orthodox Jews be expected to respond to the assertion by Rabbi Sholom Klass, editor of *The Jewish Press* of Brooklyn, that "unless you have completed the study of the entire Talmud (over 60 volumes) and its many commentaries, you are not capable of discussing our religion"? Or to the question posed by Rabbi Aaron Soloveitchick, a member of the Talmud faculty of Yeshiva University: "What kind of common dialogue can there be between Jews *shlemim b'emuna* [of perfect faith] and Conservative and Reform rabbis?" Or, finally, to the argument put forward by Rabbi Avi Shafran in an article entitled "The Perils of Pluralism": "A Jew is a Jew, no matter what he rejects of Judaism. But, by the same token, Judaism is Judaism, no matter what Jews may reject of it. The rejecters remain Jews; the rejected, Judaism. . . . Judaism has a specific historic definition. The essence of that definition has always been Jewish law."

I do not hold with the model of contemporary Jewish life that views the Jews as divided into two groups—one that is authentic, purposeful, centered, another that is ersatz, aimless, empty. While

Orthodox Jews may "speak" Jewish more fluently than most non-Orthodox Jews, that does not mean that there is no other Jewish language that might be spoken. The issue is not authenticity but fluency. And there is this, as well: the language of the Orthodox is simply not accessible to very many American Jews. It will not do for these to feel themselves wanting, to be termed, as has become modish in some Orthodox circles, the "not-yet observant." If there are other authentic languages, they should be—as indeed they often are—taught and learned without apology, without embarrassment, without the disabling sense that they are fast-food versions (or perversions) of the classical repast.

I say that the language of the Orthodox is not generally accessible because the Orthodox understanding of Revelation is very distant from where most of us are. For myself, I prefer the hazards of anarchy to the constriction of authority. I cannot believe what I cannot believe, and see no need to twist myself toward belief even if I were capable of it. "It hath been told to thee, O son of man" is not for me a way toward a usable truth. And I am troubled, as well, by Orthodoxy's preoccupation with boundaries—from the "four ells of the *halachah*," of Jewish law, to the historic boundaries of the Land of Israel, to the boundaries that divide Jew from non-Jew, to the boundaries that separate the *kosher* (the ritually acceptable) from the *treif* (the ritually unacceptable), to those that separate man from woman. It often seems to me that the purpose of much that happens within those boundaries is only to ensure their impermeability. It is as if, now that the guards on the other side of the boundary have relaxed, the great fear of the Orthodox (though again, there is much variety within Orthodoxy) is that the Jews will not be able to withstand the temptation to wander across it, there, inevitably, to be seduced. Hence the Orthodox are even more likely than the rest of us to emphasize the continuing persecution of the Jews, as if to say that the guards are only feigning inattention, that the barriers are not permeable after all. Hence the Orthodox, from the time of the Emancipation, when Jews were at last permitted citizenship, have tended to cast their lot with conservative parties. In nineteenth-century Germany, they preferred the parties that defended the old, highly structured, order, that were less sympathetic to emancipation. As David Biale observes, "From the point of view of these Orthodox Jews, such an 'unholy alliance' with anti-Jewish forces was preferable to the dubious benefits of emancipation and assimilation." And in twentieth-century America, the Orthodox remain far more politically conservative than other Jews.

Plainly, this summary of Orthodox perceptions will not please the defenders of Orthodoxy. I put it forward not in order to join a debate, but to enable the reader to know the understanding (or misunderstanding, as the case may be) I bring to these issues—and to emphasize that the quest for a unitary Judaism, a single definition against which to measure Jewish beliefs and behaviors, is pointless as well as futile.

My correspondent—he who accuses me of mere "Jewishism"— would enter a vehement objection here. He would argue that Judaism is, more or less simply, the texts as authoritatively interpreted by the rabbis through the centuries. That, and nothing more, but nothing less. Everything else about the Jews, he would continue, falls under the heading "Jewish," not "Judaic."

There is more than a semantic quibble here. If my correspondent's view is permitted to go unchallenged, then Judaism has no necessary and intimate relationship to what the Jews think and do. And if that be so, if Judaism has an existence independent of the Jews, we are inevitably drawn to a fruitless competition over authenticity. Does my way come closer to Judaism, or does yours, or does his? And, accordingly, which of us is the "better" Jew? There are the norms of Judaism—in his view, the norms Orthodoxy represents— and there are the behaviors, and those norms are the basis for judging our behaviors.

I do not propose that there are no norms, that Judaism is simply what the Jews of any age and place do. I propose instead that there are multiple norms, diverse and sometimes divergent emphases, and that Judaisms in any age emerge from the ways in which the Jews of that age struggle to make sense of—and use of—their past, a past that includes not only the texts and their interpretations, but also their memories and their histories.

And now we come full circle. For though we do not know the grammar of the Orthodox, we do know that our own language (for the most part) is less than fluent. We may reject their language, but honesty requires that we acknowledge that they, at least, have a language. And they claim it is the only language. And few of us are competent to rebut the claim. So we are left feeling inadequate.*

The issue of inadequacy is of surpassing importance; more than any ideological uncertainty or confusion, it depresses Jewish morale and discourages Jewish commitment. Though it extends far beyond the realm of religion, we can easily enter the discussion from that realm.

America, we learn from the polls and surveys, is one of the most deeply religious nations in the world. One recent survey (1981) finds that 62 percent of all Americans "know God really exists and have no doubts about it." For Jews, that number is 38 percent, suggesting that the majority of America's Jews are agnostic. Similarly, 64 percent of Americans regard religion as "extremely important" or "quite important"; for Jews, the figure is 43 percent. A 1972 study of Reform rabbis reports that only 10 percent believe in God "in the more or less traditional Jewish sense." But the data on Jewish belief are both scattered and inconsistent. A 1986 survey finds that 77 percent of America's Jews agree that "I definitely believe in God," and 62 percent agree that "I believe God gave the Torah to Moses at Mount Sinai." Hardly the views of agnostics.

The vast difference between the two sets of findings cannot readily be explained; differences in research methodology or in the wording of the questions may be partly responsible, as may the much-heralded return to religion. Nor is there much to be learned from other surveys. The curious and likely significant fact is that very few have included questions on Jewish religious belief, and those few provide a mottled portrait. So, for example, one recent survey finds that while 91 percent of its respondents agree that

---

*I have been using the word "language" here as a metaphor, of course. As it turns out, it has a literal relevance as well, one that casts light on its metaphoric use. In *Ties and Tensions: The 1986 Survey of American Jewish Attitudes Towards Israel and Israelis,* Steven Cohen examines the relationship between denomination and knowledge of the Hebrew language. Forty-one percent of his Orthodox respondents claim at least a minimal competence in Hebrew—compared to just 9 percent of Conservative Jews, 5 percent of Reform Jews, and 5 percent of those who describe themselves as "just Jewish." The Orthodox score dramatically higher on other items as well: 62 percent are in the highest category of attachment to Israel, compared to 34 percent of the total sample (and 20 percent of Reform Jews)—and 30 percent have considerable sympathy for Meir Kahane, compared to 14 percent of the total sample.

"Without Jewish religion, the Jewish people could not survive," nearly a two-to-one majority reject the assertion that "To be a good Jew, one must believe in God."

We know considerably more about ritual practice than about religious belief, but the extensive data on such practice do not provide a more consistent portrait. On the one hand, for example, two out of five Jews do not fast on Yom Kippur; four out of five do not observe the Jewish dietary laws; only about 10 percent attend Sabbath services more often than once a month. (Forty-three percent of all Americans attend religious services "every week" or "nearly every week.") On the other hand, 84 percent attend a Passover seder, and 82 percent light Hanukkah candles.

The disarray may well surprise the non-Jewish reader; we know that 71 percent of non-Jews believe that Jews are "highly religious." Presumably, they witness the intensity of Jewish affect, and (mistakenly) suppose it signifies religious fervor. But by any conventional understanding of the word "religious," it does not. It does not describe Jewish belief, and it does not describe Jewish behavior. Insofar as one encounters specifically religious fervor among the Jews, it is limited to scattered pockets of people. Some of these pockets are surprising, and we will want to have a closer look at them, but they hardly characterize the bulk of American Jewry.

Instead, it seems to me, Jews mostly have beliefs about what they are "supposed to" believe and do; when queried, their answers will reflect those perceptions rather than their own convictions. They themselves do not believe or do the things they imagine "good" Jews believe and do. Which means, obviously, that at some level very many Jews feel that they themselves are not "good" Jews.

This is, as I have said, a matter of surpassing importance. Jews see Judaism as a normative code that instructs them in proper belief and behavior. Insofar as they bother to think about the content of that normative code—beyond, say, the obvious injunction to "be nice" or "be a good person"—they become uncomfortably aware of the gap between being and believing, between their own Jewishness and the Judaism that dwells ominously off at a distance, judging them and declaring them inadequate.

This critical discrepancy runs through Jewish life today like a

massive fault line, and it is a major disincentive to Jewish commitment. Nor is it restricted to the contrast between the facts of the
"average" Jewish life and the norms of the imagined tradition. In
countless ways, the experience of Jewishness in America today is an
experience in inadequacy, an experience, therefore, in failure. Hebrew school is remembered by most Jews as the place they failed
to learn Hebrew.* Even those Jews who devote time to Jewish study
know that they are only dabbling at the edges, so vast is the Jewish
library. For that half of the Jews that contributes to Jewish philanthropy, there is only sometimes the sense of a job well and generously done; more often, they know (or are reminded) that they
might have given more, that their generosity is not commensurate
with the needs, which are constant and overwhelming.

These several examples might easily be multiplied many times
over. They skirt the edges of the renowned Jewish guilt. But it is not
my intention to focus on the matter of guilt. I mean instead to call
attention to the fact of an uncommonly successful generation, measured by the standards that are usually invoked to measure success
in America (education, wealth, status), that has not experienced
anything that feels like Judaic success. (We can, of course, speculate
that the depth of the American Jewish attachment to Israel is in part
due to the desire to experience, even if only vicariously, such success.)

All this gives rise to a peculiarly American version of the classical
problem of assimilation. Once upon a time, when legal and social
barriers blocked Jewish mobility at every turn, assimilation was
seen as one way to get to the other side, to the sweet smell of
success. (Back in the middle of the last century, a Russian Oriental-
ist named Daniel Chwolson chose to convert to Russian Orthodoxy.
The story has it that he was asked by a friend whether he had
converted out of conviction. His answer? "Yes, I was convinced that

---

*A recent study by New York's Board of Jewish Education concludes that "Conversational
Hebrew is the subject in which pupils showed the least knowledge and progress. The graph
indicates a slight increase in knowledge between Hebrew grades one and three, a steep decline
between Hebrew grades three and four and a steep drop between Hebrew grades five and
seven. There is a substantial increase from Hebrew grades seven to eight. But all that this
increase does is to bring the scores back up to the level of the first and second grade!" The
report goes on to say that pupils' scores in Jewish involvement and Jewish attitudes are
"passive and neutral," and that they decline annually. (The quotes are from the draft report
of the study.)

it is better to be a professor in St. Petersburg than a *melamed* [a schoolteacher] in Shnipishok.") Now, there are few external barriers. Yet it may be that for many Jews, being Jewish remains an impediment to success—not, in current circumstances, to secular success, to objective success, to a job in Tampa or Palo Alto, but to the sense of well-being, of internal satisfaction, they desire and to which, in the other arenas of their lives, they are accustomed.

So, for example, we remember—whether the memory is at all accurate or not hardly matters—the Passovers of our childhood. We remember the smells and the songs, the drama of the seder, the Passover meal. And we wonder why it is that our own seder seems so shriveled. We are embarrassed at its atrophy, at our awkward Hebrew and our hesitant singing. We leave the table stuffed, and empty; we know we have been poor caretakers of the tradition.

The consequence is that we look out at this vast thing called Judaism, this saga of woe and of wonder, through a lens of joylessness. We know, we have been taught, we sense, that out there, on the other side of the mist, it awaits us. But we do not know how to get from our barren place to the garden.

Some Jews, dispirited by the discrepancy they observe between their own capabilities and their perceptions of what it means to be a "good" Jew, give up, turn away. If the fact of Jewishness raises the problem of Judaism, so much the worse for the fact. They might have ignored the discrepancy, but as the Orthodox, first in Israel and now here, have become more visible and more voluble, have pressed their claim that theirs is the only authentic way, it has become impossible to ignore it. Convinced, as it were, of their own inauthenticity, but closed to the Orthodox alternative, they make themselves whole by making their Jewishness less salient, less relevant.

Others continue to muddle through, learn to live with contradiction. How is it, for example, that so many utterly secularized Jews respond generously to charitable appeals on behalf of ultra-Orthodox organizations? Even a cursory examination will reveal the gulf that separates the donor from the recipient—and a closer examination will show more than a gulf, will show that the ultra-Orthodox beneficiaries endorse a way of life that is not merely alien but wholly antithetical to the values of the secularized benefactor. So why the support? Not because "they" have the courage of "our" convictions, for theirs are not, in fact, our convictions. Perhaps, then, because yes, we accept that "without the Jewish religion, the Jewish people could not survive," and, knowing our own religious emptiness, believing, therefore, that it is they and not we who are the guarantors of the Jewish people, we wish to subsidize—to subsidize rather than to participate in—Jewish religious life. *Real* Jewish religious life, not the ersatz compromised versions we have chosen for ourselves. Participation in that real religion, the old-time religion, would ask too much of us; as we see it, even in expansive America, it would ask that we build walls we do not wish to build, that we risk closing ourselves off from America and its familiar and seductive bourgeois life, from modernity itself. Above all, it would require that we reconstruct our map of the world, placing the classic Jewish God, God the Father, the King, the supernatural, at its center. This is an option most Jews are not prepared seriously to consider, vastly preferring the confusions and compromises of an essentially agnostic Judaism to what they perceive—if they stop to look at all—as the confinements and the contradictions of traditional belief. If we have a god at all, it is not God the First Cause, but God the Last Resort, not the God of the heavens above, but the God of the foxhole below, the God to whom we turn and pray when we are sorely afraid, and only then.

So: We believe that God is central to Judaism, and we call ourselves Jews, but we are without God. This startling disjunction is a fracture of compound consequence, one that we seek to ignore but that necessarily haunts us. It is our collective secret, of which we never speak nor even whisper—perhaps not even to survey researchers. It is as if we have decided that some secrets are too disturbing to utter, as if we have agreed to live our lives as Jews in the presence of a cosmic wink.

These days, it is increasingly apparent that there are as well some Jews who will not let go, will neither abandon their Jewishness nor be satisfied with muddling through it. Their Passover seder may be disappointing, but stubbornly, they try again next year. Some even buy the books and tapes or attend the classes and workshops that will help us "renew our days as of old." If they perceive a divide between where they are and what they believe being Jewish implies, they seek to find a way across it. One way is a leap of faith, willing oneself from God as metaphor to Adonai, the Lord our God, King of the Universe. So we witness a stunning rise in neo-Orthodoxy, to the point where membership in such places as New York's (Orthodox) Lincoln Square Synagogue has achieved an almost "with-it" quality.

Another way, for those unable or unwilling to leap across the divide, is to craft a bridge. The goal is not faith but understanding, or, more often, community. One may seek to defeat the sense of inadequacy by study; the data are not conclusive, but it appears that more adult Jews participate in educational programs, often quite demanding, than attend weekly worship services. Or one may seek to defeat inadequacy by joining with others in a purposeful fellowship whose manifest function may be worship or study or philanthropy but whose latent function is community. The *havura* movement alone, which was born in the 1960s and is the most explicit institutional expression of the "bridge" of fellowship, includes some tens of thousands of Jews. (Conversations with members of Lincoln Square Synagogue suggest that community may be their principal motive, too, more important as a reason for their membership than specific religious conviction. The same likely holds as well for those who register for adult education courses.)

These are among the several ways in which America's Jews seek to formulate for themselves a meaning for Judaism in a land that is neither quite exile nor quite home, and they are an impressive testament to the stubbornness of those who pursue them. The surprising energy they reflect should not, however, be allowed to obscure the fact that it is inertia rather than an active will that moves the large majority of America's Jews. Most are carried along by meanings they cannot readily articulate; their lives as Jews are reflexive rather than examined.

Martin Buber once wrote that "We are carried along by a meaning we could never think up for ourselves, a meaning we are to live— not to formulate." But in Buber's view, to "live a meaning"—*as a*

Jew—means, necessarily, to live as a member of a community. Buber understood that the participants in a living community do not pause throughout the day to take their cultural bearings; instead, they absorb, through symbols and structures, through landscapes and language, the conceptions of their culture, its way of looking at the world.

It may be that Buber was right, that there is no other way, that without the living culture of community there is no meaning, no language, there are only slogans, folklore, and group interests. If so, we are obviously in trouble, since very few of us live within the parameters of organic Jewish communities. In our circumstances, we cannot assume that we will be "carried along" by a meaning that is implicit. We cannot take for granted that the unexamined Jewish life will, as Paul Mendes-Flohr puts it, "serve the modern Jew as a vehicle of signs, guiding his reflexes of imagination and intellect, and facilitating a meaningful organization of his passions and the ongoing experiences of his life. . . ." The Jewish culture that is available to us is too constricted and too artificial to serve so grand a purpose. More, a reflexive Judaism that is not sustained by a living culture cannot readily be passed on from generation to generation.

Therefore, Buber's advice notwithstanding, we have no choice but to try to formulate the meaning we are to live—and then to ensure, whether through the creation of community or in other ways, that it is more than a slogan. We are required to search out a vocabulary and a grammar for Jewish life that are accessible to those of us who want to talk Jewish but do not know how, and who will not accept the Orthodox claim that theirs is the sole authentic language available to us. That is no small assignment for an agglomeration of geographically scattered people of disparate backgrounds and beliefs, immersed as we obviously and necessarily are in American culture. But I do not accept that we are restricted to this thing called "Jewishism." I believe instead that being Jewish affords us the opportunity to define a Judaism that is pleasing, that can help us feel—and be—fulfilled as human beings. I do not accept that we are stuck with a joyless Judaism that comes as a reminder of our own inadequacy, that we are condemned to Jewishness as only a circumstance, an accident, a condition. I believe instead that we can find a path to Judaic achievement and success, that we can impose intention upon our condition, and find thereby sustaining—and redemptive—meaning.

The place to begin is with an examination of the implicit choices America's Jews have made, with the commitments that do, for the time being, carry us along. We cannot "formulate" a meaning in a vacuum; we must first look to the fragments of meaning that already exist. We need to know why and how they work, and what their limits are. And so we turn now to the two extraordinary events that our generation has witnessed—the Holocaust and the birth of Israel—and to the obsession with Jewish survival that is their product. These are the central reflexive Jewish meanings of our time, and we want to understand both their power and the ways in which they fall short as answers to the question of Jewish meaning.

4

Mourning as Meaning: The Holocaust

SOMETIMES I WONDER what it would have been like to grow up as an American Jew, in the second half of the twentieth century, had there been no Auschwitz. No Auschwitz, no Treblinka, no Maidenek, no Sobibor, no camps, no bunkers, no cruelty beyond the inherent cruelties of war, no slaughter of one third of my people. How would American Jewish children have been taught Jewish history had the Holocaust never happened?

For the Kingdom of Night was not the first sorrow to be visited upon the Jews. Temples had been destroyed, there'd been exiles and dispersions, rapes and burnings at the stake, the Inquisition and the Crusades, ghettos and pogroms—all these had been visited upon us long and shortly before, and were central elements of what we were taught of Jewish history.

Or were they what we remembered of what we were taught? Or were they central, whether to the teaching or to its memory, only because there had been a Holocaust, only because we knew the way the story ended and no other sequence but the stories of sorrow and suffering could anticipate, could bring us to that ending? Inevitably, we cheat when we remember the day before yesterday, because we already know and cannot forget what happened yesterday; if yesterday had been different, would we have learned and remembered other things about the days before? If there'd been no Holocaust, would we still learn that our history is one of suffering and persecution, of pogrom and travail, would coming to awareness as a Jew still seem so sinister an initiation, would we still so sharply feel ourselves a people apart?

We might; the evidence is there, after all. Yet there is reason to believe that earlier generations of Jews were considerably less preoccupied than we are with the saga of our suffering, made more out of the achievements than out of the agonies, the triumphs than the tragedies. Perhaps, without the Holocaust to work back from, to find a historic logic for, we'd have worked at explaining our durability, or our passion, or any of the other things that seem distinctive about us.

But there was the Holocaust, and now it is anti-Semitism, the fact that people have hated us, hated us enough to murder, hated us enough to be silent in the face of the murdering, that seems the most distinctive thing, the one most worth remembering and knowing. What is the first lesson a Jew learns? That people want to kill Jews. Whether the Holocaust was a culmination or an aberration makes no difference to the dead, and little difference to those who remember. Either way, the memory overwhelms.

I count myself among those who are, these days, concerned with the trivialization and exploitation of the Holocaust, disturbed by the degree to which the memory of it crowds out other memories, displaces reason, depresses hope. Yet I know as well that the world of the aftermath is not the same as the world before, cannot be. People talk about the impossibility of putting the nuclear genie back in the bottle, of pretending that we do not know about nuclear energy. As well pretend there was no Holocaust. One understands the impulse so to pretend, for to confront the truth is more sobering and more frightening than the sobering and frightening confrontation with the truth of nuclear energy. (The one is principally about danger; the other is about evil.) But we cannot, in the end, sustain our innocence. To be a Jew in America, or anywhere, today is to carry with you the consciousness of limitless savagery. It is to carry that consciousness with you not as an abstraction, but as a reality; not, God help us all, only as memory, but also as possibility.

In a remarkable passage in *The Anatomy Lesson,* Philip Roth tells how the narrator's stricken mother is asked by her neurologist to write her name on a piece of paper. And then:

> She took the pen from his hand and instead of "Selma" wrote the word "Holocaust," perfectly spelled. This was in Miami Beach in 1970, inscribed by a woman whose writing otherwise consisted of recipes on index cards, several thousand thank-you notes, and a voluminous file of knitting instructions. . . . But she had a tumor in her head the size of a lemon, and it seemed to have forced out everything except the one word. That it couldn't dislodge. It must have been there all the time without their even knowing.

How could it be otherwise? It will be said that we have tumors in our head, that we are paranoid, that we are obsessed, that we are distorted by the experience. It will be said that we are trapped by our past, that we have come to wallow in a kind of morbid fascination, that we have made ourselves into victims. After all, that was then, and them; no numbers have been tattooed on *our* arms.

Not us, but only because we happened not to be there. Not us, but our family. Not us, but the heart of world Jewry. And even if not us, or our kin, what then? We fear not only for ourselves, but also for our world, a world that now and evermore contains such horrendous possibilities, whoever is next time's victim. Before there was a Holocaust, such a thing could not be imagined; it could not happen, ever, not anywhere. But it did happen, it has happened. And if those to whom it happened most directly—indirectly, it happened to all humankind—now cry a warning, who is to say that they are excessively preoccupied?

Foreign dignitaries who visit Israel are routinely taken by their hosts to a place called Yad Vashem, a Holocaust memorial on an isolated hilltop in western Jerusalem. As such exhibits go, this one is dramatically understated, but the visitors are invariably moved. Whether they see what they are intended to see and conclude from what they have seen what they are intended to conclude, we cannot quite know. Most of them say the right words, go through the right motions. But the purpose of taking them to the place is not to elicit those words, those motions. It is to indicate to them how we see ourselves.

We see ourselves as survivors. And some of us see ourselves as victims. When they say it is over, we do not believe them. How can we, why should we? We do not understand and never will how it happened once, so there is no way for us to know, to know in our bones, that it will not happen again. We know only that for the time being, very many people are ashamed and embarrassed that it happened. So we play on the shame and the embarrassment, try to extend the time being for another day, and another. We remind people.

On January 2, 1987, John Cardinal O'Connor, Archbishop of New York, was a visitor at Yad Vashem. *The New York Times* reported that he "walked through the museum silently, nodding his head in disbelief, the pain of what he saw visible in his face." What did he see? "This is totally indescribable. I can't talk about it. It's a mystery to me." But his hosts "hoped that by understanding the history of anti-Jewish persecution and Israel's vulnerability in the Arab world, the Cardinal would appreciate why Israel finds it difficult to make such concessions to the Palestinians as the surrender of the West Bank." Yitzhak Arad, chairman of Yad Vashem: "If at that time there had been a Jewish state, things would have been different. The lesson we have learned from the Holocaust is what it means to be on the margins of mankind, to be vulnerable, to be dependent on the good will of other people."

When we remind others, we remind ourselves. And that is not always a healthy thing to do.

Leave aside the more egregious exploitation of the Holocaust. The murder of our kinsfolk within our living memory does not, after all, alter our merits and deserts at all, not an iota's worth. We do not earn exemption from tough judgment today because yesterday we suffered. So we are wrong when we claim special indulgence, as sometimes we do. And we are as wrong when we succumb to the temptation to dredge up the gory details in order to stimulate Jewish tears and Jewish solidarity, Jewish energies or Jewish philanthropy. (It is a temptation, since there is no surer device to elicit the tears and the rest.)

Should a people's fixation on its murdered children be dismissed as merely an example of morbid fascination, or as a manipulative device? And if sometimes it spills over into these, does that mean these are all there is, does that in any way diminish the sorrow, the pity, the terror?

The sorrow and the pity and the terror are internal. They are not merely a part of our baggage that we might, if we chose, discard; they are a dye that colors everything else. They are our brain tumor.

The exploitation is a device; its vulgarity condemns it, it will pass. The danger comes from the internal distortions, the ones that bend and twist us in ways that are not obvious, in ways we sometimes do not see. The danger is that we will come (have come?) to see the Holocaust as the most important thing that ever happened to us, even the richest, the one most filled with consequence and implication.

It is not just the magnitude of the event that gives rise to the danger; it is also who we are and the kinds of questions we ask.

A question Jews ask: What does it mean to be a Jew? If it means to believe in a particular doctrine, how is that doctrine defined? We look around and see a dozen different doctrines, each called Judaism; we look inside ourselves and find we subscribe to none.

Nor does it mean to live to the beat of the Jewish calendar, which once upon a time used to mark (and for a handful still does) the times of the day, of the week, of the month and the year, the times for prayer and for celebration. "Where are we?" a Jew would ask, and the answer was that we are in the week of the Sabbath on which we read this chapter or that from the Torah, and that was all the answer that was required. A very different clock now regulates our hours, our seasons.

Culture? Here and there, a shard, no more. A culture of fading memories, not sustained by living experience.

No, all we know is that we are, in some fundamental way, Jews, heirs to a legacy we cannot fluently describe, partners in a destiny we cannot define, people of a book we have not read. We yearn for some sign, some mark that will indicate to us in a way we can comprehend what it is that's special about the Jews.

Along comes the Holocaust, and makes us special. It's not the kind of special we'd have chosen, but there it is, ours by right, and awesomely substantial. If you have the Holocaust, what more do you need? Other answers may be more precise, but none is more comprehensive.

And if the Holocaust becomes a definition, then you don't have to hunt for other answers, other ways of defining yourself. Who are the Jews? The Jews are the people who, within living memory, lost a third of their number, the people who were hunted and hanged in this, the twentieth century, the people with the numbers tattooed on their forearms.

Jewish tradition has a different use for the forearm. Each weekday morning, Jewish men wind a leather thong around their arm in the course of their prayers: "And you shall bind them as a sign upon your hand." But that is a tradition preserved by very, very few Jewish males in our day. In choosing to define ourselves more by tattoo than by thong—phylactery—we reveal a powerful truth about ourselves.

For what is the thong? It is a reminder that we are to "love the Lord our God with all our heart, with all our soul, with all our might." More specifically—and more threateningly—it is a reminder that we are to keep His commandments.

But the idea of commandment is not readily available to us. In our time, we are more taken with opinion than with commandment. Moreover, classical Judaism is quite specific regarding how God is to be loved. The kind of vague religiosity that passes for loving God hardly seems an adequate expression of Judaic intention. God is to be loved through taking His commandments to heart, through teaching them to our children, through remembering them and observing them that we may be holy.

"Holy" is a very far cry from the culinary (or even the landsmanschaft) ethnicity that used to serve as our connection. (Now, of course, you don't any longer have to be Jewish to eat bagels, or smoked salmon, any more than you have to be Italian to eat pasta.) "Holy" is a very far cry from the trivial pursuits that engage so much of our energy and attention. Most of all, "holy" is plain scary. In the name of holiness, books—and people—have been burnt; in the name of holiness, souls have been snatched; in the name of holiness, ideas have been suppressed.

In the name of holiness, passions have been aroused—and disappointed. Is it not safer, perhaps even healthier, to avoid passion than to risk its excess—and its disappointment? The gods have all failed: communism failed, and secularism failed, and science failed; none has brought its promised redemption.

These sundry gods have meant much to Jews, as has their failure. But the central failure of contemporary Jewish life, hence also the central disappointment, comes out of the camps: God is the god that failed.

So what passion can there be? Utopian passion is depleted, and messianic passion, the passion for the end of days, the eschaton, is drained. Passion can, perhaps, withstand uncertainty; can it survive hopelessness?

Holiness? Where does one search it out? What prophets enjoin it? When we seek respite from the traffic of our lives, it is to Las Vegas or Vail or such other places as we can afford that we repair, not to the mountaintop. Our rabbis, the best of them, the preachers, the pastors, the pedagogues, are not holy men and women, they make no such claims and would not be hired if they did. Now and again, in the synagogue or in the woods, in the bedroom or the nursery, in the concert hall or the theater, we are visited by a moment of transcendence, but we do not suppose we might live there, the air is too thin at the peak and besides, there's bread to be earned and the Super Bowl is on this afternoon.

At the heart of holiness there is affirmation. Our problem is not that we are reluctant to affirm, it is that we no longer know what can confidently be affirmed. All our erstwhile affirmations seem to have turned to ashes in our mouths. So we save what energy for affirmation we have for a handful of ritual occasions, whose majesty we can scarcely recall, and close ourselves off to expectation and surprise, without which there can be neither affirmation nor passion. Nor, therefore, holiness.

And if, as we have been taught, there's a connection between holiness and commandment, the problem is compounded. It is not that we object to the commandments we have been given; our objection, the objection we have learned in a culture that prefers fashion to commitment, regrets to repentance, opinion to conviction, is to the very idea of commandment. Indeed, to the degree to which we still yearn for the sacred, we are inclined to speak of "spirituality," a notion that permits us to yearn vaguely, to search for the sacred outside the realm of commandment.

And what, pray tell, has all this to do with the Holocaust?

If utopian passion, the passion of secular messianism or of religious messianism, is beyond our grasp, there is apocalyptic passion to replace it. If it's transcendence you want, and the peak is inaccessible, look to the abyss. If Sinai is too remote or too mysterious, look to Auschwitz. Holy means, does it not, rare, not ordinary? (No, that is not what it means, not at all, but that is what most of us suppose.) Look, then, to the exceptional, the unique. Look to the one thing that absolutely sets the Jews apart, that makes them special. Look to the chimneys, o the chimneys.

So we look. For a generation, we averted our eyes. Now we are far enough away that we can risk it, we will not be blinded if we enter, as connected visitors, this Kingdom of Night. Now, indeed, we can no longer tear our eyes away.

We do not know what it means, nor do we truly need it to mean anything. It is enough that it makes us feel, and beyond ourselves; it divests us of roles and routines, it puts us in touch with awe, with evil, with the absolute. It is a history we can almost touch, and it is so vast, and we so tiny, that to touch it, or even to nearly touch it, enlarges us. And the facts are on our side. The tragedy can be exploited, manipulated, trivialized; it cannot be exaggerated.

Nor, for that matter, can it be understood, though there is no lack of effort at understanding it. Did God die at Auschwitz, or did Man, or neither, or both? Was it a quirk, the product of one deranged hypnotic mind, or was it the victory of rational bureaucracy—or both, the achievement of insane goals by precise and orderly means? Was it banal, or horrific—or both? Could it have been prevented?

Could it have been interrupted? What should the Jews appointed by the Nazis to make up the lists for the deportations have done? Refused, thereby condemning their own families, thereby inviting the Nazis to name others, perhaps less decent, less fair, less able to negotiate an extra life here, an extra life there? Refused, thereby denying the executioner the complicity of his victim, disturbing the system's efficiency if only for an hour, a day? And what should the worker with the critical skill, offered an extra pass, either for his wife or for his daughter, have done? (Before this was Sophie's choice, it was another's, whose testimony was offered in a Jerusalem courtroom at the trial of Adolph Eichmann.) Refused the pass, condemning both wife and daughter, or chosen, condemning one—and, in a different way, himself? Where the most important thing, more important than compassion, is that the trains run on time, is it inevitable that the trains will come to be filled with boys and girls bound for slaughter?

And where was God? For the dying Jews, God's absence a terrifying rebuke; for those who survived, God's absence a grim riddle.

It does not derogate from the pain that others have suffered if we assert that the Holocaust was unique, remains unique. For this is not, withal, the slaughter of the Armenians, nor of the Cambodians, nor of the Biafrans. Grotesque, cruel, tragic beyond measure though these mass killings were, the Holocaust stands apart. There are Armenians and Cambodians and Biafrans alive today because their murderers won what they had set out to win, and then there was no "need" to kill more. There are European Jews alive today—not very many—only because the Nazis were defeated. Alone among the victims, the Jews were slaughtered for no reason at all. There was no dispute between the Nazis and the Jews over land, over jobs, over power, over anything. There was only the fact of the demonic Nazi purpose, to kill the Jews in order to make them dead.

How do you contend with such a fact? Where in your consciousness do you tuck away the awareness that just yesterday a normal people, a people in whose midst you'd lived, a people, so we say, of culture, resolutely managed so vast an industry of death, an industry whose explicit purpose was to "exterminate" each and every Jew? You tuck it away there, in the space reserved for tumors.

And you refuse to "understand" it. There is a danger in claiming it can be understood, in regarding it as merely an unusually tragic event, yet within the normal categories of history. When a mass audience watches "Holocaust" on television, a Jew who watches wonders: Will people whose memories and experiences are limited to the "normal" not wonder whether, for all that the Nazis were plainly beasts, the Jews must not have done *something* to bring this horror upon themselves? We have no categories for national madness, after all; we are taught that everything has a rational explanation, if only we search for it with sufficient energy and intelligence. Might not one such explanation be that the Jews were—how shall we put it?—not entirely innocent?

Some deeply Orthodox Jews, who see God's hand in every detail of the human experience, believe that the Holocaust was a divine punishment. But in the more conventional historical view, the view that is rooted in experience rather than theology, no Jew is prepared to accept the notion that the Jews were, in any sense at all, accessories to the crime. We may chastise ourselves for our sloth, for our naivete, for our passivity, for all manner of human failing. But even if all the criticisms are warranted, we will not accept that the victim is to be blamed.

Instead, our scholars chronicle in considerable detail the roots of the thing: the tradition of Christian anti-Semitism, the specific circumstances of Germany from 1879 on, the particulars of the Jewish experience in Germany and throughout the West in the wake of the emancipation—and then they fold in the madness. In short, they identify the circumstances in which madness may flourish, may be transformed into public policy. They engage in rational analysis of irrational behavior.

But the madness is not a deus ex machina, a random variable that drops in to explain that which cannot otherwise be explained. And there is danger in holding, as some of us do, that it is. For then the Holocaust stands outside history, cannot be adequately understood by reference to history. How, if that be so, guard against its recurrence? (Ironically, the separation of the Holocaust from history is precisely the goal of the most virulent current anti-Semites, who do not assert—whatever they privately believe—that the Jews deserved what happened to them. Instead, they argue that it never happened at all.)

But we, who have been its victims in more modest ways through the centuries, recall, or should, that madness—and not just the madness of anti-Semitism—is ever-present, is history's warp, that it lurks just beneath the surface, and that although we may not yet know how to expunge it, we do know how to restrain it, how to inhibit its expression. We, for whom such madness is inevitably both memory and possibility, must insist that it *is* history, and that the polity must guard against those conditions that might ignite it, that shape madness into social doctrine.

We resent, of course, the efforts to universalize the Holocaust, whether by including it as one in a long and still growing list of this century's depredations, or by including it as just another in the long (and growing?) list of calamities the Jews have experienced, or by mourning, in the same breath, all the civilian dead of World War II.

Part of our resentment is instinctive, and easily understood. It is no consolation to the bereaved to observe, while they are still in mourning, that others, too, have been killed. There is no comfort in such grim statistics. People are entitled to experience their grief as a unique event; so, too, a people. Humankind knows tragedy; it is *we* who know *this* tragedy.

And part of our resentment derives from the analytic ways, limited though they be, in which we comprehend the event. The other civilian dead died in other ways and for other reasons, more often than not sporadically, randomly, sometimes for no better reason than that they were in the wrong place at the wrong time. But for Europe's Jews, there was no place that was not wrong.

And part of our resentment derives from the fact that we are obsessed by the Holocaust. It cannot be understood, but we cannot stop trying to understand it. Somehow, it *must* mean something. We will wrestle the meaning out of it.

And then, only then, only after all the natural instincts and the unavoidable obsessions and the thoughtful analyses are done, there is also the fact that we resent those who would take it away from us. We need it. We need it not only because every people needs all its history, the good and the bad, but also because this people, the Jews, no longer knows where else to look for its connection. We need it as motive.

So Emil Fackenheim, distinguished and eloquent theologian, proposes that we must add to the traditional list of 613 commandments a 614th: "The authentic Jew of today is forbidden to hand Hitler yet another, posthumous victory." And we come to see the living of a Jewish life as a form of defiance. So we engage in a veritable orgy of Holocaust museum construction—and learn that it is far easier to raise money for the construction of such museums than it is, say, to offer higher wages to the scandalously underpaid teachers in Jewish schools. So the announcement by Jewish organizations of "missions" that include a visit to the death camps in their itinerary has become commonplace. So the Simon Wiesenthal Center for Holocaust Studies, in Los Angeles, an institution that at the time of its creation was widely viewed as entirely redundant with existing efforts, has become (by far) the most successful solicitor of contributions of any domestic Jewish organization.

These activities are all, of course, well intentioned. My point here is not that one ought not visit the death camps or build museums. My point is that the explosion of Holocaust-related activities tells us something about how we have come to understand Jewish history. The problem here is that in the absence of more comprehensive understandings, the Holocaust now threatens to become the starting point for Jewish life. And the Holocaust is simply not where Jewish life begins nor where it ends. Auschwitz is not our switching station, to which all roads lead, from which all roads go out. It is not the most important or even the most interesting thing that ever happened to us.

Sinai, whether or not it happened, and whether or not we can cope with it, is the most important thing that ever happened to us.

But the Holocaust is relentlessly perplexing, and—in our present circumstances, so very distant from the mountaintop are we—the most riveting.

The fact that we cannot understand the Holocaust, and may never, does not inhibit our effort to find some purchase, some fragmentary wisdom we can grab hold of and use to keep our balance.

So we make our sociological and political assertions, so we debate the response of American Jewry between 1933 and 1945, so we shout a warning and tell a cautionary tale to all who will listen.

Here is an understanding to grab hold of: The evil genius of the Nazis was not in their invention and perfection of instruments of mass extermination. Were that all that set them apart, they would long since have lost their status as the most sinister slaughterers of our time. Alas, our technical efficiency at causing mass death has long since surpassed their achievements, which now seem quite old-fashioned.

What sets the Nazis apart—one hopes, despairingly, for all time— is their dehumanization of their victims before killing them. Here is Abba Kovner, poet, hero of the Vilna Ghetto resistance: "The most appalling thing in the Ghetto was not death. It was infinitely more terrible to be defiled to the depth of your soul every hour of the day for twenty-five months—and to wait . . . to look at life by the mercy of the butcher."

Note, please: Kovner is not making the conventional sermonic point that it is easier to kill people if you do not perceive them and relate to them as human beings. He is not asserting that a society that permits dehumanization will, sooner or later, come to genocide. While these connections may exist, he is making a rather different point. He is saying that the dehumanization, in and of itself, is worse than death—or, at least, more appalling, more terrible, than death. This will doubtless seem a touch hyperbolic to many of us, for our usual assumption is that death by violence is the most terrible thing there is. But those who have read of those days, those places, will readily understand what Kovner intends and that he does not exaggerate. Death is worst only because it alone is final, not because it is most terrible.

Nor can I conclude this thought without adding that it was not only the victims who were dehumanized. Those who gave the orders, those who pulled the triggers, those who smashed the babies' skulls, yes, and those who idly watched—not all, not even very many of them, were monsters. In order to do what they did, they had to close down large parts of themselves.

The appropriate sermonic conclusion, which I note only in passing, is that one need not be a Nazi to defile people to the depths of their souls. The ovens of death are cold, for now, but families are still forced to stand naked before each other.

The non-sermonic conclusion, the conclusion wrested from out of the depths, belongs to a survivor. It is Primo Levi's, in his *Survival in Auschwitz*. A week after his own arrival in Auschwitz, Levi encounters his friend Steinlauf in the washroom. Steinlauf is vigorously washing himself, though there is no soap and the water is brackish. Levi cannot understand his purpose, his waste of energy and warmth, and Steinlauf explains:

> It grieves me now that I have forgotten his plain, outspoken words, the words of ex-sergeant Steinlauf of the Austro-Hungarian army, Iron Cross of the '14–'18 war. It grieves me because it means that I have to translate his uncertain Italian and his quiet manner of speaking of a good soldier into my language of an incredulous man. But this was the sense, not forgotten either then or later: that precisely because the Lager was a great machine to reduce us to beasts, we must not become beasts; that even in this place one can survive, and therefore one must want to survive, to tell the story, to bear witness; and that to survive we must force ourselves to save at least the skeleton, the scaffolding, the form of civilization. We are slaves, deprived of every right, exposed to every insult, condemned to certain death, but we still possess one power, and we must defend it with all our strength for it is the last—the power to refuse our consent. So we must certainly wash our faces without soap in dirty water and dry ourselves on our jackets. We must polish our shoes, not because the regulation states it, but for dignity and propriety. We must walk erect, without dragging our feet, not in homage to Prussian discipline but to remain alive, not to begin to die.

And here is another small piece of understanding: What happened to us did not make us into saints. It conferred no moral distinction upon us. It did not even earn us the right to tell the story, for the story belongs to anyone who takes it to heart. The only difference is that where others have the right, we have the responsibility—"to tell the story, to bear witness."

The temptation runs in a different direction. Beleaguered still, we invoke the memory of the Holocaust to stifle our enemies. When the foreign dignitaries are taken to Yad Vashem, we are not clear whether we want them simply to understand, in a very literal way, where we are coming from, what events have helped shape us, or whether we mean to inhibit their response to us by presenting ourselves as a people of convalescents to whom one speaks gently. We are not clear because we ourselves do not know.

It is time for us to begin knowing. The routine invocation of the Holocaust, for whatever instrumental purpose, is no longer (if ever it was) an acceptable form of argument, whether the argument is for the purpose of raising money for Jewish causes or for the purpose of winning friends for Jewish interests. The issue here is not time, not the fact that more than forty years have passed since the camps were liberated and the remnant that was left began the work of reconstruction. The issue is, instead, that we risk the dilution and distortion of the tale's significance if we use it to draw attention to our special circumstances. Our cautionary tale is more likely to be heard, attended, if it is seen not as special pleading but as testimony. We, the living, the survivors and their kin, are witnesses, not victims.

Not victims.

Sometimes we forget that, and our forgetting is not merely for purposes of eliciting the sympathy of others. We sometimes forget it even when we are with each other, or alone. Often, we perceive Jewish life as a succession of calamities, either actually experienced or only narrowly averted. Each year at our Passover seder, we read that "in every generation, our enemies rise up to destroy us," and that is part of the consciousness we carry with us, part of what we are taught, part of what we believe we cannot afford to forget.

So Nelly Sachs, Nobel Laureate in Literature, 1966, could write, "We rehearse tomorrow's death even today while the old dying still wilts within us."

If there is recurrent evidence of anti-Semitism, we are perversely comforted; the world remains familiar, this is the world as we have come to understand it. We do not know what tomorrow will bring, but we can make an educated guess; underneath our street clothes, we imagine a shroud.

Is that not the reasonable response of a people that knows "it" can happen anywhere—the more so if we do not fully understand why it happened when and where it did? Yet it is not merely a demoralizing response, it is also an inadequate response. Is our purpose to prepare for the next holocaust—or to prevent it?

And it is a distorted response, for it omits the central post-Holocaust fact of Jewish life. Here, in Nelly Sachs's "Chorus of Comforters," we learn what the Holocaust *might* have meant for us, forever:

> We are gardeners who have no flowers.
> No herb may be transplanted
> From yesterday to tomorrow.
> The sage has faded in the cradles—
> Rosemary lost its scent facing the new dead—
> Even wormwood was only bitter yesterday.
> The blossoms of comfort are too small
> Not enough for the torment of a child's tear.
>
> New seed may perhaps be gathered
> In the heart of a nocturnal singer.
> Which of us may comfort?
> In the depth of the defile
> Between yesterday and tomorrow
> The cherub stands
> Grinding the lightning of sorrow with his wings
> But his hands hold apart the rocks
> Of yesterday and tomorrow
> Like the edges of a wound
> Which must remain open
> That may not yet heal.
>
> The lightnings of sorrow do not allow
> The field of forgetting to fall asleep.
> Which of us may comfort?
> We are gardeners who have no flowers
> And stand upon a shining star
> And weep.

Yet precisely between our yesterday and our tomorrow, there where the lightning of sorrow is ground, there in the barren defile, Israel has happened.

I must be careful here, very careful. I do not want to suggest, not at all, that Israel is the Redemption, or even, as our prayer puts it, "the beginning of the flowering of our redemption," much less that it is in some way a cosmic compensation for the loss we suffered. My concern here is not with the vast cosmos, but only with gardening and seeds, and then with flowers.

I do not accept that Israel exists in spite of the Nazis; no seeds grow where spite is the gardener's fertilizer. Nor do I accept that Israel exists because of the Holocaust. This common view derives from the belief that only the sympathy of the United Nations, in the aftermath of the Holocaust, caused it to endorse the idea of an independent Jewish state. But the British, then the mandate authority in Palestine, were in any case withdrawing from their imperial responsibilities around the world, for their reasons, not for ours. Their timing might have been different by a year or two, but they'd surely have left, and we'd have made a state out of what was already our home. And had there been no Holocaust, that state would have been able to draw on what was then the largest and richest pool of human resources in Jewish life, on European Jewry, to help in the work of nation building.

I reject the "from ashes to rebirth" metaphor not only because it seems to me wrong, but also because it leads in perverse directions. There are those who to this day deny Israel's legitimacy as a nation state. As they read—or misread—history, they conclude that a sudden and perfectly understandable wave of sympathy for the Jews led the nations of the world to impose upon the Middle East an alien presence. Why, they ask, should the Arabs be made to pay the price for Europe's sins?

But modern Zionism began in 1881–82, not in 1945. It was Zionism, and not the world's sympathy, that brought forth a Jewish state. Without the sympathy, the details of the story would have been quite different, but its central fact would almost surely have been the same.

The confusion here is plainly the result of the temporal association of the two events. Scarcely three years after the liberation, the Jewish state came into being. The interesting, the compelling question concerning the linkage is not about its politics; it is about its poetry.

How could a people so brutally cast down, a people without

flowers, take up again the work of gardening? How could a despondent people find room for hope?

Here, then, is the last small piece of understanding: If we are a witness people, what we can attest to is not only man's capacity for evil but also man's capacity for hope.

Without Israel, the evidence for futility would have been unrebutted. To be a Jew, part of this stiff-necked people, is to know that the seeds you plant in the morning may well be trampled before night; that is surely the lesson of our tragedies. But it is also to know that you must go back the next morning, and plant yet again, though your anxieties are entirely intact, while your heart is still breaking; that is surely the lesson Israel brings to us.

It is, in any case, the lesson American Jews learned. Without Israel, it is hard to imagine how we would have rejected despair. And that, of course, is why we have invested such grand hopes in Israel. It is not "merely" home to nearly 4 million of the world's Jews, it is our best evidence for the reasonableness of hope. It is a garden, after all, with a profusion of flowers—and, inevitably, some weeds.

Of the flowers and the weeds and how we perceive them, I will say some things in the next chapters. But first, a final word here.

It is exceedingly painful to write of these things. The pain is not only because the events to which I have alluded are so wrenching; it is also because there is no one who writes of them who does not know his or her own inadequacy. We do what we can to contain it within our notions and our syllables, but what we can do is never nearly enough. For this reason, I conclude not with a summary thought to cap this discourse. I conclude, instead, as discussions of these matters must conclude. Here is a poem by Dan Pagis, himself a survivor; its title is "Written in Pencil in the Sealed Railway-Car":

> here in this carload
> i am eve
> with abel my son
> if you see my other son
> cain son of man
> tell him i

5

Israel as Meaning: The Faith, the Place

If they show me a stone
And I say stone
They say stone.
If they show me a tree
And I say tree
They say tree.
But if they show me blood
And I say blood
They say paint.
If they show me blood
And I say blood
They say paint.
—Amir Gilboa

MY EARLIEST MEMORIES of Israel antedate the day in May of 1948 when Israel became again an independent state. I know where I was and what I was doing on November 29, 1947, when the news came that the United Nations had voted to partition Palestine into two states, one Arab, the other Jewish. I remember, even earlier, joining with my boyhood friends in Baltimore to paste stickers on every lamppost we could find: "Get the British out of Palestine."

And I remember, some weeks before Israel's independence—I was then not yet fourteen—my first introduction to the problematic of a Jewish state.

I was walking with my father, and we were talking about the imminent event. I imagine—I have no specific recollection—that I thought it an unmitigated and uncomplicated blessing. Were those hardy swamp drainers and tree planters, those heroic kibbutz builders and freedom fighters, not entitled? Had they not earned by their sweat and their blood, by their passion and their purpose, the right to independence? And were we not, as a people, owed?

And then my father asked: "Do you think that the president of Israel must be a Jew?"

I tried to bend my child's mind around the question. I do not know whether my father was expressing his own sense of the contradictions inherent in the Zionist endeavor or whether he was merely trying to exercise my mind. Nor do I recall how, if at all, I answered his question, how I tried to sort out the different meanings of Israeliness and Jewishness. I remember only my sharp sense of frustration, as if an ominous cloud had suddenly blocked the sunlight.

That cloud has stayed with me through nearly forty years and more than forty visits to Israel. Often enough, the sunlight breaks through, or at least illuminates its edges. But the cloud is always there, a warning that nothing is quite so simple as we might wish, as our sunlit illusions imply, as a thirteen-year-old might believe— or as a veteran Lover of Zion might wish to believe.

If our problem in dealing with the Holocaust is how to come to grips—and to terms—with its reality, our problem in dealing with Israel is how to come to grips—and to terms—with its illusion.

The vagueness of the boundary between illusion and reality has auspicious roots. The Jewish tradition has long distinguished between the heavenly and the earthly Jerusalem. For most of the early Zionists, and for many of their offspring, the Zionist effort was not merely intended to "normalize" the Jewish condition, but to create, in the tangible hills of Judea, a heavenly city. Even the most pragmatic, the least traditional, Zionists were interested in far more than a refuge for the persecuted of their people; they, too, harbored utopian aspirations. Normalization was a means, utopia (variously defined) the end. I have already cited the words of one of the best-known songs of the pioneering generation, "We have come to the land to build it—and to be rebuilt by it." Though the pragmatists spoke of making in Israel "a nation like all the nations," none truly believed that the Jews were an ordinary people. This was, they supposed, an extraordinary people—or, at the very least, an ordinary people to whom extraordinary things keep on happening. And they fully intended that the Zion they were pragmatically building, one dunam at a time, be a "light unto the nations."

This transcendental view of Israel has fared somewhat better here in America than it has in Israel, where it is harder to ignore the sweaty facts of daily life. Here it has withstood nearly all the assaults of these past four decades; in the mind of most American Jews, the imagined Jerusalem has overwhelmed the data from the earthly Jerusalem. Indeed, much of the story of how American Jews have sought to fit Israel into their lives has to do precisely with the interaction between the two Jerusalems, with the ways in which we have managed—or failed to manage—the tensions between the Israel of our dreams and the Israel of our experience, between the ordinary and the extraordinary Israel.

The story is inherently intricate, for Israel's history has been so frenetic, so dense with development, that there is no obvious point of entry to it, no coherent outline for it, no paradigmatic event that can serve as symbol for the whole of it. Instead, we watch—and respond—as a dozen different slide projectors, set to different speeds, some in perfect focus, some badly blurred, cast their dizzying images on the multiple screens. And the screens are not across two oceans; they are inside our heads, our hearts.

In the fall of 1985, there was a tragic accident near Petach Tikvah, a town outside Tel Aviv. A school bus was hit by a train, and twenty-two children were killed. The news made the morning broadcasts and papers in America, and the Jewish response here—as in Israel—was acute grief.

School bus accidents are no novelty in America; once or twice a week, it seems, usually in some faraway place, such tragedies occur. We hear the news, and there is a fleeting—very fleeting—sympathetic response. Unless the tragedy is personal, we go about our business.

And that is precisely the point: Israel is not a faraway place to us, and Israel's tragedies—and triumphs—are personal for us, even when the victims are nameless. A 1983 survey of American Jewish opinion* confirms the more general context: 77 percent of the respondents agreed that "if Israel were destroyed, I would feel as if I had suffered one of the greatest personal tragedies of my life."

Yet when I ask my friends to explain their reaction—and mine—to the Petach Tikvah bus tragedy, they have little to say, beyond acknowledging the deeply personal sense of loss they experienced.

How shall we try to understand it? What makes so faraway a place so near to us?

There is, first, the association of Israel with the Holocaust. Whether or not that association is perceived in theological terms, the coincidence in time between our learning the full dimensions of the European tragedy and our rejoicing at Israel's independence has irretrievably linked the two events. As I suggested at the end of the last chapter, one need not impute a causal connection of any kind, metaphysical or empirical, in order to experience the linkage between the ashes and the rebirth. It is enough to know that on the morrow of our misery we ascended the mountain. And so it is that we say to one another, and often, that Israel is our response—to God, to the nations, to ourselves—in the aftermath. We bled, but did not break. We found the strength to plant again. Israel becomes our best evidence that, in spite of everything, hope is not absurd: Israel as affirmation.

And then there are the photographs, the tens of thousands of photographs of Jews disembarking from the boats, from the planes, and falling into the arms of their loved ones. There have been other photographs since, including the stunning one of the young soldier,

---

*The survey was sponsored by the American Jewish Committee and directed by Steven M. Cohen. It is one of an annual series, to which I henceforward refer as "Cohen" followed by the appropriate year.

fully armed, leaning in ecstatic exhaustion against the Western Wall just hours after Jerusalem's reunification in 1967. But none speaks as clearly, as unambiguously to American Jews as those earlier pictures, those of Jews coming home, coming home from the Kingdom of Night, coming home to hope. The first truth is that before it is anything else, Israel is haven.

And it is opportunity as well. We will never know whether or not some of those who perished might have been saved if American Jews had more vigorously protested Germany's treatment of the Jews from 1933 to 1945. In the event, our protest was muted, at best. The full recognition of how shameful our silence was has come upon us slowly; the more we have found the strength and the voice to press our diverse concerns in the years since 1945, the more we have come to realize how wrong we were to be so passive in the years before.

The homecoming to Israel has given us, as it were, a second chance. Meir Kahane did not invent the slogan "Never again," nor will it disappear when he has finally become merely a disturbing footnote to the Jewish history of our time. For American Jews "Never again" means quite simply never again to be silent in the face of threats to Jewish safety. Whatever the subsequent facts of Israel's development, its prior significance to American Jews is in those tears of reunion and salvage, and in the opportunity Israel affords us to do what we did not do when Jewish life was last in jeopardy.

And there is also this: Israel captures perfectly our understanding of the great themes of Jewish history. On the one hand, it is proof of Jewish virtue; on the other, it is proof of Jewish vulnerability.

Jewish virtue? What of the spies and the cover-ups, what of the religious fanatics, what of the tawdry politics, what of all the lapses, the sins of omission and yes, of commission, too? Is it not by now plain that the children of Berl and his friends in fact have faltered, have come to hunt, have even perhaps become hunters?

To a new generation, not insulated by memory, that may be the way it appears. The rest of us still remember what we were taught, and what we saw: The Israelis wanted peace, the Arabs chose war; the Israelis planted, the Arabs uprooted; when the Israelis killed, they wept, but when the Arabs killed, they exulted. Golda Meir once said that she could forgive the Arabs anything, even their killing, but she could never forgive them for having forced us into killing. It is likely that at the time she said it, she meant it. We, in any event, took her remark as yet another confirmation of our moral superiority, of our redeeming virtue.

I reread these words, recall these sentiments, and realize how much has happened these past years, or how much we have learned. Once, days after the Six Day War, I traveled to Jericho, a lush oasis in the Jordan Valley rift, now for the first time since 1948 accessible from Israel. Across the road, just outside Jericho's city limits, were two abandoned refugee camps, home until just days earlier to some tens of thousands of Palestinian Arabs. Here and there, a shack of corrugated tin; for the most part, adobe huts, sand growing out of sand. And nowhere, nineteen years of time after the camps were established, nowhere a tree. A half-hour's drive away, in Israel, a society that had for decades engaged in an orgy of tree planting, that had embraced its refugees and provided each with warmth, with shade. And here, no tree. The evidence of my eyes supported the categories of my mind: To us, each human life is precious; not so for them.

That visit was more than half Israel's history ago; since 1967, Israel has been master of the West Bank. Whether my conclusions of 1967 were warranted even then, I can no longer say with any confidence. Golda Meir's sentimentalism notwithstanding, I have by now seen too many weeping Arab mothers to believe, as once I did, that our children are more precious to us than theirs to them. I do not mean that all the moral categories and distinctions have collapsed; I mean instead that after two decades of Israel as occupying nation, the categories are much less compelling, the distinctions not nearly so precise and reassuring.

But that is my own view, and for all that America's Jews may lately have come somewhat closer to it, it does not capture the competing truth to which many, perhaps most, still cling. *That* truth is that Israel's flaws, such as they are, are the consequence of Arab enmity, its imperfections the fault of others, that Golda was right, that left to its own devices, Israel would have been and one day yet will be a light unto the nations. And that if for now it's not, that's more because the nations are blind to Israel's light than because the light itself has dimmed. For these, Israel is virtue, and vulnerability; beloved of God, rejected by man, Israel is Jewish history encapsulated. Israel is confirmation.

And there is also and again Sinai, and our continuing effort to avoid and evade it. Israel has become for us a binding Jewish cement, a powerful explanation of the Jewish connection. So long as Israel is imperiled, we need not search any farther—or so we suppose—for a rationale that will justify our persistence as Jews, will provide a collective Jewish purpose. And we prefer it that way, for to resume the search would mean once again to confront the possibility that it will lead us to the base of the mountain, where, according to our tradition, all of us—the dead, the living, the still unborn—stood as the earth trembled, as the mountain itself shook, as we became a covenanted people. The secular covenant—our oath that Israel shall live—is far more suited to the modern temper, far more easily accessible, far less mysterious and threatening.

I have been saying "we" throughout these paragraphs, using the pronoun indiscriminately to refer both to American Jews (enthusiasts and skeptics alike) and to Jews both here and in Israel. That is also part of the story. For an American Jew, the choice of pronoun is both revealing and unsettling. The level of identification with the ongoing saga of our kinsfolk in Israel makes "we" the preferred pronoun—until we arrive as visitors in Israel itself, where suddenly the "we" becomes inappropriate, an unseemly presumption.

We say "we" for good Zionist reasons. Israel is conceived as the possession of the Jewish people, not only of its inhabitants, and the conception has practical implications. In the first decade of this century, for example, the Jewish National Fund was created in order to purchase land in Palestine. Funds were solicited from Jews worldwide, not as charity for the Jews of Palestine but as a way of giving concrete expression to the traditional understanding that this place was the trust of our entire people. To this day, the resettlement of Jewish refugees in Israel is a responsibility not of Israel's government but of the Jewish Agency, an institution that is formally a creature of the people, worldwide—and whose leaders, in terms of protocol, rank at a level equal to that of the leaders of the Israeli government. So we are formally implicated in Israel's saga.

But the more interesting implication, by far, is considerably less formal than that; our "we" is hardly because of a theory or an institutional framework. When we mourn in the wake of a distant bus accident, it is for other and richer reasons. We mourn, as I have said, because of the Holocaust/Israel association: the lives of Jewish children are doubly precious to us because so many such lives were ended so brutally, because Jewish life in general is so very vulnerable. We mourn as well because we recognize just how tiny Israel is, and how intimate; loss there is a family affair. We read the words of S. Y. Agnon, Israel's Nobel Laureate, and we take them as our own, seeing nothing exceptional in them:

> A king of flesh and blood who goes out to war against his
> enemies
> Brings forth his force to kill and be killed.
> There is doubt whether he loves his soldiers, whether they
> are important in his eyes
> Or whether they are not important in his eyes.
> And even if they are important in his eyes, they are no more
> important than corpses.
>
> But our king, the king of kings, the Holy One, Blessed be
> He,
> Desires life, loves peace and pursues peace.
> Loves Israel His people and has chosen us from all the
> nations,
> Not because we are greater in number, for we are the least in
> number.
> And because He loves us and we are few in number,
> Each one of us is as important in his eyes as a whole
> regiment.

If we were to stop to think on these words, our liberal sensibilities would surely be offended. But the point, of course, is that we do not stop to think. The familiar sentiments do not enter the mind, they enter the heart, and coddle it. This house, the tiny House of Israel, is our home; it is family. And so we mourn when tragedy befalls it.

We mourn also because of our sense of equity: Is not Israel already beset by more than its share of crisis and death, must it now suffer common tragedy as well?

And we mourn because of the very banality of the tragedy. It comes as a disturbing reminder that Israel may be, after all, an ordinary place, a place where lives are lived and lost not only in heroic ways, but in the very ways in which our lives here are lived and lost.

We prefer—who would not?—the mythic realm, the extraordinary Israel of Entebbe. When, in 1976, an Air France airliner was hijacked and forced to land in Uganda, at the Entebbe airport, and when the passengers were subsequently separated into two groups—Jews and non-Jews—Israel staged a stunning raid and rescued all but one of the hostages.

The next day, I had to take my car to the repair shop. The owner, a Greek immigrant to the United States, gave me a lift back to my office in his Mercedes. While we were riding, he tried to persuade me to trade in my car—its visits to the shop had become all too frequent—and buy "a real car, a Mercedes." "Nick," I replied, "I have a problem with buying a German car." "Oh," he said, "you must be a Jewish person." I told him I was, and he said to me, "Listen, let me congratulate you on what you people did yesterday in Uganda."

At which point my ears heard my mouth say, "Thank you very much."

If I can bask in the glory of Entebbe's heroes, and even be thought in some sense related to them, why not? American Jews have learned from both their texts and their experience that military prowess has not been—how shall we say it?—our long suit. On the contrary: A generation of American Jewish boys was urged by its parents to stay out of fights, to avoid contact sports, to think of our bodies as useful mainly to prevent our heads from rolling around on the ground. (As a kind of compensation for these anti-physical teachings, we were given books with such titles as *The Jews Fought, Too,* and we knew the names—there were not that many—of every Jewish sports star.) Our grandparents and theirs, we knew, were scholars, merchants, poets, beggars, and bookkeepers—but hardly ever generals, or even sergeants. We are not from the iron-pumpers; brain, not brawn, and all that.

And then, overnight, Entebbe, the Six Day War, a reputation as the world's fourth or fifth most mighty military power, a reputation earned not by mutant Jews, but by our own cousins—meaning, obviously, that we too are capable of such deeds. Of such strength.

I leave to others the exploration of the psychoanalytic possibilities of such a transformation in the cultural code. I allude to the transformation here only to suggest, in yet another way, how very profound is our attachment to Israel, for reasons obvious and for reasons mysterious. Israel enters our lives not only as refuge and promise but also as opportunity for vicarious fulfillment. In our classrooms, we were taught more of Jewish tragedy than of Jewish triumph. And, in any case, the triumph was chiefly theological, abstract, the tragedy historical, concrete. And now comes Israel, a place where Jews have done and do things that do not fit with what we have been taught of Jewish history—or with how we perceive ourselves. Its triumphs, of which excellence in war is only the most dramatic—the swamps were actually drained, and the desert was truly made to blossom—help compensate for our failures in the history we've been taught and for our own inadequacies. They help bring us, as survey after survey shows, a new sense of self-respect. Of course, then, we will say "we," and mean it.

And the tragedies? When we grieve over a bus accident, our grief is not only for Israel's loss but also for our own. There, it is sons and daughters that have died; here, it is a dream, a myth—the myth that Israel and its people are extraordinary, that the history of our people is now redeemed—that is undermined. Israel is reduced to a place.

And how much more corrosive the tarnish when it is not a bus accident we are trying to process but a rising crime rate, or the latest evidence of political incompetence.

Lately, as I have already suggested, it has become difficult to ignore these things, to avoid the place, to insulate the myth. When I was a graduate student working on my dissertation on Israeli politics—the year was 1961, thirteen years after Israel's independence—there were no more than half a dozen books in English, and not many more than that in Hebrew, that dealt with the subject directly. Except when a significant event warranted their presence, foreign correspondents were rarely assigned to Jerusalem, then very much a backwater town, for all its religious distinction. Back then, what American Jews who had not visited there knew of the place derived mainly from speeches by visiting Israelis at fund-raising events or similar occasions.

Today, of course, Israel is no longer the private preserve of a few tens of scholars, or of a few thousand adventuresome tourists, or even of just the Jews. Informed people everywhere feel obliged to know what is happening there, and the considerable media coverage Israel is accorded renders such knowledge easily accessible. Today, my library overflows with a hundred and more volumes on Israeli politics and society—and it is very far from a complete collection. Today, Israel is a nation of global consequence—and of global concern.

Still, for a generation of Jews who were witness to its birth, the pictures on our television screens and the articles in our newspapers and magazines cannot entirely displace those photographs of reunion. Inevitably, we know more and more facts, facts of all kinds, some of them merely prosaic, some of them deeply disturbing. But much of what we know is prior to all the facts; it is a knowing that is essentially unimpeachable. Neither all the years of war, nor all the calumny, nor even the growing awareness of Israel's ultimate ordinariness, can refute it.

There is a name for a belief that is essentially immune to the facts, that lives independent of them; its name is "faith." And there is no understanding of the meaning of Israel to American Jews without appreciation of the degree to which Israel is for us first a faith, and only then a place.

It was Arthur Hertzberg who observed most precisely that Israel has become the religion of America's Jews. "One can," he wrote, "no longer be excommunicated in modern America for not believing in God, for living totally outside the tradition, or even for marrying out. Indeed, none of these formerly excommunicable offenses debar one today from occupying high offices in positions of Jewish leadership." Opposition to Israel and Zionism, on the other hand, does result in debarment, and not only from leadership positions, but from "any participation in Jewish life on any issue. . . . The yearning for Israeli leaders with charisma on the part of American Jews, and the emotions they pour into United Jewish Appeal missions, are to be understood as part of a religious phenomenon, the modern equivalent of *hasidim* traveling in exaltation to see their rebbe and to spend some time in the uplifting precincts of his court."

Faith: Think what it means that in a recent study of the attitudes of students in New York City's afternoon Hebrew schools, one of the ten items used to measure "Jewish attitudes" was "The State of Israel is the most important country in the world for Jews." Students who agreed with that statement were given points for a "positive attitude"; students who disagreed had points deducted. Again, were we to pause and think through the implications of such a statement we would likely have serious problems with it. There is something strange about teaching nine- and ten-year-olds in Queens that Israel is the *most* important country in the world. On its face, such a teaching means that Jonathan Pollard, an American Jew convicted of spying for the State of Israel, may be thought a success story. And if the reply is that what they are being taught is only that Israel is the most important country for Jews *as* Jews, that to Jews as Americans the United States is, of course, the most important country, confusion is compounded: Do we mean to teach our children that they are half Jew, half American, rather than teaching them that there is such a thing as a whole American Jew?

The point is that we rarely think such things through. Statements such as the one I have cited (albeit usually less blatant) are part of the unexamined assumptions of Israel-as-religion, the catechism we are taught and we recite without serious reflection.

Faith: Imagine what it means to an Israeli archeologist to unearth and unravel an amulet from the days of King Solomon's Temple, and then to decipher the very faint words etched thereon, to realize that he has dug up the most ancient text of a Biblical verse thus far discovered, and not of a peripherally significant verse, but of the priestly blessing itself, *y'varech'cha adonai v'yishmerecha* . . . , the same words—may the Lord bless you and keep you—the archeologist had spoken to his son on the day his son became a bar mitzvah.

That happened in 1986. And something like it will happen next year again, or the year after. Does it matter that the archeologist is himself a secular man? It does not to him, it does not to the reader of the story, thousands of miles distant, who has spoken those same words to his children. Does not the fact that this is where these words were written—and etched, and recovered—have its place on the scales, along with all the confusion and all the rot? The question, then, is how we weigh things up, how we sort out the confusions, how we manage the inevitable collision between the faith and the place, between the Jerusalem of our imagining, that Jerusalem we have dreamed for 2,000 years, and the Jerusalem of our experience, the Jerusalem that can no longer be ignored.

Take war, for example.

Israel's excellence in war is both the most surprising and, potentially, the most disconcerting of its achievements, war having been so peripheral an element of the historic Jewish experience. (Peripheral, and devalued. No holiday marks Joshua's conquest of the Land, even though that conquest, we are taught, was at God's behest and with His active cooperation; nor do we mark David's conquest of Jerusalem, for all that Jerusalem means to us.)

The long war that began even before the day of independence and has continued, more or less actively, ever since, so long now that it seems part of Israel's destiny, has helped, in very many ways, to shape our attitudes toward the Jewish state. Back then, at the time of independence, no one imagined that the conflict would be without end; by now, few can imagine its conclusion. Peace has become a prayerful yearning, not a serious anticipation. The state of war has become as well a state of mind.

That state of mind is captured by a common experience of American Jews: When we awake in the morning, we hold our breath as we turn on the radio or television to learn whether we have made it through another night, or whether, instead, the terrorists have struck yet again, or the next round of the war begun. The truth is not pretty, but it is the truth. If the broadcast begins, "Six people were killed last night when a bomb exploded," we tauten—and when the announcer continues, "in Sri Lanka," we experience relief.

That is a measure of the depth of our connection, but not of its texture. Dazzling military achievement is, after all, hardly what we anticipated from the heavenly Jerusalem. (Nor, for that matter, is chronic anxiety.)

Still, the faith can accommodate war at a distance, the more so if the war fits traditional religious metaphor—David and Goliath, for example—or has about it the aspect of a miracle—the Six Day War, for one. We accommodate the revolutionary innovation in Jewish life by sharing the accepted understanding that Israel's wars have been forced upon it by its enemies. That was plainly the case in both the 1948 War of Independence and the 1973 Yom Kippur War. It was not so in the 1956 Sinai Campaign, but that is the least remembered of Israel's wars. As to the Six Day War, its causes have lately become a matter of some debate, both political and scholarly. Menachem Begin and Rafael Eitan (chief of staff of the Israel Defense Forces during the Lebanon War), seeking to find precedent for the Lebanon War, argued fiercely that the Six Day War, too, was "optional," and there are some historians who are inclined to agree with them.

But here in America, until the Lebanon War, Jews preferred to be less analytic, to accept that Israel fought only because there was, as the Israeli slogan goes, no alternative. And, further, that it has fought not only with uncommon skill, even heroism, but also with remarkable restraint, killing gently, as it were.

There is a factual foundation to these perceptions. Israel's doctrine of *tohar haneshek*—the "purity of arms"—is, quite likely, unique. After the Sinai Campaign of 1956, for example, two young battalion commanders met with the chief of staff and urged the removal and prosecution of their brigade commander on the grounds that he had not taken due care to protect his men and civilians in the battle area. (The two men were Motta Gur and Rafael Eitan, both later chiefs of staff; the commander against whom they complained was Ariel Sharon.)

Or, more tellingly, the IDF delayed its entry into Tyre and Sidon during the Lebanon War of 1982 in order to give the civilian population time to flee. Israeli planes dropped leaflets over the cities indicating routes to safety that would be free of fire. So, too, Israeli soldiers moving into built-up areas were forbidden the standard military technique for house-to-house combat, which is to begin by throwing hand grenades or satchel charges, or at least to enter firing. The examples can easily be multiplied, and they provide substantial justification for the view that Israel's army is as "special" as Israel itself.

The specialness is expressed in other ways, too. Here, for example, is a report from *The New York Times* of November 9, 1983, describing then Prime Minister Shamir's visit to Israeli positions in Lebanon:

> In a freewheeling question-and-answer session between the soldiers and Mr. Shamir and Defense Minister Moshe Arens . . . one soldier stood to challenge the validity of Israel's continued presence in Lebanon.
>
> "Sometimes when I'm riding on the roads of Lebanon," the tall, bearded kibbutznik said in an impassioned voice, "I feel like an actor in a movie about the Germans in Europe during World War II or a Russian in Afghanistan.
>
> "I feel like an occupier in a foreign country," the soldier said as a hushed silence fell over the group of more than 200 soldiers in the tent at a forward armor camp about four miles from the Lebanese-Syrian border. Both Mr. Arens and the Israeli Chief of Staff, Lieut. Gen. Moshe Levy, stared hard at the soldier as he talked.
>
> "My hope," the Israeli said, "is that more and more soldiers will refuse to serve in Lebanon and that they will put more pressure on the government to pull out entirely."
>
> There was a moment of strained silence and then Mr. Shamir, his face impassive, coldly dismissed the comparison.
>
> "We're nothing like the Germans in Europe or the Soviets in Afghanistan," he said. "We're not here because we want to be here or because we have any intention of ruling the people. We're here to insure the safety of Israel, and once we've accomplished that, we'll leave."
>
> It was obvious that the soldier felt no need to apologize to anyone for his views and no doubt about his right to express them.

Perhaps the most poignant and telling illustration of the character of Israel's citizen army, as we here have come to understand it, was in the form of a book that appeared soon after the Six Day War. The book is called *The Seventh Day: Soldiers Talk About the Six-Day War.* It is a compilation of interviews with veterans of the war, probing their feelings in the wake of Israel's stunning victory. Its power derives both from its honesty and from the virtually total absence, throughout its pages, of any sense of postwar exultation. Instead, it reads as if written by a company of poets suddenly called to arms in order to defend their homes and their families:

> Those who survived the Holocaust, those who see pictures of a father and a mother, who hear the cries that disturb the dreams of those close to them, those who have listened to the stories—know that no other people carries with it such haunting visions. And it is these visions which compel us to fight and yet make us ashamed of our fighting. The saying "pardon us for winning" is no irony—it is the truth. Of course, one may say that our doubts are only hypocrisy and nothing more; that we deck ourselves out in morality, perhaps even that our behavior is contradictory. But who says that war can be anything but contradictory?

Or:

> Those first days [after the war] were very difficult. . . . Everything you'd ignored previously, all the corpses: you suddenly start thinking about them and you ask yourself, while everyone's rejoicing over this great victory, what it's all about. It cost us dear. And this time, when you say dear, you take the enemy's corpses into account as well as your own. I begged them not to ask me so many questions, not to think so much of me, to tone down all the rejoicing over the victory. The feeling I had was that this wasn't the moment for rejoicing, for victory, for celebrations; it was the moment for some sort of mourning.

Moving sentiments, these—and feeding precisely into the image of our Israeli cousins we here would like to preserve: farmer-soldiers, poet-soldiers, citizen-soldiers; anything but soldier-soldiers. Soldiers both cruelly miscast and utterly competent.

(One lazy Friday evening, some years ago, I lay on the lawn of an old kibbutz with a boyhood friend who had lived in Israel from the time he was seventeen. He is now the father of three sons, and one of them had just completed a highly specialized army training course. My friend interrupted his description of the course to say, "Strange, isn't it? If I'd stayed in America, and we were getting together like this on a Friday night, we'd be talking about what colleges our kids have applied to, where they've been admitted. And here I am, instead, telling you about my boy's military prowess. Yes, he was graduated first in his class, summa cum laude, from the Harvard of war making. And yes, I am terribly proud of him. And yes, so long as we are in the position we are, I am mighty glad we do war so well. But dear God, I hope we never forget that this isn't what we are about.")

Israelis, just as we in America, search for exoneration, for reassurance that they have not gone military. But they are at a disadvantage: the battlefield is near to home, it is their fathers, husbands, sons, who go off to war and come back with the stories of blood, not paint; it is their lively press that reports war's myriad details. So in Israel itself, *The Seventh Day* is by now a piece of quaint history. There was an effort to produce a similar volume after the Yom Kippur War, but it was plainly a contrived undertaking, soldiers seeking to echo the virginity of their predecessors six years earlier. And after Lebanon, the books and the articles had a very different tone. They were more political, less existential; they were analytic, not poetic. After Lebanon, a new version of *The Seventh Day* would have been pointless, or worse; it would have been not a contrivance, but a fraud.

Here, the distance permits us to pick our facts, and there are sufficient facts, by and large, to support our imagination, to leave it intact; the others we try not to notice. The testimony of *The Seventh Day* suits us so well because of all the things we hope for and expect from Israel, none is more important than that it help sustain our sense of moral distinction.

It is time to recall the story with which I began this book, the story of Berl and his friends, and to propose a somewhat different context for it.

The sense of moral superiority that is the story's heart did not end with Berl and his friends in 1860. We are their heirs, and though it is awkward to announce it, most of us were raised to believe that the Jews, on the whole, are indeed more moral than most others. Jews don't hunt.

Which is to say, Jews—we have believed—are partners in an ethical culture, heirs to and practitioners of a set of values that derives from the early prophets and is the heart of our instruction to this very day. We don't hunt, and we clothe the naked and feed the hungry—we are *rachmanim b'nai rachmanim,* compassionate children of compassionate parents—and we pursue justice, too.

As I observed at the outset, this sense of who we are was much easier to sustain before we came to power—to wealth, to status, to office, to guns. But though it has since become more problematic, we continue to cling to it, for it has long since become a central aspect of our self-portrait. In the meantime, the other aspects have blurred. Language and belief, calendar and culture—all these are in massive disarray. Yet to be a Jew by more than inertia requires some definition of our collective identity. There is our history of suffering; there is our concern for Israel; and there is, finally, our sense of moral—let us say "ambition," since "superiority" is so odious a word. That sense, in short, is more than a simple belief, susceptible to proof or disproof according to accepted canons of evidence. It is bred into our very definition of collective self, it is part of our collective identity, it is at the very heart of our collective motivation—and the sovereign State of Israel is where that self, that identity, are most manifestly on the line. Here in America, when a Jew errs, his error belongs mostly to him; there, when the Jews err, the error belongs to us all, threatens us all. The threat is not that others will think ill of us; the threat is that the very foundation of our self-understanding will be eroded.

So, again: What happens when unpleasant facts insistently intrude? What happens when our attachment to Israel and our moral conceit collide? What happens, for example, when Israeli bombs fall on an apartment building in Beirut? What, in fact, happened to us during Lebanon, when the war was no longer war at a distance, but war transmitted by satellite to our living rooms? What happened when we learned that Israeli soldiers stood idly by while hundreds of people were being slaughtered by the Phalange in Sabra and Shatilla?

Between September 16 and September 18 of 1982, the Christian Phalange in Lebanon killed some hundreds of inhabitants (Israeli intelligence estimates between 700 and 800)—including women and children—of the Sabra and Shatilla refugee camps, situated in West Beirut. The news was widely and extensively reported around the world, with special attention accorded the role of the Israeli army.

The Israeli army, we later learned authoritatively, controlled entry to the camps during the entire period and provided the Phalange with diverse services, including nighttime illumination. Most important, there is no question that responsible Israeli officers knew at an early stage, at least generally, what was happening.

News of the massacre began to reach the world on Saturday morning, September 18, the first day of Rosh Hashanah, the Jewish New Year. For most of the ensuing ten days—the period between Rosh Hashanah and Yom Kippur—the front pages of virtually all daily newspapers reported additional gruesome details of what had taken place.

The initial response of the Begin government was to express its regret over the incident and to deny any Israeli responsibility; indeed, the government resolution on the matter falsely asserted that the Israel Defense Forces intervened to put an end to the killing as soon as they learned what was happening, that without that intervention the losses would have been far greater, that to accuse the IDF of responsibility for the tragedy was "a blood libel against the Jewish state and its government." "No one," the resolution concluded, "will preach to us moral values or respect for human life, on whose basis we were educated and will continue to educate generations of fighters in Israel."

The event, and the government's response to it, touched off a furor within Israel and around the world. The daily *Ma'ariv,* a middle-of-the-road newspaper, editorialized that "This whole affair, which outrages and disgusts, cannot be ended by a simple statement of sorrow. Someone is responsible here and has to take the consequences. Somebody failed, and he should not be allowed another chance to repeat his failure." And *The Jerusalem Post,* a frequent critic of the Begin government, wrote that "Rosh Hashanah 5743 has become the Rosh Hashanah of shame. It is the shame of the state, of the Government, of the army. It is the shame of every individual citizen. For we have all been made accomplices to the horrible Rosh Hashanah massacre in West Beirut."

Meanwhile, in America, *The New York Times* reported that the Conference of Presidents of Major Jewish Organizations—the most auspicious aggregation of Jewish leadership in the American Jewish community—"stressed that their strong support for Israel and the administration of Prime Minister Menachem Begin had not decreased because of the massacre." The *Times* report was entirely accurate. Yet so also was the *Boston Globe* headline, during the same week, that read, "Jews in U.S. Decry Massacre," and was followed by a subhead asserting, "Leaders pray for slain Palestinians, criticize Israeli Prime Minister."

The fact that Israel is a faith to American Jews does not mean that its leaders are perceived as gods, or even as prophets. It does mean, however, that criticism of Israel is perceived as an assault on our faith, the more so as there are those among Israel's critics who—to pursue the metaphor—see Israel itself as a heresy to be uprooted. Once the criticism begins—among its authors are inevitably enemies, not merely dispassionate critics—we move instinctively to defend the faith. This instinctive defensive response often confuses our friends, who know us in other contexts to be cautious, analytical, reasoned. They do not understand that even as our public posture is to stand with Israel, and with its leaders, against the critics, privately we share our anguish with one another. This is hardly a rare phenomenon. We have seen it with Jesse Jackson, who is defended publicly by black leaders who excoriate him privately; we see it with lapsed Catholics, who may mock the Church when out of earshot, but who will leap to its defense when it is attacked by strangers. The fact is that by coming together to defend against a common enemy, we help define who we are. And if the enemy rises up to attack us when we are internally in disarray, his attack is all the more welcome, since it is precisely at such times that we most want a reminder of our underlying solidarity. Who are we? Notwithstanding our divisions, we are the group the others are attacking. Anger becomes our connection to each other, pride our motive.

And if the external threat the group faces is, more or less, constant, the defensive posture becomes so routine that the habit of evaluation, of judgment, of discrimination, atrophies.

Yet during the week before Prime Minister Begin reversed himself and agreed to appoint an official commission of inquiry, during the same week in which the official response of American Jewish leaders was to assert that their support for the prime minister had not lessened at all, urgent messages were reaching the prime minister from many of those same leaders pleading with him to acknowledge and rectify his error in refusing to appoint such a commission. The events of Sabra and Shatilla were simply too large to be contained within our routine forms of response.

And that is why American Jews have rarely experienced so profound a sense of relief as we did on the morning of September 26, when we learned that some 400,000 Israelis—well over 10 percent of Israel's Jewish population—had rallied in Tel Aviv the night before to protest Israel's involvement in the massacre and to demand that a commission of inquiry be appointed.

The relief was about the image of the Jew, now redeemed, and about the self-image of the Jews, now restored. Poet-soldiers, after all. A cleansing, a catharsis: no need any longer to twist, to rationalize, to search for alibis. Quite the opposite, in fact. Now we could turn the episode to our advantage, claim that Israel had vindicated our confidence in its high ethical standards, merited particular respect for the courageous honesty of its citizens. Our faith was intact, our god had not failed.

Tangled, all this. And more tangled still when a footnote is added: In due course, the Commission of Inquiry was appointed, conducted an investigation, and issued a report. In its discussion of then Defense Minister Ariel Sharon's responsibility for the events in Sabra and Shatilla, the commission had this to say: "It is impossible to justify the Minister of Defense's disregard of the danger of a massacre." And this: "The sense of danger should have been in the consciousness of every knowledgeable person who was close to this subject, and certainly in the consciousness of the Defense Minister, who took an active part in everything relating to the war." And this:

> As a politician responsible for Israel's security affairs, and as a minister who took an active part in directing the political and military moves in the war in Lebanon, it was the duty of the Defense Minister to take into account all reasonable considerations for and against having the Phalangists enter the camps, and not to disregard

entirely the serious considerations mitigating against such an action, namely that the Phalangists were liable to commit atrocities and that it was necessary to forestall this possibility as a humanitarian obligation and also to prevent the political damage it would entail. From the Defense Minister himself we know that this consideration did not concern him in the least.

And, finally, this:

> We have found, as has been detailed in this report, that the Minister of Defense bears personal responsibility. In our opinion, it is fitting that the Minister of Defense draw the appropriate personal conclusions arising out of the defects revealed with regard to the manner in which he discharged the duties of his office—and, if necessary, that the Prime Minister consider whether he should exercise his authority under Section 21-A(a) of the Basic Law of the Government, according to which "the Prime Minister may, after informing the Cabinet of his intention to do so, remove a minister from office."

There was no ambiguity in the commission's recommendation: Ariel Sharon was to resign as minister of defense or Menachem Begin was to remove him. After a time, and with ill-grace, Sharon did resign—and was appointed minister without portfolio. In the Government of National Unity that came to power in 1984, the Likud Party insisted that Sharon be appointed minister of industry and trade and be a member, as well, of the inner cabinet, the group of ten ministers who form the core group of Israel's government. And so it came to pass.

Such are, evidently, the exigencies of politics in Israel. But that does not explain why or how it is that when Ariel Sharon comes to the United States and seeks a platform within the Jewish community, he is rewarded by packed houses and standing ovations.

Perhaps it is only that there are nearly 6 million of us; in so large a community, any view has its supporters, more than enough to pack a hundred halls. Surveys of American Jewish opinion show that Ariel Sharon is the least admired of Israel's leaders. But "least admired" is a relative measure. While Sharon earns a higher unfavorable rating than any of his colleagues—41 percent—52 percent of us view him favorably.

Or perhaps what I wrote a month before Sabra and Shatilla explains our ambivalence:

> There are two kinds of Jews in the world. There is the kind of Jew who detests war and violence, who believes that fighting is not "the Jewish way," who willingly accepts that Jews have their own and higher standards of behavior. And not just that we have them, but that those standards are our lifeblood, are what we are about. And there is the kind of Jew who is convinced that it is time to strike back at our enemies, to reject once and for all the role of victim, who willingly accepts that Jews cannot depend on favors, that we must be tough and strong. And the trouble is, most of us are both kinds of Jew.

Perhaps, too, Israel has now become the Jew among the nations. That, of course, is the great irony. Israel was meant to "normalize" the condition of the Jews. But whatever Israel's achievements, "normalcy" remains elusive. Instead, Israel is hated, hunted, singled out. As Henry Kissinger once observed, Israel did not solve the problem of the ghetto; instead, it is the largest ghetto of all, surrounded as was the ghetto of old by enemies, dependent for its survival, as was the ghetto of old, on the power of a distant prince.

The stunning difference, however, is that this Jew knows how to fight. Some Jews in America find this Jew, this fighting Israel, an offense against Jewish history. No matter that the world is carnivorous; Jews are to be strictly vegetarian. To have and use a gun means to be a hunter, no matter what the provocation. For these few, Israel is not dream but nightmare. Show them paint, and they say "blood." The sharpest and saddest example of such distortion comes, as it happens, from the pen of an Argentine Jew, Jacobo Timerman. Timerman's book *The Longest War* is hardly about what it purports to be about, which is the war in Lebanon, the manifestly bloody war; instead, it is about Timerman's own disappointment in an Israel that does not live up to his moral demands. Writing from Israel, where he was then living, Timerman, a wonderfully passionate and blunt man, concluded that it is "the diaspora Jews who have maintained the values of our moral and cultural traditions, those values now trampled on here by intolerance and Israeli nationalism." Here there is no tension between fact and faith; if the two collide, the faith is abandoned, Israel becomes betrayal.

Plainly, however, it is not a dream that has collapsed but a fantasy, the Jerusalem of Minsk or of Buenos Aires, not the Jerusalem where real people live and laugh and cry and sometimes make terrible mistakes and sometimes even commit crimes. (And is it less a fantasy to believe that in Buenos Aires or New York, all those noble moral and cultural traditions are intact?)

The preference of most American Jews when fact and faith collide has been to abandon the fact. We have not written of Israel's flaws in our journals or spoken of them from our pulpits. And when the news of them has been so insistent that we could no longer pretend to ignorance, we have blamed the messenger. Ask an American Jew about Israeli excesses during the war in Lebanon—excesses widely discussed and debated within Israel—and you will most likely hear a lament—or a diatribe—on the bias of the media.

The fact is that there was media bias—and there were excesses. The fact is, as most Israelis now accept, that the war itself was ill-conceived. But we here have too much at stake to wrestle with such facts. Our dream, too, is a fantasy, and we will search and find ways to insulate it. We will plead self-defense on Israel's behalf, we will plead intolerable provocation, we will plead, if we must, temporary insanity. Thinking about the West Bank, we will remember that the Palestinians who live there enjoy a higher standard of living and, indeed, more rights than do many citizens of Arab countries—and we will forget what freedom and independence mean to people, and to a people. (Our self-serving assessments are made considerably more plausible by the grotesque excesses of Israel's enemies. Once it is declared, for example, that Zionism is racism, we all rally round Zionism's flag.) Better that than to relinquish the pride we have felt in Israel's achievements, the achievements of the Jewish people, by extension our own achievements. Better that than to revise our understanding of who the Jews are and what we are about. Better that, and easier, than to wrestle with the evidence of Israel's ordinariness and with our own capacity to be lovers not only of Zion, but of the place called Israel. Better that than heresy.

Such are the complex implications of Israel as faith and as motive. For sooner or later—and there is reason to believe the process is already under way—the disenchantment (I use the word quite literally) must come. And then? We have no right to blame the Israelis for encouraging our enthusiasm for magic, for make-believe; who, in their position, would not? (Yet what must they think of us, they for whom the houselights never dim?) The danger, of course, is that when the magic's over, we will feel that we've been had, duped, betrayed; again, a god that failed.

Earlier, I cited a survey research finding: 77 percent of America's Jews agreed that "if Israel were destroyed, I would feel as if I had suffered one of the greatest personal tragedies of my life." That was 1983. In 1986, the question was asked again; this time, 61 percent agreed—a decline of 20 percent. How can we account for the fact that in three years, one in five Jews appears to have stepped away from Israel?

Beware an intimacy that depends on innocence; with disenchantment comes disappointment, then distance. Our attachment to Israel is born out of all the themes of our people's history that Israel represents; beware an attachment that requires of Israel that it remain wholly a representation, a symbol. Do not suppose that if faith is vulnerable to fact, the remedy is an infusion of faith, much less a denial of fact; the remedy may be to disentangle faith from fantasy, still more to know things by their right names. Where love of Israel grows organically in the soil of Jewish understanding, there is no need to fear the facts, the complex truth. Where it is planted away from that soil, it will not take root.

Another statistic: In the same 1986 survey I cited a paragraph back, Steven Cohen finds that those American Jews who are most deeply attached to Israel are also those most likely to agree that "I am often troubled by the policies of the current Israeli government." That, plainly, is as it should be; that is what real caring is about.

6

Israel as Meaning:
Where Is Jerusalem?

IT IS NOT ONLY the facts that intrude on our faith; it is also the anomalies of our situation. Each year, at Passover, we begin the seder meal by reciting, "This year, we are here; next year, may we be in the Land of Israel." And we conclude the seder with the same sentiment: "Next year, in Jerusalem."

Yet, though Jerusalem is now infinitely more accessible to us than it was to our ancestors, who recited the same words, we are here, not there, and the odds are overwhelming that next year we will still be here. In the years since the founding of Israel, only 60,000 Americans—just about 1 percent of America's Jews—have taken the words sufficiently to heart to make the move. (Several times that many Israelis have chosen to move to the United States, where presumably they too now recite the ancient formula.)

It is tempting, therefore, to interpret the words as an expression of idle—very idle—sentiment, if not anachronistic hypocrisy. The archaic formula appears to have nothing, or very nearly nothing, to do with either our lives or our intentions.

Yet the words cannot be so quickly dismissed. The fact is that not only do the government of Israel and the agencies of the Zionist enterprise urge American Jews to make their home in Israel, but American Jewry is formally responsive to their demand. The Jerusalem Program of the World Zionist Organization—an organization that nominally includes some millions of American Jews in its ranks—asserts that the aims of Zionism include, among others, "the unity of the Jewish people and the centrality of Israel in Jewish life" and "the ingathering of the Jewish people in its historic homeland, Eretz Yisrael, through *aliyah* [immigration] from all countries." *All* countries.

Somehow, we must understand how a people that resolutely refuses to be "ingathered" is at the same time prepared to endorse its own ingathering, to sit through speeches exhorting it to *aliyah*, to fund Israeli emissaries whose task it is to promote *aliyah*, to establish local committees whose mandate is to encourage *aliyah*. Or to hang on the wall of a B'nai Brith Hillel Foundation at a large state university a poster, in the form of a letter, that reads:

Dear Son:
Come back home.
ISRAEL

And the place to begin such an inquiry is with the peculiarity of the expectation. On the surface, it would seem outlandish to suppose that any significant number of citizens of the United States, with all its wealth, power, and opportunity, members of a well-established and uncommonly affluent community, should be expected to pack their bags and move off to a tiny and beleaguered country in the Middle East, there to learn a new language and sink new roots. Yet that is precisely what is asked of American Jews, repeatedly. And when so importuned, American Jews do not reply, "That's absurd," or, "What chutzpah!" Instead, they accept the call as entirely legitimate, if also essentially ritualistic.

Plainly, then, there is more here than meets the eye. What is it that leads Israelis to care so much for American Jewish immigration, and what is it that induces American Jews to hear the Israelis out—and then do nothing?

Look to the language: the word for immigration in Hebrew is *hagirah*—but the word for immigration to Israel is *aliyah*, which means, literally, ascent. From the time Abram "went up out of Egypt" to Canaan, that has been the way Jews have described the act of coming to dwell in the Promised Land. In our own time, the great waves of immigration that define the modern Jewish settlement of Palestine are referred to by the same term, and an immigrant—a Jewish immigrant—to Israel is called an *oleh,* one who ascends. And yes, one who leaves Israel is called a *yored,* one who descends.

Israel's classic religious significance to the Jews cannot be overstated. From the very beginning of our people, it has been so. It starts with Abraham, to whom, just thirteen verses after his name first enters the Biblical account, God promises: "Unto thy seed I will give this land." It continues through the texts that include the ultimate threat, exile from the land, and beyond the texts, to the liturgy and the life of the people. As much as some have tried to make of the geography a mere metaphor, no reading of Jewish religious history and understanding that does not acknowledge Judaism's specific territorial dimension can be taken seriously. The fact—though it may well offend the modern sensibility—is that to the Jewish people, throughout its history, it was simply inconceivable that the separation of the people from the land was permanent. To have acknowledged such a possibility would have meant to have lived a story without a point, an option that Jewish teaching did not—and does not—permit. With the exceptions of Job and Ecclesiastes, Judaism utterly rejects absurdity, insists instead on meaning, on causal connection, on intention.

And the point of the Jewish story has always been that one day the people would return. Whether its restoration to its natural and promised home would be a gift or a reward, whether it would be through God's grace or through the people's merits, through the Messiah or through the Zionists—all this might be debated, and was. But that no matter how long delayed, the return would come— of that there was never the slightest doubt.

This fundamental religious perception informed even the most secular among us. Zionist ideology, for example, sought to liberate itself from the mysteries of faith and religious doctrine. As mainstream political Zionism saw things, the problem it had come to solve was principally the problem of anti-Semitism in the nineteenth and then the twentieth century, not the problem of exile. Yet when Theodor Herzl, the most consequential of the early Zionists, sought to persuade his colleagues to accept an apparent British offer to permit Jewish settlement in what was then a portion of Uganda (now Kenya), he was rebuffed.

Imagine: Here is Herzl, in the wake of the shock of the Kishinev pogrom, Herzl the Central European aesthete, pleading with his East European colleagues to save themselves and their brethren before it is too late, at least temporarily to accept Uganda as a substitute for the Holy Land, for Palestine. "Let us save those who can be saved." And here are the representatives of persecuted Jewry, the delegates to the Zionist Congress from Russia, from Poland, refusing to hear of it, embarking on a hunger strike to resist it. Secularized socialists though they were, their Zion had a specific geographic location, and it was not Uganda.

Imagine: Here is Herzl, playwright and journalist and secular gentleman, Judaically virtually illiterate, seeking at the Congress's closing session to make amends for his misreading of Jewish sentiment. He takes the podium, in his morning coat, explains again that Uganda is only a temporary expedient, then raises his right hand and recites, "*Im eshkachech Yersuhalayim, tishkach yemini*—If I forget thee, O Jerusalem, may my right hand forget its cunning."

"Exile," Ben Halpern writes in his *The American Jew*, "is essentially a religious idea. Exile is something God imposed upon the Jews, not Roman Titus." And Zionism, Herzl's version of it notwithstanding, was not merely a program to save the Jews from anti-Semitism, from Titus; it was a program to save the Jews from Exile, to restore the Jews to their land and thereby to renew God's relationship with His people.

Hence, *aliyah,* ascent.

Hence also—implicit in the word, often enough explicit in the discourse—Zion's elevation above all other places. In the second-century words of Rabbi Simeon bar Yochai,

> The Holy One, blessed be He, considered all generations and He found no generation fitted to receive the Torah other than the

generation of the wilderness; the Holy One, blessed be He, considered all mountains and found no mountain on which the Torah should be given other than Sinai; the Holy One, blessed be He, considered all cities, and found no city wherein the Temple might be built, other than Jerusalem; the Holy One, blessed be He, considered all lands, and found no land suitable to be given to Israel, other than the Land of Israel. [Lev. Rabbah 13:2]

And that is why, even to the most secularized Jews of our time, a faint smell of failure clings to those who remain, willfully, outside the land. So, for example, the Israeli philosopher Nathan Rotenstreich contends that Israelis must distinguish between understanding the Jews of the Diaspora and approving them:

It is one thing to feel loyalty, solidarity, affinity and the like towards Jews everywhere; it is quite another to concede that two different modes of Jewish existence—Diaspora and the Jewish State—are historically of equal importance. . . . The sense of affinity with the Jewish people—which has to be part of the awareness of an Israeli—cannot suppress awareness of the singularity of the State of Israel. That singularity is not smugness on the part of Jews who live in Israel but is rooted in the point of departure which underlies Zionist ideology.

The curious aspect of the matter is that very many American Jews would share Rotenstreich's conclusion. They would not necessarily accept his reasoning, nor are they, for the most part, familiar with the content of the diverse Zionist ideologies. Still, "the singularity of the State of Israel" is part of their conceptual baggage, too, and so, therefore, the critical assessment of the Diaspora self.

I say this even though there have been elaborate efforts through the years to find meaning and purpose, even theological purpose, in the Diaspora. But by and large, those efforts have not "taken"; all Zionist theories, to a greater or lesser degree, assert or imply *shlilat hagolah*—the "negation of the Diaspora" that Rotenstreich does. Rotenstreich is hardly exceptional in this regard. Yet most American Jews call themselves Zionists. The explanation for this anomaly goes beyond the fact that we impute transcendent significance to Israel; it suggests that we have no analogous sense of our own significance. We are, that is, without an accepted theory of American Jewish life, a theory that would make of American Jewry more than an accident.

Before we come back to this curious and somewhat disturbing matter, it will be helpful to see how Zionism has understood the imperative for *aliyah.*

Classic Zionism, beginning in the middle of the last century, had both a predictive and a normative aspect. Observing Diaspora life, it held that the Jews were now caught between two equally distasteful dangers. On the one hand, it was plain that anti-Semitism was endemic to the societies where Jews lived. Sooner or later, the Jews would be pogrommed to death. And, on the other hand, if they somehow managed to escape the pogromists, the open society would get them; they would be assimilated to death.

No one has made the case more succinctly than Jean-Paul Sartre, who, in his *Anti-Semite and Jew,* argued that,

> For a Jew, conscious and proud of being Jewish, asserting his claim to be a member of the Jewish community without ignoring on that account the bonds which unite him to the national community, there may not be so much difference between the anti-Semite and the democrat. The former wishes to destroy him as a man and leave nothing in him but the Jew, the pariah, the untouchable; the latter wishes to destroy him as a Jew and leave nothing in him but the man, the abstract and universal subject of the rights of man and the rights of the citizen.

The Jews of the Diaspora, in other words, might be raped, or they might be seduced; either way, no good could come to them. Many Israeli Zionists cling to that prediction. After all, both parts of it have a good deal of dismal evidence in their favor. The pogromists did kill one third of all the Jews, and assimilation has depleted the Jewish population by millions more. Given the current circumstances of nearly 3 million Soviet Jews, as well as the continuing evidence of assimilation in the West, it is easy enough to sustain the gloomy prognosis.

Here, for example, is Hillel Halkin, writing from Israel in 1975:

> The same classical Zionist beliefs that justified modern Jewish settlement in Palestine, and that justified the establishment of a

Jewish state, justify this country to this day. These are so simple that they can be presented in an ordinary syllogism:

1) It is natural for a Jew who is committed to his Jewishness to seek to perpetuate Jewish life in himself and in his people.

2) For objective historical reasons, Jewish life in the Diaspora is doomed; and, conversely, such life has a possible future only in an autonomous or politically sovereign Jewish community living in its own land, that is, in the State of Israel.

3) Therefore, it is natural for a Jew who is committed to his Jewishness to desire to live only in Israel.

This, I suggest, is the essential faith of this country, and when I say that a Jew who visits here from the Diaspora is necessarily a person on trial, I mean that his visit is an evasion if it fails to compel him to confront these articles of faith in all seriousness and to take a stand in relation to them.

But the excerpt from Halkin also indicates the normative orientation to *aliyah* that characterizes much of the argument, classic and contemporary. It is not just that the Diaspora is doomed; it is also that a Jew—at least one who wants to be a Jew, one to whom Judaism matters—*belongs* in Israel. It is, as Halkin observes, "natural"—and to resist *aliyah* is, accordingly, perverse.

Halkin argues from a secular perspective. So, in a different formulation, does the North African Jew Albert Memmi, in his remarkable book *The Liberation of the Jew:*

It is always possible to reassure oneself with money, science, honors, universality, but without liberty all these things will give forth the tenacious odor of death. Neither the perpetuity of an improved Diaspora, nor Socialism, nor a more adaptable religion, more easily tolerated by others, nor a modus vivendi with the Christians, nor even an amiable pro-Israelism—Jaffa oranges and Tel Aviv singers—are real solutions. They are at best compromises which do not fundamentally change a condition which demands a radical transformation.

And that radical transformation, of course, is Israel itself. "Only the territorial solution, a free people on a free territory—a nation— is an adequate solution to the fundamental and specific deficiencies in the Jewish condition."

Memmi, according to his own testimony, is not certain that it was wise to choose Palestine as the site of the transformation. "Since it was necessary to start from scratch in any case, why didn't they choose some fertile-soiled, perhaps subsoiled, Eldorado, uninhabited, rich in deserted expanses?" But he recognizes, as well, that there was no choice, no alternative myth that would galvanize the needed energies: "the oppressed's first need is to return to himself, in other words to his language, be it sick, to his tradition, be it a phantom. In this restoration of himself he is obliged to utilize the stones of his past. It is as much a question of reconstruction as of construction."

And when the stones of the past are not buried under mountains of debris, but are turned each day in the hands of the people, when the myth does not require artificial infusion, when it is not merely an available myth but the prevailing myth—how can it be abandoned? Here is Yehuda Halevi, writing in the twelfth century: "If only all our people had willingly returned then to our land with a glad heart, the divine promise would have kept faith with us as it had before. . . . Had only we unhesitatingly gone forth toward the God of our fathers, we would have been accorded no less of His wonders than were our ancestors."

To all these historic arguments, secular and religious, a newer argument has lately been added, an argument with special poignancy: "We need you." We need you, the Israelis say, because we need more people, and because we specifically need more people experienced in liberal democracy, and (sometimes) because we need more people from the West to serve as a counterweight to all those Eastern Jews who now outnumber the rest of us. "It is," an Israeli friend told me not long ago, "monumentally unfair. We here have all the problems—and you have all the human resources."

How could American Jews refuse to be an audience to such weighty arguments? Even were Israel not, as I have argued it is, the binding element of the contemporary Jewish understanding, the raison d'etre of very many Jews, even if we had not been taught to "place Jerusalem above our chiefest joy," most of us are not entirely certain that the Zionist prediction is wrong, nor do most of us have a coherent ideological view with which to counter the ideological argument for *aliyah*. So we listen, and feel discomfort, sharp or vague, feel ourselves slothfully wanting, Jewishly inadequate. We accept, most of us, that we are here principally because this is where the fleshpots are; we are here because we are not sturdy enough to be there, where we belong. We listen in mild embarrassment, we nod reluctant agreement, and we stay where we are and recite again, "Next year, in Jerusalem."

Not very much, it would seem, has changed in the 700 years since Yehuda Halevi concluded the remark I quoted above with these words: "But all our repetition of such verses as ... 'He who restoreth His glory to Zion,' and others like it, [is] as the starling's caw, since we say them without thinking."

I have made it seem as if American Jews wander about their daily lives with a profound sense of guilt. While some us do, my sense of the matter is that the more general feeling is of a mild discontinuity, not especially germane to our self-understanding as Jews.

The part of the Zionist argument we generally accept was expressed by the Israeli novelist Amos Oz in 1984, during a lecture tour in America. Oz told his audiences that Israel is the living theater of Jewish life today, that we in America are at best a museum, where a smattering of the old is preserved and nothing new is created. The three great creative achievements of the Jewish people in our time, he argued, are the rebuilding of Jerusalem, the resurrection of the Hebrew language, and the development of the kibbutz. What, he asked, have we that can compare to any of these?

The fact is that in each of his audiences, there were those who took sharp issue with him. They acknowledged, in effect, that Israel is indisputably the standing-room-only Broadway hit show of this Jewish time, but they insisted as well that American Jews are busy mounting modest productions of their own. Many are painfully amateurish, but now and again there is one that offers promise, that might even be regarded as, say, solid Off-Broadway material.

Still, very many American Jews are content to perceive themselves as living out their Jewish lives in the role of ticket takers, ushers, stagehands, angels, or audience to Israel's drama. Here are roles we can comprehend, here is a definition of what it means to be a Jew that is straightforward. No matter that we here may have done more than the Israelis with regard to the role of women in

Judaism, that we may have produced a group of native-born scholars that can hold its own, quantitatively and qualitatively, with
Israeli scholars, that we may have given more creative thought to
matters religious; we are pleased and relieved to acknowledge that
Israel is the main stage of Jewish life in our day. That takes the
pressure for definition—and for performance—off us.

At the same time, however—and here is the source of the discontinuity—we resist the historic claim of *aliyah*. It is not merely that
inertia holds us back, keeps us where we are. It is also that we lack
the essential sensibility that makes *aliyah* plausible: we do not feel
ourselves to be in exile.

I do not mean by this merely that it is difficult to sustain the sense
of exile in Scarsdale or Beverly Hills, although there is much truth
to that. I mean that here in America, we feel ourselves at home. And
Zionist theory did not really foresee such a possibility—nor, indeed,
does it readily acknowledge that reality even now.

At home. Consider how different that is from the common experience of the Jew, even in the West, even in our own time. In the
old joke, one Jew says to another: "I'm leaving for South America."
"Really," his friend replies. "That's very far away." "From what?"
the first responds.

That is a Jewish joke, a Jewish perception. It mirrors the non-
Jewish perception, which is hardly a joke: On December 26, 1894,
the leading French anti-Semite, Edouard Drumont, wrote in *La Libre
Parole*, the paper he had founded, "[Dreyfus] has committed an
abuse of confidence, but he has not committed a crime against his
country. In order for a man to betray his country, it is necessary first
of all that he have a country."

The conviction that Jews are inevitably alien is not restricted to
anti-Semites. A half-century after Drumont wrote, Jean-Paul Sartre
had this to say of the Jew in France:

> In a bourgeois society it is the constant movement of people, the
> collective currents, the styles, the customs, all these things, that in
> effect create values. The values of poems, of furniture, of houses,
> of landscapes derive in large part from the spontaneous condensa-
> tions that fall on these objects like a light dew; they are strictly

national and result from the normal functioning of a traditionalist and historical society. To be a Frenchman is not merely to have been born in France, to vote and pay taxes; it is above all to have the use and the sense of these values. . . . A Jew is a man who is refused access to these values on principle . . . there is formed around him an impalpable atmosphere, which is the genuine France, with its genuine values, its genuine tact, its genuine morality, and he has no part of it.

But however it was or is in France, in America, this land of immigrants, the WASP no longer reigns. The Jew is not refused access to America's values; he is invited to help shape those values, and has accepted that invitation with vigor. Now and again, he of course encounters resentment, or worse. In 1985, one Dr. Robert L. Simonds, a member of President Reagan's Task Force to Implement the National Commission on Excellence in Education Report: "A Nation at Risk," and president of the National Association of Christian Educators, published a pamphlet entitled "How to Elect Christians to Public Office." There he observes that "All citizens should elect someone who represents their philosophy on vital issues. Only Christians can truly represent the Judeo-Christian views." Or we may recall Reverend Bailey Smith's unforgettable "God Almighty does not hear the prayers of a Jew." (Smith was president of the Southern Baptist Convention.)

But the consequence of being at home is that when Bailey Smith said what he did, the Jewish response was to declare Smith's perception illegitimate, not to doubt Jewish legitimacy. It is no longer the case, as it was until recently, that America's Jews are prepared to defer to others' definition of American values.

Or is it? When Jonathan Pollard was convicted in 1987 of spying for Israel, American Jewish leaders openly expressed their anger at Israel's behavior. Such public and vehement criticism was unprecedented, and was susceptible of two very different interpretations. On the one hand, it could be seen as the response of Jews who felt themselves quite comfortably American, and who therefore doubly resented Israel's behavior: as Americans, because Israel encouraged treachery, and as Jews, because Israel, in exploiting Pollard's Jewish loyalty, had challenged the essential proposition on which their comfort as Americans was based. That proposition, quite simply, is that Jewish loyalty and American loyalty are entirely compatible, that Justice Brandeis was quite correct when he said, back in 1915, that no American should think that "Zionism is inconsistent with Patriotism." Pollard notwithstanding, the great surprise of America, indeed, is that the dual loyalties of the Jews do not need to be suppressed; one can live with both, and never have to choose between them.

On the other hand, the open anger could be seen as a response to classic Jewish insecurity. That is how Professor Shlomo Avineri of the Hebrew University chose to interpret it, in a remarkable and widely publicized letter "to an American Jewish friend." Avineri professed to see in the Jewish response to Pollard "a degree of nervousness, insecurity and even cringing . . . which runs counter to the conventional wisdom of American Jewry feeling free, secure and unmolested in an open and pluralistic society." He is, he writes, "reminded of some Jewish reactions in France during the Dreyfus affair: 'He is guilty—we are not, we are good French patriots.' " And then comes the classic Zionist attack:

> This anxiety is deep in your soul, and it is in the soul—and not in external circumstances—that *Galut* [exile] resides. *Galut* is ambivalence, alienation, homelessness. . . . Zionism grew out of the cruel realization that for all their achievements and successes, when the chips are down Jews in the Diaspora become vulnerable and defenseless, are seen as aliens—and will see themselves as such. . . . [The] truth of the matter is . . . you in America are no different from French, German, Polish, Soviet and Egyptian Jews. Your Exile is different—comfortable, padded with success and renown. It is exile nonetheless. [The letter was published in *The Jerusalem Post International Edition* of March 21, 1987.]

Although Avineri's brutal analysis was not echoed by others, it was a reasonable summary of the traditional Zionist view: You in America are victims of a delusion. Anti-Semitism is everywhere latent, and you are irretrievably alien. Judaism outside the land is doomed, and if you imagine yourselves at home in America it is only because you mistake grudging tolerance for genuine acceptance and because you have only the foggiest sense of what being

Jewish is really about. You speak a foreign language, you think foreign thoughts, you are the real Levantines of our time, covering your empty selves with an American veneer that no "real" American takes seriously. You are the most pathetic Jews we have had, for you live in exile and you don't even realize it.

For their own reasons, Israel's Zionists are almost invariably drawn to such views. In an American Jewish Committee symposium on "Zionism Today," Avraham Harman, for many years Israel's ambassador to the United States, later president of the Hebrew University, makes those reasons clear:

> The Jews of Israel are being told today by certain schools of opinion in American Jewry that the Jewish world is not to be conceived as a circle with Israel as its growing center but as an ellipse with two centers, one in Israel and one in America. If this is the case, then surely it means that for the individual Jew it is immaterial where he lives. The two centers are of equal value for the Jewish future. Why then would the individual Israeli not say to himself that what is good for the American Jew is also good for him? He, too, can be a full Jew and make an equal contribution to Jewish existence and the Jewish future in New York. Why should he stay in Israel and do his annual reserve duty and worry about terrorist incidents and pay high taxes? . . . For the Israeli to live a harsh and at times dangerous life he must surely feel that Israel is indispensable to Jewish existence and to the Jewish future, that there is a radical difference of Jewish significance between living as a Jew in Israel and living as a Jew in America.

One understands such views, and respects the context from which they arise. But the conclusions to which they lead are both harsh and problematic. We live in a world of facts as well as of theories, and the growing disposition of American Jews to point with some measure of pride to the facts of American Jewish life does violence to the classical Zionist theory. Accordingly, Israeli Zionists reject the facts. At the same symposium, the Israeli scholar and Zionist historian Anita Shapira asks rhetorically,

> What is there to hold [American Jewry] together, to keep the spark in the next generation? . . . A bit of nostalgic shtetly history, the plight of the first-generation immigrants, bits and pieces of Jewish traditions which, not observed, will soon be forgotten. This

is not enough to keep Jewish identity alive. The only subject that
carries a real meaning to the secular Jew is Israel. . . . If American
Jews want to retain their Jewish identity, they have to recognize the
centrality of Israel.

Israeli demographers join in the battle, predicting a steady decline
in the number of American Jews (a prediction rejected by virtually
all American Jewish demographers), seeking thereby to fit the facts
to the theory. And so do Israel's political leaders and newspapers,
reflecting what is, in effect, the trap into which Zionism stumbles
when its adherents come to assess American Jewish life.*

There is, in the end, only one way for American Jews to "win"
the argument, and that is for them to live richly Jewish lives, not
in order to show that the Israelis are wrong, but because they want
to, because, having established (at least to their own satisfaction)
that Jews can be at home in America, they now want to test whether
Judaism, too, can be at home here. Whether it can, whether such a
thing as an authentic American Jewish culture is truly possible—a
subject I take up in a later chapter—we do not yet know; save for
pockets of people here and there, we have not yet tried, the argument is not yet truly joined. Our effort, until very recently—and
much of it still—has been invested in establishing the safety of the
Jews. Whether the fact of that safety is yet adequately appreciated
by America's Jews, and, more important still, to what uses, Judaic
and/or other, we shall put it—these questions are what the coming
decades of American Jewish life will be about.

But one thing is clear even now, and that brings us to a second
critique of our "at-homeness." The American Jewish reaction to the
Avineri letter was less one of fury than it was of wonder: What can
that man possibly be talking about? At home in America, we do not,
by and large, retain the sense of exile; surely, in fact, many of us
are offended when Israelis use the word to describe our home. For

*The only major exception is Abba Eban, who has criticized Avineri for his "refusal to look
at American Jewry in its own terms" and, more generally, has argued that in terms of Jewish
history, the rise of American Jewry should be regarded as one of the "two towering events"
of the twentieth century. (The other is, of course, the emergence of the State of Israel.) In
Eban's view, what we call "Zionist ideology" is more nearly "a body of writing that is
fundamentally about Russian Jewry" and that did not envision the American experience. But
here, as in so many other respects, Eban's is a lonely voice.

does not our history teach that it is possible for Jews to be Jews anywhere, whether or not we weep when we remember Zion? The Torah, after all, is portable.

But there is exile, and there is Exile—and a Jewish community that has lost the sense of Exile cannot live a richly Jewish life.

Ben Halpern cites the "many great ideas in Judaism" that make it "one of the great influences and lasting monuments of all human civilization." These, he observes, can be and have been "transplanted, cherished and made fruitful" by others. But, "In the system of Jewish ideas, Exile is the inalienably Jewish idea, the most intimate creation of the Jewish people, the symbol in which our whole historic experience is sublimated and summed up. . . . Live under the sign of Exile—your life as a Jew is an ever-present tension. Cut that idea out—and you cut out memory, identification, and drive, substituting a dull adjustment."

Halpern's statement will surely come as a puzzle to very many American Jews, to whom the distinction between exile and Exile is not immediately comprehensible, to whom the idea of Exile is unfamiliar. At its core, Exile is not an idea that has anything to do with geography. What is it about? Here is how Halpern explains the distinction:

> We in America are not in exile, we say, because nobody keeps us here, nor does anyone keep us out of Israel. The argument is sound—but it is not an argument. The debate is not about exile; it is about "Exile"—Golus, Galut. "Exile" does not depend on the United States Congress nor on the Israeli Knesset. "Exile" means a disordered condition of the Universe as a whole, which is epitomized in the fact and symbol that the Jewish people live outside their own proper place, the land of Israel.

What is required, then, to sustain the sense of Exile is not continuing persecution, or even alienation, but a world view that is essentially independent of personal condition or geographic location. Restore the Jews to their proper place, and you end their exile—but the Exile persists; the world remains fundamentally disordered.

A Jew, then, is in Exile not because of Titus or because there are

Cossacks—though Titus and the Cossacks are part of it—but because God's world is not working the way it was meant to work. The acknowledgment of Exile is equally available to the bag lady and to the billionaire, to the illiterate and to the laureate. It is not linked to one's personal condition, but to the condition of the world.

And on this reading, a Jew is also in Exile whether he lives in Boston or in Jerusalem. A Jew is not *supposed* to feel at home.

But if Exile is not a place, if Exile does not mean anywhere that is not Israel, in what sense does Zion come to redeem it? The Exile Halpern describes is an existential condition, not a geographic location. How then can the place heal the condition? The Exile Halpern describes is not about the dispersion of the Jews; it is about the fracture of the universe. How then can it be supposed that the mere fact of the ingathering of the Jews will finally repair that fracture?

What, in short, are the links between Return and Redemption, between Exile and Dispersion and Diaspora, between Zion and the Land of Israel and the State of Israel? Or: Where is Jerusalem?

There are countless stories of Jerusalem, and they point us in different directions. It is not at all clear from the sources—from the Biblical texts, the Talmud, the poems, and the folk tales—whether the Jerusalem, the Zion, of our millennial longing is the earthly Jerusalem or the distant and inaccessible heavenly Jerusalem. It is not clear whether our expression of hope for redemption is a ritual hope or a lively anticipation. It is not clear what the relationship is between the two Jerusalems, nor which of them is truly Zion.

The stories can support and have supported a variety of conclusions. True, the central story, the one story from which all the rest derive and descend, is crystal clear:

> I call heaven and earth to witness against you this day: I have set before you life and death, blessing and curse. Choose life . . . by loving the Lord your God. . . . For thereby you shall have life and shall long endure upon the soil that the Lord your God swore to Abraham, Isaac and Jacob to assign to them. (Deuteronomy 30: 19–20)

Or again:

> And when Moses finished reciting all these words to Israel, he said to them: Take to heart all the words with which I have warned you this day. Enjoin them upon your children, that they may observe faithfully all the terms of the Teaching. For this is not a trifling thing for you: it is your very life; through it you shall endure on the land which you are crossing the Jordan to possess. (Deuteronomy 32: 45–47)

Or most starkly:

> Should you, when . . . you are long established in the land, act wickedly, and make yourselves a sculptured image in any likeness . . . I call heaven and earth to witness against you this day that you shall soon perish from the land which you are crossing the Jordan to take possession of; you shall not long endure in it, but be utterly wiped out. The Lord will scatter you among the peoples, and only a scant few of you shall be left among the nations to which the Lord will drive you. . . . But if you search there for the Lord your God . . . with all your mind and being . . . the Lord your God will not fail you nor will He let you perish; He will not forget the covenant which He made under oath with your ancestors. (Deuteronomy 4: 25–31)

Still, the history of the people is, as I have said, an ongoing commentary on the original text, and in the Jewish imagination over the centuries, elaborate theologies of Exile were developed that sought somehow to *justify* the continuing separation of the Jews from the Land, to overcome the grim perception that the Jews were doomed to live out an unending punishment. How, after all, could it have been otherwise? Cast out, as we saw it, from our sacred space, we sought desperately for some other mode to experience the sacred, to understand the grand purpose of our election—and of our rejection.

So we learned to make do with what we had. The Land, for the time being, was not ours, nor were the lands of our wanderings. What we had, and what no one could take from us, was memory and dream; what we owned, instead of space, was time; not today, but yesterday and tomorrow.

At Sinai, we heard; at Zion, we saw; removed from Zion, we became auditors again—prayer substituting for sacrifice, the Word, the Torah, the Teaching substituting for the Land. Prayer and Torah exist in time, not in space. And what began as a consolation became, in due course, a vocation, with a life and a thrust—and even a vocabulary—of its own. So it was that Zion transcended itself, became a location not only in space—that it never ceased to be—but a location in time as well. Time's Zion was not vulnerable to the oppressor; it would happen on the day that is neither day nor night, the day that is the end of days, in the world to come, the world that is entirely Sabbath. It would happen outside history.

In the meantime, what to do while waiting? How to explain the travail, to infuse it with purpose? For some, it was a test, and the challenge was to continue to believe, to hold on to the dream in spite of its repeated denial by the experience of Exile. For most, the meaning of the thing—again the meaning, always the search for meaning in the midst of madness—was not punishment but mission.

The nature of the mission was variously defined. The Kabbalist Isaac Luria believed that the Exile commenced with the Creation itself, that the sparks of God, of the Divine Presence, are scattered throughout the earth and that it is man's task to recover them; thus does man engage in the work of *tikun* (repair), of redemption. And the people Israel? It has been scattered among the nations in order to fulfill its special task, the work of *tikun,* the gathering of the sparks.

For Luria, the work of *tikun* was essentially the pursuit of piety; for Reform Judaism, emerging two centuries later, it was the work of what we now call social action, no less a mission, no less messianic in its intention.

The understanding that the world is fractured, in desperate need of repair, and that the Jews are implicated in the work of repair, called to that work, has been a very widely shared way of coming to terms with the Diaspora. At the heart of that understanding is, as Halpern puts it, the belief that Exile is not merely the condition of the Jews, but their *commitment.* Jews—whether because they were chosen for the task, or because of their own condition—were understood to be especially, perhaps even uniquely, sensitive to the pain of a world disordered.

But to pain of such magnitude, the Land could be at best only a partial response. Israel might "cure" the dispersion of the Jews; it could not cure the Exile. (Indeed, one might observe that it is precisely the introduction of a messianic agenda into the Israeli political debate that distorts political life in that country.) Jerusalem restored would surely be a blessing, but could not yet be the promised Jerusalem; Zion remains an aspiration.

In the Zionist view, the promised Jerusalem remains an aspiration principally because the Jews, in their vast majority, have stayed where they were before Jerusalem became available—or even worse, have chosen to move from Moscow to Milwaukee. But in the Diaspora, it remains an aspiration for two entirely different reasons. First, the particularity of Israel cannot satisfy the universality of the mission. Israel may be—is, surely—haven; it cannot be, quite, home, for no place can be in a world of pain. And second, the nature of the Diaspora experience has caused the Jews to invest so heavily in the eschatological "ought" that they are at something of a loss in dealing with the geopolitical "is," with the fact called Israel. Judaism, as the Jews have perforce come to understand it, is wrapped up in the days that were and in the end of days, in the past and in the future. Against these, the present is empty, a burden and a bore.

Zionism came, it announced, to bring the Jews back into history. For centuries, however, the Jews had sought not to retrieve history but to abolish it; that is what messianism, religious or secular, promises, and it was messianism that was the balm to the pains and punishments of the Diaspora. It takes considerably longer than 40 years of stormy national independence to work 2,000 years (and more) of utopian orientation out of a people's psyche.

The more so in America, for here the dispersion has been most benign, the geographic Zion therefore least urgent; here the Jewish understanding came still more emphatically to emphasize the Redemption rather than the Return. Here, where the fact of exile has been least relevant, the Jewish vocation has been to bear witness to the persistence of Exile.

But can we truly say of America's Jews that they retain a lively sense of Exile, that they stay where they are, reject the return, because they await the larger Redemption?

In his essay "Are We in Exile?," Jacob Neusner attacks this notion with a vengeance. It would be, he says, "pretentious" to impute metaphyiscal significance to so "banal" and "boring" an ethnic group as ours. "American Jewry simply does not add up to much. Its inner life is empty, its public life decadent. So to whom shall we ask the ultimate questions of meaning? To what shall we apply the transcendent symbols of exile and alienation? To Bar Mitzvah factories and bowling clubs? It would not be merely incongruous but derisive."

I believe Neusner is mistaken, though his evidence cannot casually be dismissed. It is not just the "Bar Mitzvah factories and bowling clubs"; one could easily expand the evidence of triviality, of vulgarity, yes, of decadence. So very much at home have we come to be that even the literature of alienation now seems nostalgic rather than descriptive. Exile? Where, whether in the synagogue or the boardroom, in the country club or the patio, can one encounter the chaos that, Nietzsche wrote, is required "to be able to give birth to a dancing star"? Instead, "one has," he continued, "one's little pleasure for the day and one's little pleasure for the night: but one has a regard for health."

It is true, I suppose, that there are Jews who have forgotten how to feel the world's pain, who know little of chaos and less of dancing stars. They inhale the perfumed anesthetics of our time and forget the language of the Jews, the language of memories and dreams, of Exile; they are satisfied, at ease. Some even come to hold high position in Jewish life, secular and religious.

We have no public opinion surveys that might tell us how many there are of this kind, how many of that. I cannot, therefore, offer hard proof with which to rebut Neusner's perception. I can only assert what seems to me the larger truth: Away from the marketplace and the mirrors, from the hustle and the hype, most Jews remain accessible to the language, to its message. For every half-million-dollar bar mitzvah party on the *QE2* (talk about splashy!), for example, there are five, ten, fifty "parties" of the kind described on the invitation that now lies before me:

> Share with us and increase our joy as Stephen H. King and Yuri Varvac, Kiev, USSR [in absentia] are called to the Torah as B'nai

Mitzvah. . . . As our home abounds with love, excitement and thankfulness at this special time in our life—so we think of those who are homeless and impoverished and have so few times for rejoicing. If you so desire, in lieu of gifts, please join Stephen in bringing non-perishable foods and/or a donation to Covering Wings [an organization that supplies blankets for the homeless]. Please join us for Kiddush following the ceremony. At Stephen's request, in place of a reception, we will be hosting families from the Orange County Interfaith Shelter for the Homeless at the Angel-Royal baseball game that evening.

Not proof, merely an anecdote. But so, too, is the *QE2* bar mitzvah. Neither, alone, is the whole of the story. Most Jews—even the ones who join the bowling clubs, even the ones who golf their days away—remember about pain. Not all, never all. (If it had been all, against whom would the prophets have railed?) Just most.

Which is to say, they have not forgotten Jerusalem, though they are here at home.

Where is their Jerusalem? Over there, and everywhere. There is the Jerusalem of the King David and the Hilton hotels, of Yad Vashem and of the Arab market, the earthly Jerusalem, troubled and troubling answer to our dispersion, haven. For the sake of that Jerusalem, most American Jews are prepared to walk through fire. And there is the other Jerusalem, the heavenly Jerusalem, the Jerusalem that remains a yearning, answer to Exile, home. For the sake of that Jerusalem, many American Jews are prepared to live their lives.

From the earthly Jerusalem where they live, Zionists resist and resent the doctrine that there is purpose to Judaism outside the Land. Israel, as they see it, is not merely the center of Jewish life; if it were only that, they might be prepared to indulge those who choose (however shallow the choice) to live at the periphery rather than at the center, in the heart of the maelstrom. No, Israel as they understand it and live it is the very *purpose* of Jewish life. To claim that there can be Jewish purpose outside it is to imply that the Jews of Israel must go out to kill and be killed, must live out their hemmed-in lives in Beersheba or Kiryat Shmoneh rather than in

Chicago or Miami, because of nothing more than an accident of fate, that they live the beleaguered lives they do in the name of geographic coincidence rather than in the name of God or some other transcendent aspiration.

It is hard not to sympathize with the Zionist perception. Unless life in Israel can be justified in cosmic terms, why endure its stress? And the cosmic terms are not hard to come by: Here Abraham walked, there Jeremiah preached; here the Temple stood, there, on the way to the beach, the Essenes lived. Nor need one turn to distant yesterdays to feel it: modern messianists roam the streets and the halls of Parliament; public rhetoric is riddled with metaphysical reference.

The Jews of Israel know, of course, that ever since the beginning of the modern resettlement of the land, most Jews on the move have preferred to move elsewhere. Though their hearts might lie in the East, their feet moved resolutely westward. Between 1881 and 1930, nearly 4 million Jews left Russia, Poland, Rumania, and a handful of other European countries; just 120,000 of them moved to Palestine—roughly one of every thirty-three Jews en route. And since statehood? By and large, those Jews who could go elsewhere did. From Algeria they moved to France, from the Soviet Union to the United States. In South Africa, perhaps the most intensely Zionist community in the Diaspora, some left for Israel, more for the United States (and lately Australia), and most have stayed put.

The Israelis will not concede that all this is for high-minded purpose, in the name of a universal messianism. To make such a concession would be to call into question the assumptions on which their enterprise rests. Better, then, to look to inertia, to indifference, or to ignorance as explanation, to faint-heartedness, to assimilationism.

And what of America's Jews? Easy enough to bring them into the embrace of the same explanation: Look at the rate of intermarriage, look at the apathy, look at the emptiness. And easy enough, too, to deprecate it all: a case of matter over mind, the victory of history's most seductive fleshpot.

Except that some American Jews don't fit that explanation. They study texts and light the Sabbath candles, they chain themselves to the gates of the Soviet Embassy in protest against Soviet treatment of the Jews, and they lobby their congressmen for increased aid to Israel; they care, and deeply, about the quality of their lives as Jews, and they claim that in Denver, too, one can find valid Jewish purpose, even if they cannot quite define that purpose. It may be accident that brought them here and inertia that keeps them here, but it is not fair or accurate to conclude that because they are here they are condemned to live without meaning, even without Jewish meaning.

But for the Jews of Israel to acknowledge that would be for them to admit not merely injury but insult as well. It is one thing to consider how different Israel's history might have been had only 2 or 3 more million Jews chosen to come; it rankles in a different way to accept that Jewish life in America may actually be a valid alternative. So Israelis, by and large, do not accept that it is.

Here is how one Israeli put it in a letter he wrote to me in mid-1987, commenting on the large proportion of Soviet Jews who, once permitted to leave the USSR, have chosen to come to the United States rather than go to Israel:

> If the United States is not a place of dispersion for the Jews, what is it? Zion? The Second Jewish Homeland? If America is not Dispersion, why is Soviet Russia Dispersion? They are both quite definitely dispersion and you must understand our insult at being used by cynics to facilitate the exchange of one diaspora for another, feeling quite safe about the whole affair knowing that there's a bunch of suckers here in Israel sitting on the borders and fighting the wars to save a place for them in case something should go haywire.
>
> As you well know, but obviously refuse to admit, the American Jewish community will self-annihilate within the next few decades, and along with it the remnants of Soviet Jewry to the land of wonders. Of course you'll be very comfortable doing it. We, in the meantime, will continue to fight for the existence of the Jewish people.

And, truth to tell, more than a few of America's Jews would be sympathetic to these ardent—and quite typical—Israeli views.

Again, discontinuity.

*   *   *

In the 1960s, as I tried to show in the first chapter, America stopped being the New Jerusalem. Though the Jewish attachment to this country remains passionate, the illusion that this was or could be Zion—as some Jews had insistently maintained—was shattered by assassins' bullets, incinerated in the burning cities here and in the napalmed villages there.

In the 1980s, as the facts of Israel became more turbulent and, yes, more disturbing, many of us came to see another Zion, too—the original Zion—as somehow tarnished. It was inevitable, of course. It would be wrong to conclude from what I have been saying that there is a radical distinction between the heavenly and the earthly Jerusalems, between Zion as time and Zion as place. That was never so (except in some ephemeral fringe ideologies). The two are inevitably intertwined; in the popular perception, the one below has been kissed by the one above. And which of us, even of the most secularized of us, can resist the power of the ashes-to-rebirth metaphor that has attended Israel's emergence into modern statehood? To be a lover of Zion has been to experience the transcendent, not as hope but as event.

And, therefore, to experience disappointment. That is what happens on the eighth day, always, everywhere. Against the background of Jewish history, Israel's birth was bound to be perceived as "the beginning of the flowering of our redemption"; against the background of such a perception, each weed was bound to come as a derogation of Israel's promise. (To say nothing of the theological problems implicit in regarding the creation of a state—as distinguished here from the return of a people to its land—as a theological event.)

In the real world, there are always weeds. And that, of course, is the point I seek to make here: Only now, a generation after Israel's rebirth, are American Jews beginning to understand that it exists in the real world. For many of us, the advent of that understanding is accompanied by stress, by frustration, by disappointment, sometimes even by resentment.

How do we handle the consequent tensions? I have been writing here as if all American Jews were of one mind on these shadowy matters. Obviously, we are not. There are those who now seek some

distance, begin a process of emotional disinvestment and detach-
ment. Israel is the tie that has bound them to Judaism; in order to
protect themselves from fierce disappointment, some of them now
search for other ties. They turn more energetically to religion, or
they study Yiddish or the Holocaust, or they redouble their commitment to secular social action. Some are so embittered that they
abandon the whole of the Jewish enterprise.

Still others, victims of organizational and sometimes personal
inertia, cling to the older understanding. They place the disconcerting facts, unopened, in dead storage, and gambol through the groves
of myth. (I will have more to say, later on, about the specific ways
in which we manage—or fail to manage—Israel's reality, and the
debate within our own community—the problem, as it is called, of
"dissent"—that reality sometimes provokes.)

But most of us are too preoccupied with the defense of Israel—
and of our own categories—to spend much time thinking through
such delicate matters. Heavenly or earthly, gold or dross, no matter;
the enemy is at the gates. Later, we think, there will be time to make
distinctions, to sort out the emotions and conclusions of this new
time in Jewish history. Later there'll be time, if there's still need, to
deal with disappointments and the like; for now, to work.

But if it's until the enemy is gone that we must wait, later may
be very far away. Later may be after a new generation has tried—
and failed—to make sense of an apparently ordinary faraway land
in which its parents seem to invest quite extraordinary emotion. If
the generation that witnessed the rebirth seeks to bequeath its commitment to Jerusalem to its heirs, if it wants them to follow in its
heartbeats as Lovers of Zion, it must learn to teach both the realities
of the place and the reality of the dream. It must itself learn to
nurture both, and the synapses that connect them, learn to say yes
to the ordinary, a wholehearted yes—and never to let go the dream.

In his *In the Land of Israel,* Amos Oz wrote:

> Perhaps we bit off too much. Perhaps there was, on all sides, a
> latent messianism. A messiah complex. Perhaps we should have
> aimed for less. Perhaps there was a wild pretension here, beyond
> our capabilities—beyond human capabilities. . . . Perhaps we should
> take smaller bites. . . . Concede heavenly Jerusalem for the sake of

the Jerusalem of the slums, waive messianic salvation for the sake of small, gradual reforms, forego messianic fervor for the sake of prosaic sobriety. And perhaps the entirety of our story is not a story of blood and fire or of salvations and consolations but, rather, a story of a halting attempt to recover from a severe illness.

There is no shortcut to the building of the city of our longings— nor to understanding the intricacies of the Jewish response to Israel. For there is another element here that I have so far only hinted at. A. B. Yehoshua, the Israeli author who has lately emerged as the harshest critic of the Diaspora, argues that we Jews outside the Land have "fallen in love with the Diaspora," have found the fleshpots irresistible.

The fleshpots cannot be discounted, but there is more to it than Yehoshua allows. Yes, we have fallen in love with the Diaspora, but we have fallen in love with it quite as much because of Woody Allen as because of the fleshpots. We have, that is, learned to live at the margins, where for so much of our history we were forced to live. And we have learned to feel at home with our marginality, to accept it as our distinctive condition, a central ingredient of our identity, an explanation of our creativity.

Life in a sovereign Jewish state comes as a puzzlement to Jews who have learned to depend, even to thrive, on marginality. Here, it is easy enough to dismiss the rednecks with contempt; they are not, after all, *our* rednecks. But in Israel, they *are* our rednecks. What are we to make of them? Here, we can stand with one leg outside the circle; in Israel, there is no such option. Here, we can take comfort in the feeling that our liability is limited; there, there is no such limitation.

Limited liability? Quite; that is the lesson of 2,000 years of wandering. It is not a question of loyalty withheld, of patriotism attenuated. It is, instead, the knowledge that the nation is not the end, no matter how glorious its achievements. Our theology teaches that, of course: there is only one King, and our loyalty to Him antedates and supercedes our loyalty to even the most compelling princes, let alone to run-of-the-mill idols. And our experience teaches it as well: so often we have let ourselves believe that if only we would enter with whole heart, we would be received with open arms—and so often, we have learned that we are strangers after all. Better not to invest it all, lest we again experience disappointment; so we hold back, we keep a part of ourselves in reserve.

Israel asks for, insists on, everything. It exhausts its citizens. It offers no place to hide. And we are not used to that and not comfortable with it.

So we make an ideology out of Babylon. We remind ourselves that the Torah was given and the Covenant struck in the wilderness, outside the Land. We recall that it was not the Zealots of Masada, who committed suicide rather than be taken into captivity, who ensured the survival of our people, but Rabbi Yochanan Ben Zakai, who left the burning Jerusalem to establish a house of study in a non-sacred place. We believe that such genius as we possess is a cosmopolitan genius, honed on the hard rock of Exile, whetted at the margins where we have dwelt.

We love Israel, Zion, Jerusalem, but that is not all we love, not even as Jews. We may not be—we are not—terribly articulate about the rest of it, not just now, but we know that our nostalgia is not for the days of David and Solomon, nor are our dreams of the Temple restored. Our nostalgia is for our grandfathers and grandmothers who managed, somehow, to thrive in all the wilderness of our people's sojourning.

And our dreams? Our dreams are not of another place but of another time.

7

Survival as Vocation: The Voyage of the Damned

SHARED EXPERIENCE and shared concerns are among the things that connect people—and also a people—and surely both the Holocaust and the saga of the State of Israel provide America's Jews just such grounds for connection. But I have been arguing that there are limits to the connective value of each, that they have become substitutes for the shared meanings that once defined and informed the Jewish connection.

I do not mean to suggest that there was a time—the good old days, presumably—when Jews were a tight ideological cadre of explicit conviction and exquisite commitment. And even if there was such a time—so what? It is not merely 200 years that separate us from the end of the eighteenth century, when there were altogether 2.5 million Jews in the world. Two hundred years ago was before the nation state happened, and before the Enlightenment took root, and before the Jews discovered America; it was before the Holocaust and before Israel. Two hundred years ago, being Jewish (whatever one chose to make of it) was in fact a condition, not an option, the product of *descent,* not *consent.* So much has happened during these last two centuries that comparisons between then and now, especially if intended to demonstrate this generation's relative inferiority—which is their usual purpose—are an exercise in mindlessness.

So perhaps it is a mistake to assert, as I have, that in our time we have developed "substitutes" for the old connections; perhaps what we have are simply our ways of connecting, as they—200 or 2,000 years ago—had theirs.

The problem here, it seems to me, is that we need to go beyond the obvious notion that "the times, they are a-changin' "; we need to inquire into the nature of the change. And when we do, we encounter a powerful distinction between connections defined by descent and those defined by consent. In pre-modern times, personal status was fixed by heredity; that is to say, by descent. Blood and biology mattered more than ambition and achievement; covenant was prior to contract, natural law to positive law. With modernity, a whole and largely new set of categories became available: citizenship, government by the consent of the governed, and, most of all, individual choice. Suddenly, one could choose not only a geography and a career; one could choose a future, one could even invent an identity. (Who, 200 years ago, had so much as imagined the concept of identity, let alone the possibility of defining it for oneself?)

The idea of the individual as a free agent, entitled to shape his/her own future, is a newish idea. Indeed, it is an idea not yet readily available to most of the world's people, whose economic, political, and psychological circumstances keep them, both objectively and subjectively, objects of destiny more than authors of decision. Our circumstances are different: the idea is available to us, and we have taken it up with great enthusiasm.

But the Jewish tradition, for its part, draws heavily on *both* descent and consent: we are Jews because Abraham and Isaac and Jacob were our fathers and Sarah, Rebecca, Rachel, and Leah our mothers, because we are, by name, the Children of Israel, and because we are heirs to God's promise to the descendants of our ancestors. We are Jews, at the same time, because we accepted—that is, consented to—the covenant; the very idea of covenant makes us citizens rather than subjects.

There is room, then, in the tradition for both the blessing and the ballot. Yet the Jews are an enthusiastically modern people; we *believe*—most of us—in consent. We would likely believe in it even if we had not, so often, been the victims of those who did not stop to ask what it was we had consented to, those for whom the fact that we were Jews, descendants of Jews, was a sufficient indictment. As modern people, we have been taught to make of our lives an intention, not to permit the accident of birth to become our destiny. We have been taught to follow the commitments we have chosen, not the categories we have been assigned. So Judaism's continuing emphasis on descent makes us uncomfortable.

Yet we cannot say that the conflict is wholly between tradition and modernity. Even the earliest Jews, and the most traditional, acknowledge the priority of commitment: one can, after all, no matter one's biological background, convert to Judaism. And even the most modern Jews, and the most secular, acknowledge the continuing relevance of descent: the mere self-identification as a Jew is not enough.

What is it that a convert to Judaism Jew commits to? Traditional conversion involves a commitment to "the yoke of commandment" and, at the same time, the acceptance of what might be called "constructive descent." The would-be convert is renamed, becoming either "son of Abraham" or "daughter of Sarah," and if a male, undergoes symbolic circumcision. Henceforward, there is no distinction of any kind between the person who came to Judaism from the womb and the person who came to it from the word. But the person who comes to it from the womb need not commit to anything, ever. The tradition teaches that one who is born a Jew always remains a Jew, no matter how rebellious, how heretical. (For that matter, a convert who undergoes a "relapse" is also nonetheless and forever a Jew.) So heredity is a sufficient, but not a necessary, condition—and commitment is neither necessary nor sufficient.

These days, there is even a growing debate on how "born a Jew" shall be defined. According to Orthodox belief, a Jew is a person born of a Jewish mother. But recently, the Reform movement has ruled that a Jewish father will do, a ruling that has evoked intense and often vitriolic debate. The Orthodox contend that the acceptance of patrilineal descent means there will soon be children of Jewish fathers who will grow up thinking themselves Jewish, only to learn that because their mothers were not Jewish they themselves are not Jewish—according to Orthodox belief—and therefore cannot marry anyone who hews to that belief (unless, of course, they are prepared to convert). And, to confuse matters still more, the Reform movement does not rest on one-parent descent alone; it insists as well that to be considered a Jew, the child of one Jewish parent must make some public assertion (bar or bat mitzvah, confirmation, ill-defined alternatives) of his/her Jewishness.

Does this mean that Reform is trying to combine elements of both consent (an act) and descent (a parent)? Not quite, since Reform acceptance of patrilineality leaves the child of two Jewish parents at rest; he or she is still under no compulsion to consent to anything, is automatically a Jew, independent of behavior.

These curious backings and forthings actually play themselves out in the real world, where they sometimes lead to bizarre conclusions. Thus, a prominent Reform family recently asked its rabbi to officiate at the wedding of their son to a young woman they represented as Jewish. In fact, she was the daughter of a Jewish mother and a non-Jewish father. The rabbi met with the young couple, and then informed the family that he would not be able to officiate. Why? Because the young woman had never made public acknowledgment of her Jewishness. If such an acknowledgment is required of the offspring of a Jewish father, then why not also of the offspring of a Jewish mother? (To which, of course, the detached observer might well ask, and why not of the offspring of two Jewish parents?) The family, upset by the ruling, approached an Orthodox rabbi—who had no problem at all in officiating, since the young woman was, according to the traditional matrilineal perspective, entirely Jewish; a Jewish mother is all that is required.

Yet even the Orthodox view is not quite so straightforward as at first it seems. The complexity of technology disturbs the simplicity of biology. Now that we engage in in vitro fertilization, in which an ovum can be fertilized outside the womb and then be implanted into a surrogate womb, what does matrilineality mean? Is it the ovum that must be Jewish, or the womb? (This is not an academic question; it confronts the administrators of Israeli hospitals today, and will surely soon be raised in the United States as well.)

There's considerable discomfort here, for we lack not only a binding definition of descent, but also a tidy theory that can help us sort out the competing claims of descent and consent. Apparently, despite all our modern enthusiasms, we are not prepared to turn our backs on descent. But where do we make room for its implications? Intellectually, most of us perceive them as mere vestiges of a less enlightened time. Yet "pure" modernity doesn't make it for us: we need help in coping with its evident sterility, with its rootlessness, its chilling anomie. We need, among other things, a past.

We cannot invent that past. For a time, we may try; we may assert the irrelevance of our grandfathers. After all, if we can make of our lives and of ourselves whatever we choose, then we can be our own fathers. (Erik Erikson, pre-eminent analyst of identity, not only invented his own name but named himself his own father.) But even so, we cannot go farther back than that. Some years ago, Edward G. Robinson starred in a television drama in which he played a retired toy manufacturer from New York City, a man who had rejected his immigrant forebears and had come to live in a Vermont village. There he purchased a home and sought, with middling success, acceptance from his Yankee neighbors. Wanting more, wanting, finally, to *belong,* Robinson sought to negotiate with the former owner of his house the purchase of the family burial plot that lay behind it. But he discovered, of course, that grandfathers are not interchangeable. If you want one, you have to take the one that's yours, the one to whom you've been assigned. As Horace Kallen put it, "men change their clothes, their politics, their wives, their religions, their philosophies, to a greater or lesser extent; they cannot change their grandfathers."

Modern Jews, like many modern others, have lately come, to their own surprise, to want their grandfathers and grandmothers. There is a veritable run on roots, a rush to remember before memories fade, before the grandparents die. We have learned that there is a sense in which we *need* yesterday, in which we remain bound to our biology, our own specific history. What draws us—and most others, apparently—to *Fiddler on the Roof* is that it recapitulates our own experience. The first daughter rejects the marriage that has been arranged for her; consent has begun to matter. The second daughter takes consent a step farther; she chooses a heretic. But her heretic is still a Jew; the past still matters. The third daughter rejects descent completely; she marries out of the faith. (And Tevye, who has bent to the earlier innovations, now announces: "When you bend us too far, we break; there is no other hand.") Had the play been conceived today, there might well be a fourth daughter, one whose marriage would end in divorce, thereby signifying the desacralization of the formerly covenantal relationship. We want the right to divorce, but we do not want the attendant loss, the sterilizing awareness that nothing endures, that nothing is sacred, that everything reduces to contract, to exchange.

Because we are children of modernity, we want to say that anyone who calls himself, herself, a Jew shall be considered a Jew—but we want, as well, some criteria beyond self-proclamation. (Though we may have been discomfited by Israel's refusal to accept the Black Hebrews, a self-defined group from Chicago with no Jewish past, most of us were not opposed to the decision.) We know that Jews are not merely a group of people who agree with each other, more or less, are not a church, a faith; Jews are a family. True, we want to be free to be Jewish or not to be Jewish, and if to be Jewish, to define for ourselves what being Jewish shall mean. But we know also that we are heirs. When we are named, as also when we are called to chant the blessings over the Torah, it is as (given name) the son or daughter of (father's name, these days mother's name as well) that we are called. And for most of us, it is as the son or as the daughter that we rise; that is the largest part of the reason we are there. As the old Yiddish folk song has it, "*Vos mir zeinen zeinen mir, ober Yiden zeinen mir*—We are whatever we are, but we are Jews."

Which is to say that we cannot readily explain just what it is that we as Jews have consented to, save that we acknowledge the relevance of our descent. It is relevant not because we live in a traditional society, although even here, in this most modern place, descent is not entirely irrelevant. (So, for example, a non-native-born American cannot become president. Naturalization—consent—is not quite the equivalent of descent.) It is relevant because we have so willed it, because we have chosen to make it relevant.

But we do not know how to make it relevant. We cannot, after all, cross the street and enter a house of relevance where Jewish culture, however defined, prevails. Outside the enclaves of the Orthodox, there is no such place. So we link ourselves to the grand themes, the things we suppose Jews know in ways that others do not, perhaps even cannot. The Holocaust and Israel give us both past and purpose; obviously, they are legitimate and authentic concerns, the real stuff of connection. Together, they give us both a motto—"Never again!"—and a method—the nation state. But at the end of the day, "Never again!" tells us only what to avoid, not what to embrace. It raises the fact of Jewishness to something more than a mere nametag, but it falls far short of offering a way of life, a source of identity. It suggests an agenda, not a culture; it is a way of saying where we are *not* and will not let ourselves be, but it does not tell us where we are and want to go. And the nation state? Its defense points to a politics, not to a value system.

So is a religious civilization reduced to a political action committee.

That is what I mean when I say that we have come to depend on substitutes for the ligaments of Jewish life. Casting about in the tangled space between our discomfort with descent and our confusion with consent, we grab hold of each other as best we can. And often enough, we hold tight; there is real passion to the connection. It may be—it is—a connection radically diminished in its scope, but it is not without drama, nor does it lack intensity. And it works.

Yet it seems to me that a tradition or a culture—call it, for the time being, what you will—that asks so much of its members (adherents?) as ours does, and in particular that wants, so insistently, to be transmitted to the next generation and the next, must be able to say not merely that "it works," but also why it *wants* to work, why it warrants the effort. Utilitarian goals may be sufficient for a time, but if and when one stumbles into an oasis where the temporal agenda is suspended, there needs to be a sustaining understanding to fall back on. Inertia may carry us for a while, but what if a sudden rise in the investment that is asked of us prompts us to step outside the habit and assess its value, its rationale? Our truths are not self-evident; if one lives, as we do, in a culture of consent, there must be a way of defining what it is that, as Jews, we have consented to. For no matter how the puzzles of descent are resolved by the rabbis, the people are more interested in and confused by questions of meaning. Zionist theory holds that American Jewry is an accident. In order to rebut that view, we must have a theory of our own; it is not the origins of Jewishness but its purposes that we need to work through.

If that is indeed our haunting question, why have so many of us so assiduously avoided the search for a rationale, for a clearer definition of consent? Why have we settled for slogans and substitutes? (Nor are the Holocaust and Israel the only such substitutes. There is also nostalgia, a kind of sentimentalization of memory; there is guilt; there is inertia, too; there is, given the Jewish past, fear.)

There are two reasons to avoid the search for purpose. The first is the fear that were it to succeed, were we, that is, to discern a definition, it would require of us an assertion of difference we are not prepared to make. It is one thing to "feel" different, special; it is another to give a name to the difference. We want it—why not?—both ways: we want to see ourselves as different, but not to be seen as different; we do not want others to see us as we see ourselves, not at all. For if they did, we fear that we might be marked as outsiders, breachers of the American ethic. America indulges, even endorses, superficial difference, difference in style, but it frowns upon substantive difference. The Judaism America endorses is a Judaism "for purposes of identification only." Identity is something else again.

And the second is the flip-side fear: knowing what we know, many Jews are afraid that the search for a rationale, a definition, might prove fruitless. For so many decades now, we have been satisfied to speak vaguely of the "Judeo-Christian ethic," to imagine that there is no contradiction, nor even conflict, nor even tension, between our Jewishness and our Americanness. At the beginning, the claim was a convenient fiction, a useful deception; by now, it has become an article of faith. Hence to search for a distinctive Jewish connection may mean to search in vain, which is, in its way, as threatening as to search successfully, for if there turns out to be no compelling rationale for Jewish continuity, no way of defining our consent, nothing much beyond inertia, why all the fuss? Why the urgent symposia on the threats to Jewish survival, why the concern about intermarriage and assimilation, why the chronic sounding of the bugle? If all that "Jewish" proves to be is a nametag (because everyone in this oh so heterogeneous America must have one, not for his/her own sake, but for the sake of the neighbors), then is Jewish continuity worth the effort it requires? For a name-tag? For "customs and ceremonies"? If all it comes down to in the end is "In God We Trust," if all we are is a sect that worships on Saturday rather than on Sunday—why bother? Worse yet: if that is what we are left with, does it not follow that we, the Jews of modernity, are Jews only atavistically, Jews by descent and no more, hence not fully modern?

On the one reading—to search and to find—a subversive doctrine, to be shunned lest it rock the American boat, our lifeboat; on the other reading—to search and not to find—a barren doctrine, to be avoided lest it make a mockery of our passion, lest it betray our emptiness. Best then simply to avoid the search, and its twin dangers; focus instead on the immediate needs of Jewish survival and evade the question of Jewish meaning. Be Jewish, but not "too" Jewish.

I want now to turn, briefly, to those many American Jews who appear to have, as it were, kicked the Jewish habit, withheld their consent—and to the characteristic ways in which they are rebuked by those who remain committed to Jewish continuity. For it would surely be a mistake to imply that all Jews seek connection. Jewishness has become, as I have said, an option, and there are, despite the renewed interest in roots, significant numbers who choose not to exercise the option.

It does not seem to me that those who opt out do so because the costs of being Jewish are onerous; in America, they very rarely are. It is, instead, the nature of the benefits that has escaped them. The call to Jewish arms is almost always a call to responsibility rather than to reward, to burden rather than to benefit. The claim on Jewish attention is a claim on one's instincts, not on one's philosophy (much less theology). And if the instincts have atrophied, the call is no call, but a whine.

It will be said that community itself is a benefit, that we really have no need to search for a philosophical underpinning, for a definition of consent. Why not simply acknowledge that people's capacity to cope is enhanced by the experience of community? Everybody has to be somebody, and Jewish is what Jews are. Why feel obliged to say or to search for anything more? We know, after all, from both anecdotal and sociological sources that most Jews, no matter the state of their ideological conviction, prefer the company of other Jews. Over and over again we find that Jews, though they may both live near and work with non-Jews, have mostly Jewish friends. Is that not a clue to the importance of community?

Of course it is. The problem, however, is that while people may well be eager for the experience of community, such experience does not follow either automatically or necessarily from the fact of being Jewish. For the time being, Jews in search of community may turn more frequently to other Jews. But absent some sense of shared situation and/or purpose, absent a shared language, there is no intrinsic reason for their search to take this direction. Even now, Jewish musicians may find their instincts for community more fully satisfied with other musicians, Jewish women with other women, what have you. Speak to them of the importance of community, and they will not disagree; they will merely assert that they have found their own community elsewhere. They need not and do not announce their abandonment of the Jews with a formal statement or act of renunciation; they merely slip quietly away, making of their Jewishness first a residual and then an irrelevant category. Now and again, perhaps when the family gathers or when Israel is sharply threatened, there may be some guilt or some covering of the tracks of their exit; there may even be, if the occasion is sufficiently urgent, a brief return. But on the whole, they have made what seems to them a reasonable choice.

A generation or so ago, there was typically more bite to the defection. Back then, it was fashionable to suppose (as did Isaac Deutscher, whom I cited earlier) that humankind's tribalism was a burden to be overcome, that in the name of progress, universalism must defeat particularism. Permit the persistence of units smaller than the whole and those units will tie a tattered cloth to a gnarled branch, call it a flag, and march off to do battle with the other clans.

Some of the Jews who accepted this view—and many did, for it seemed the only way to put an end to anti-Semitism—did not merely slip away; they rebelled. They saw Judaism as an impediment to human progress, and their own Jewishness as an embarrassing legacy.

These days, there is much less of that. The pendulum that swings between universalism and particularism has shifted quite dramatically toward particularism (and not just among Jews). It is an ill-calibrated pendulum; it does not rest at the midpoint but more often careens from one extreme to the other, each new generation over-correcting for what it perceives as the excesses of its predecessor. So now, though the numbers of those who leave may be no smaller, no sparks fly, there is little argument, it is all quite anemic.

Yet the choice that seems reasonable at the private level still seems subversive at the public level. Those who care for the welfare of the Jewish community cannot be indifferent to private choices, whatever their motive, that plainly weaken it. So they will argue the matter, and the shrillest part of their argument tends to be some form of "You can't do this to us."

The problem, of course, is that from the perspective of the defector, he/she is not doing it "to us," there has been no defection—not, in any event, from anything that matters, not from anything more than sentimental attachment. The fact that private choices have public consequences is obvious, but unless the Jewish community can go beyond the mere recitation of those consequences, can say not only that Jewish survival itself is at stake, that with the next defection, Jewish history will come to its end, but can also say *why* that survival matters so, its argument is not telling.

There is, of course, an alternative position, which does away with the difficulty of saying why survival matters. In the Orthodox view, one does not quit because to quit would be to break the Covenant. Why survive? Because that is how we do God's will. But it is doubtful that very many Jews are slowed by such talk; the matter and meaning of Covenant are too far from their lives to give them pause.

The Orthodox—not more than 10 percent of America's Jews—are

in many respects a special case, to whom much that I have been saying does not readily apply.* But with regard to the matter at hand, the rationale for the Jewish endeavor, the sobering truth is that even they, in making their case, are not very likely to argue from God; like almost all others, they rest their case on the idea of survival itself. No word, no theme, is more often invoked by Jews, of whatever denomination, none more solemnly proclaimed. When young people are asked to "stay" Jewish, despite their proclaimed indifference, they are not asked to do so for God's sake or for their own but in the name of Jewish survival. And what gives the invocation of survival meaning is the axiom that it cannot be taken for granted, that it is always and everywhere in jeopardy. From this follows the appeal to guilt as Judaism's claim on its young; from this follows that it is dishonorable to quit.

The uncertainty of our survival has in fact informed Jewish life since very nearly its beginning. The late scholar Simon Rawidowicz, in his essay "Israel: The Ever-dying People," chronicles the ways in which each generation of Jews has seen itself as the last, citing, inter alia, the extraordinary passage with which Tractate *Sotah* of the Talmud concludes:

> When Rabbi Meir died, there were no more makers of parables. When Ben Azzai died, there were no more diligent students. When Ben Zoma died, there were no more expounders. When Rabbi Joshua died, goodness departed from this world. When Rabbi Simeon ben Gamliel died, the locusts came and troubles grew many. When Rabbi Eleazar b. Azariah died, wealth departed from the sages. When Rabbi Akiba died, the glory of the Law ceased and the fountains of wisdom were stopped up. When Rabbi Hanina b. Dosa died, men of good deeds ceased. When Rabbi Jose b. Ketanta died, there were no more saintly ones. When Rabbi Yohanan b. Zakkai died, the splendor of wisdom ceased. When Rabbi Gamliel the Elder died, the glory of the Law ceased and purity and abstinence died. When Rabbi Ishmael b. Piabi died, the splendor of the priesthood ceased. When Rabbi [Judah ha-Nasi, the compiler of the Mishnah] died, humility and the shunning of sin ceased. (Sotah 49b)

---

*It is worth noting that although only 10 percent of America's Jews are Orthodox, the Orthodox make up a far higher proportion—at least 20 percent—of those who are in any way affiliated with an explicitly Jewish community or institution.

So also in later generations. Rawidowicz wisely recalls that while Chaim Nachman Bialik, who was to become the major poet of the Hebrew revival, was still a child, Y. L. Gordon, the leading poet of *his* day, was writing, "For whom do I labor? Who will tell me the future, will tell me that I am not the last poet of Zion, and you my last readers?" And years later, Bialik in his turn referred to himself as "the last of the last."

This apocalyptic sense comes, evidently, with the Jewish territory. In my own childhood, it was made crystal clear to me by my teachers that mine was the last generation of Jews—and not because of the Holocaust, but because my generation could not possibly remember as lavishly as its parents, could not sigh as deeply, could not care as passionately. We were, in a word, inadequate. Only later did it dawn on me that my parents' generation had been taught of their inadequacy by their parents, and so all the way back to the time when troubles grew many, when there stopped being diligent students and goodness departed from this world. (And later still, I was relieved to find myself learning new Hebrew songs from my children. I am not the last, after all.)

For 4,000 years, we have been dying. Which means, of course, that we are a remarkably hardy people. Perhaps our durability comes from never taking our survival for granted. Yet there is something anomalous, even perverse, about a people manifestly so competent at enduring that is at the same time so reluctant to shake off its embrace with death.

A well-known Hasidic story takes what is, in this context, an optimistic view of the Jewish prospect:

> When the founder of Hasidism, Israel Baal Shem Tov, sought to avert a threatening misfortune, he would go to a certain place in the woods, and there light a fire and utter a special prayer—and the misfortune would be averted.
>
> When his successor, the Maggid of Mezeritch, sought to accomplish the same purpose, he, too, would go to that place in the woods and there light a fire, and he would say, "Master of the Universe, I no longer recall the prayer, but this is the place and here is the fire, and that will have to suffice." And suffice it did.
>
> In due course, it fell to Moshe Leib of Sassov to intercede in

behalf of his people. And he, too, would go to that place in the woods, and there say, "Master of the Universe, I do not recall the prayer and I cannot make the fire, but at least I remember where it was done." And again, the evil decree was averted.

Finally, the task fell to Israel of Rizhin. And the best that he could do was to say, "Master of the Universe, I know not the prayer, nor the fire, nor even the place, but I can still tell the story, and that must suffice." And it did.

A charming story, told and retold often in our day, and, as I have said, intended as a comfort. Even though each generation is only a shadow of its predecessor, we endure; we peter down, but not out.

A comfort? What, then, of Israel of Rizhin's successor—or does the attrition finally stop? And even if it stops, how much of a comfort can it be that we have to settle for the telling of the story? Can it be thought that the telling alone will forever suffice? Can it be that a people that once knew the words with which to pray, that once knew the secret place, that once knew how to kindle the fire, can get by with the telling of how these used to be done? If what we have to say to our children amounts to a series of "once upon a time" stories, will our children not notice how much our today suffers by comparison with our yesterday, how much we have become shadows of our forebears? "Please come survive with us," we say, "even if by survival all we mean is remembering some stories to tell." Who would favorably reply to such a stingy invitation? "We are, after all, the people to and through whom God once spoke." Then what has happened since? The thunder of the prophets has shriveled, become toothless reminiscence. Can it be that when we speak of and urge a commitment to Jewish survival we do so out of stubbornness alone, with no sure sense of what, beyond the telling of stories, our survival is intended to achieve? All this a comfort?

I am mindful here that the survival of a people whose survival has been so regularly threatened may in and of itself be thought a worthy goal, a goal that under the peculiar circumstances of Jewish history requires no justification beyond itself. Moreover, sophisticated survivalists would not accept that the survival they seek is without purpose. Thus, Jonathan Woocher, in his recent book *Sacred Survival:*

> Critical observers . . . have at times expressed concern that Jewish survival has become an end in itself for the Jewish polity. The critics have asked, to what end? and have decried the absence of answers in much . . . Jewish rhetoric. . . . [But] the survival of the Jewish people is a consuming passion because the Jewish people plays a unique role in history as the bearer of Jewish values. In the work to insure the perpetuation of these values, the survival of the Jewish people and the Jewish community becomes a value in its own right. . . . Jewish survival is not . . . survival for its own sake. It is a purposive continuity.

Perhaps. I am, however, inclined to think that most Jewish survivalists would be hard-pressed to name (beyond a mouthful of unexamined slogans) the Jewish values our survival is meant to ensure. Instead, the means have become the end, and we are left, as Rabbi Dov Marmour puts it, with "a sense of duty to carry on Judaism and a deep resentment at having been landed with it in the first place. The 'compromise' has been to limit one's personal Judaism to a minimum, but to insist on collective survival."

The fact that survival has in our time come to replace the values it was meant to defend is yet another example of the lengths to which Jews are now prepared to go in order to avoid the challenge of Jewish meaning, of Jewish consent. (And again, who can blame them? In the aftermath of the Holocaust there is, after all, sufficient reason to believe either that there is no meaning, or that, if there is meaning, it is grotesque.) The elevation of survival to the principal consensual aim of the Jews may, indeed, be the distinctive "contribution" of this generation; recall the argument of Emil Fackenheim that Jewish survival is now a theological mandate. We must, says Fackenheim, add to the traditional list of 613 commandments a 614th: "The authentic Jew of today is forbidden to hand Hitler yet another, posthumous victory."

To people less thoughtful than Fackenheim—and that includes most people—the message of the 614th commandment is likely to be read as instructing us to be fruitful and multiply out of spite; to "teach them diligently unto thy children" out of stiff-neckedness; to make of our trauma a testament, of our resentment a religion. We are enjoined, in short, to commit ourselves to commitment.

That is what it comes down to. Nor does it surprise, for over and over again, as we have seen, the Jews of this generation twist and turn to assert Jewishness while avoiding Judaism, vastly prefer stance to substance, sentimental affirmation to serious confrontation. They want, by and large, Jewish identification, but not Jewish identity. They want, as I have suggested, to be Jewish—but not "too" Jewish.

I intend no disrespect. Given the options and the temptations, the intensity of devotion one encounters among the Jews, the sheer stubbornness of their commitment to Jewish survival, are truly impressive, even moving—the more so because they so often rest on entirely visceral foundations. My purpose is not to condemn the attenuated Jewish identity and ambition of American Jews, still trying to find a balance between descent and consent, between the claims of the Jewish past and the claims of the American Jewish future, still trying to apprehend the implications of the Holocaust and the complications of the State of Israel. My purpose instead is to suggest once again that we cannot expect an identity that is not nourished by distinctive ideological and cultural commitment to be passed on from generation to generation; not enough remains out of which to mold an enduring identity. My purpose is to suggest that the preoccupation with survival for its own sake is not merely redundant, but self-defeating, for it reflects both confusion and shallowness so blatant that it may (must?) eventually disenchant, demoralize, distance those it seeks to persuade. My purpose is to suggest that far from assuring the Jewish future, the survivalist obsession betrays it. (And yes, I am aware that I am merely fashioning yet another way of saying that this generation may well be the last. The difference, if there be one, is that I do not recommend survivalism as the remedy.)

Survivalism: Writing in Russia toward the end of the nineteenth century, the Hebrew poet Yehuda Leib Gordon (he who wondered who would read his poems) urged the Jews to participate fully in Russian society. "Be a Jew in your home and a man in the street." Like so many of his comrades of the Haskalah (the Jewish Enlightenment of the nineteenth century), he was impatient with Jewish separatism, and in the wake of the liberal reforms of 1861 he came to feel that it was their own instinct for isolation that barred the Jews from full participation in the larger society. In the early decades of this century, many American Jews took Gordon's counsel to heart, came to see Judaism as a private matter, to believe that "out there" the rule was to be a man, to pass. Change your name, get rid of your accent, become a Yankee, a WASH (that is, a white Anglo-Saxon Hebrew).

Since then, we have learned two lessons that point in a very different direction. First, we've learned that no matter how hard we try, there are still barriers; by the Yankees, we're not Yankees. (Irony: In Israel, the first housing project built chiefly for American immigrants came to be known as *shikun Anglo-Saxi*—the "Anglo-Saxon housing complex." For an American Jew finally to become an Anglo-Saxon, he had to move to Jerusalem.) And second, we've learned not only that are there really very few penalties for staying a Jew in the street, but that there are ways in which the street *expects* us to be what we are, to be Jews.

So it was that in the wake of the Pollard affair of 1987, Arthur Hertzberg could say, in commenting on fears that the case of a Jew recruited by the State of Israel to spy against the United States on its behalf would inevitably lead to anti-Semitism, "The non-Jewish American majority has always known that Jews are different from all other Americans. Jews are unique in their ways, as blacks or Orientals are unique in their different ways. . . . The American majority understands that Jews have a special passion for Israel, that this is the issue which unites the American Jewish community, and that Jews are, at the same time, among the most dedicated of American patriots."

And we, the children of those who stayed quiet in the 1930s, know now that there are Jews elsewhere—in the Soviet Union, in Ethiopia, in Israel of course—who depend on our noise, who count on us to take to the streets, to assert, not deny, our Jewishness. All of which leads us to a precise inversion of Gordon's maxim: here in America, we are Jews in the street, men (and women) at home.

At home, we watch the same programs on television (adjusting, of course, for socioeconomic status), we play the same games and eat the same foods. When we lock our doors, it is against the

criminals, not against the Inquisitor. We become advocates of Judaism, energetic, passionate advocates—and we cease to be its practitioners. More precisely, we presume that the practice of Judaism
begins and ends with its advocacy. We will vigorously defend the
right of the Jews to be Jews. But we ourselves will not exercise that
right. And our obsession with survival enables us to believe that our
defense and our advocacy are the substance of a Jewish life.

A Judaism so understood requires for its persistence, as I have
already suggested, either the real or the imagined hostility of others,
for if our Judaism is a thing to be defended, it must be seen to be
under attack. Such a Judaism, then, is fundamentally *reactive,* takes
as its basic inspiration its threatened status. "Scratch a *goy* and you'll
find an anti-Semite," the vulgar folk saying has it, and it reflects not
merely an inherited perception of history but a deeply rooted intui-
tion regarding how things still work. Never mind that there is daily
evidence that points in a different and more benign direction. Never
mind that were the world indeed so bleak a place as our stingy
perception suggests, we'd have no chance at all. There are, lamenta-
bly, enough current data to support the dreary perception. And if
not, we will dredge out the old data. (A new book by Simon Wiesenthal is entitled *Every Day Remembrance Day: A Chronicle of Jewish
Martyrdom.* On its flyleaf, we are informed that "This book is not a
calendar in the ordinary sense. . . . It is a book commemorating
horror, arranged by date: it is the story of Jewish martyrdom, of
suffering. . . . This calendar relates the atrocities committed against
the Jewish people over two thousand years." As promised, the book
tells us, for any given day of the year, the horrors visited upon the
Jews on that day in years past.)

But think what it means to be recruited by a tradition that presents itself as one part bloody memory and one part grim forebod-
ing. Think what it means to be pressed toward identification with
a people that—mind you, after standing at Sinai and after crossing
the Red Sea, after authoring the Talmud and recreating the state,
after 4,000 years of odds-beating—now lives cramped between pogrom and pogrom. Think what it means to need Pharaoh. Consider
what it means to invite people to a partnership in persecution, an

endless voyage of the damned, its sails filled with the winds of others' hatred: What it means is that when the winds die, the vessel will stall.

What happens when Jewish identity is reduced to a response to anti-Semitism? What happens is this: those embattled few who have made the welfare of the Jews their mission look out upon a Jewish community whose members are Jewishly available only to protect a right they themselves do not (and do not want to) enjoy, only to defend a way they do not (and would not) walk; in order to move them to action and commitment it appears necessary to invoke the imminence of the anti-Semitic threat. And so anti-Semitism becomes a motive, perhaps even *the* motive, for Jewish life. How else engage the attention of those whose fundamental commitments lie elsewhere? The threat may or may not be real; the purpose of invoking it is not to describe reality, but to get Jewish juices flowing. And it works, sort of. For even those who cannot bring themselves to say yes to Judaism's claims will mount the barricades to refuse others, them, the right to say no.

Evidence or allegation that Jew-hating is still alive and well has still another function. How do we infuse contemporary Jewish life, so thoroughly bourgeois, with the high drama that will link it to the tales of tragedy and triumph we recall? How shall we shade the boundaries between then and now, between the prophetic and the pedestrian, prove that we, too, are worthy actors in Jewish history, not merely its passive witnesses? Announce that the threat is here and now, that the vandals march again, march still, that we, too, no less than our ancestors, are called to defend the honor, even the life, of our people. And if the evidence of anti-Semitism is simply too thin, find another enemy and impute to it all the sinister, the deathly qualities of the classic enemy.

Do I overstate? Here are some excerpts from a recent fund-raising letter of the National Council of Synagogue Youth:

> In the 1940's Jews faced annihilation. In the 1980's we face it again!
> This time, however, we face a much more insidious enemy. This time you and I face the scourge of assimilation. Dare I call it a second holocaust in the making?

. . . There are no longer Nazis to fight. There is no single force to battle—except—ourselves. If you believe and understand that, you will realize that I am not overstating the problem.

Announcement of imminent threat, whether from within or from without, has become a familiar routine of Jewish life. It comes not as an intrusion, an interruption of our "normal" pursuits, but as an accepted ritual. Nor do I mean to suggest that a devious group of professional Jews foists an exaggerated threat upon an unwilling and unsuspecting mass. The routinization of threat is by mutual, if uninformed, consent. Indeed, I recall that in the early 1980s, I was invited to address the biennial convention of the National Jewish Community Relations Advisory Council—an "umbrella" organization of all the national and local agencies charged with defending against anti-Semitism. My assigned subject was the nature and extent of the anti-Semitic threat in the United States. In order to ground my remarks in the actual data, I spoke with half a dozen of the more thoughtful directors of NJCRAC's affiliated organizations, and asked them for their professional assessment of the threat. To a person, they reported that anti-Semitism in the United States was neither a clear nor a present danger to Jewish safety. And to a person, they went on to say that they could not persuade the members of their boards to accept their encouraging assessment. For if the assessment is correct, if the anti-Semites have indeed been beaten back, what is left to connect us? If Jewish survival is assured, what is left for us to be about? More precisely, if the threat to Jewish survival does not come from without, we who profess to care for that survival must turn inward. And that is something we prefer not to have to do.

In 1977, Elihu Bergman published an article entitled "The American Jewish Population Erosion." In it, he predicted that by the year 2076, there would be no more than 944,000 Jews left in the United States, and perhaps as few as 10,420. The very demographers whose projections Bergman cited in his article repudiated his forecast within a year, in the pages of the same magazine (*Midstream*) where his article had appeared. Yet, as Charles Silberman correctly observes, "American Jewish leaders have embraced Bergman's dour vision as if it had been carved in granite." My own experience confirms Silberman's observation: Some years after the Bergman article appeared, I visited the Jewish Community Center in New Orleans. In the lobby of the building there was a good-sized bulletin board devoted to "News from Around the Jewish World." On that bulletin board was tacked exactly one item: a by now yellowed news bulletin summarizing the Bergman article. That and only that, though years had passed.

So also we find, when we examine the public opinion surveys that deal with the matter, that Jews consistently and persistently misapprehend the perceptions and overstate the bigotry of others. In one especially intriguing study in 1982, conducted by the Daniel Yankelovitch organization, a sample of Jews was asked whether or not they thought that a majority of non-Jews agreed with various statements—and then a non-Jewish sample was asked whether or not they in fact agreed with those same statements. One such statement, for example, was simply, "Jews have too much power in the United States." Fifty-three percent of the Jews thought that most non-Jews would agree with that statement. In fact, however, only 20 percent agreed with it. Do Jews have too much power in the business world? Seventy-six percent of the Jews thought that most non-Jews would say yes; in fact, 32 percent did. Would non-Jews be bothered if their political party were to nominate a Jew as its candidate for president? Seventy-eight percent of the Jews thought they would—but only 21 percent of non-Jews said they would. How would non-Jews respond if one of their own children wanted to marry a Jew? Sixty-two percent of the Jews supposed that most non-Jews would object. In fact, 28 percent said they would.

And should such data be called to the attention of the Jews, no doubt many would argue that non-Jews dissemble. Better to reject the data than to question the very foundation of their Jewish understanding. (A man appears in a psychiatrist's office. The psychiatrist, looking up from his desk, asks, "Can I help you?" "No," says the man, "I am dead." "I find that rather hard to believe," replies the psychiatrist. "So do most people," the man says, "but it doesn't alter the fact. The fact is that I am deceased." "Are you sure?" "I am so sure that if I were alive, I would stake my life on it." "Interesting," the psychiatrist says. "Tell me, what do you know about dead men?" The man thinks for a moment and answers, "One thing I know is that dead men don't bleed." Whereupon the psychiatrist takes a razor blade from his desk drawer and nicks the man's finger. A drop of blood appears. The man looks at it in astonishment, and says, "How about that! Dead men do bleed!")

By calling anti-Semitism a "substitute," I do not mean to suggest that the fears of the Jews are without foundation; Jewish history and Jewish memory provide the foundation. But the American Jewish experience does not rest on that foundation. Here, the fears do not come to summarize the reality; they come, instead, to sustain the notion that the Jews are special. They enhance the drama, they feed the survivalist obsession, they establish our interdependence by dividing the world into "us" and "them." Most of all, they tell us that we are still worthy, for we remain, after all and even here, the hunted—and "they," of course, remain the hunters.

Max Weber once wrote of "the theodicy of disprivilege," by which he meant the ways in which people come to explain their lower status. For many centuries, the Jews were experts at that kind of theodicy, teaching and writing and learning that those rejected by man were chosen by God, that their suffering itself was sufficient evidence of their virtue. (The way you know you are a good people is that bad things keep happening to you.) What term would Weber have coined to describe a people freed from the burden of disprivilege yet unwilling to let go the sense of it, unable therefore to shape a new meaning to suit its new circumstance?

We dare not let go our fears, for they confirm our peoplehood, our election, our virtue—ultimately, our meaning. And were we to let go of them, what would become of us, what would be left for us? But when faith is replaced by fear, the claims of an informed Jewish life are obscured. Whether survivalism is intended as evasion or merely has that effect scarcely matters; either way, Jewish life is impoverished, cheapened, misguided.

PART II

8

The American Jew: Text and Context

THE JEWISH TEXT is not a bound volume shelved in a central archive; it is an unfinished manuscript, passed from hand to hand. Its last pages are blank, and whoever writes on them must be sure to add new blank pages, to make room for those to come, scribblers and scribes alike. The reader who begins at the beginning and reads straight through will note the continuities, the words and hopes that make all the different pages belong in this one book. The reader will see, as well, that there are distinct stories within the whole. There are, suddenly, new words, not encountered before; there are shifts in emphasis, occasionally subtle and occasionally marked. Sometimes, these amount to no more than marginal notes, historical curiosities. But sometimes, the changes are sufficiently compelling and sufficiently enduring to mark the beginning of a new chapter.

We have been examining the confusions and the commitments of America's Jews, the reflexive meanings by which they are "carried along." The "ashes to rebirth" metaphor and all that flows from it are powerfully compelling, but, as we have seen, they are ultimately inadequate. They serve, for the time being, to connect people whose earlier connections have crumbled in the wake of a series of fracturing discontinuities. But for all the energy they evoke, and even passion, they only paste us together. An empowered Jewry must dig deeper into the layers of meaning that are available to it, must hazard the move from reflexive meanings to what Martin Buber called a "formulated meaning."

Up to this point, our search for meaning has taken us through ancient religious understandings and recent historic experiences. We have reviewed Judaism as both catechism and culture; we have sought to eavesdrop on the voices Jews hear, to chronicle their gropings and their wrestlings. All these, I have said, are part of the American Jewish text. But we have so far paid only passing attention to the American Jewish context—that is, to America. And that will not do. A Judaism that is about God and the Holocaust and Israel and survival is not yet about *us,* we who are not merely Jews *in* America, but Jews *of* America. To put it bluntly, there can be no authentic Judaism in America that is not an American Judaism.

So long as the experience of America's Jews was largely the experience of Jewish immigrants and their children, the theme of the American Jewish story was adaptation: how were we affected by America as we learned the ways of this new place? Now we must move the discussion beyond adaptation, for however colorful the old story is, there is a fresh story being written. It is not the passive story of how a people transplanted from the Old World to the New learned to get along, of how we absorbed the language and the habits of America. It is the dynamic story of how, having mastered that language and those habits, we have integrated them into our own understanding—and of how, in turn, we have helped shape and expand them. For though we are an ancient people with a vast wisdom literature, we have understood that there are valuable new lessons for us to learn here. Nor have we been content to memorize America's lessons verbatim; inevitably, we have rewritten them along the way. The story of America's Jews is, therefore, a story of synthesis, of how people who were once Americans *and* Jews have become American Jews.

*   *   *

And so we come to the American context, hence to pluralism. For, as Martin Marty puts it, "Pluralism is the obvious fact about America."

America is, of course, a radically imperfect place. (Which place is not?) But this nation is also a place where the commitment to pluralism runs very deep. That does not mean that it flows unimpeded; American history can be (and has been) written as the story of our nation's continuing ambivalence toward the consequences of pluralism. Surely the persistent inadequacy of America's response to its black citizens is a measure of how incomplete our acceptance of pluralism remains. Yet there is much evidence on the other side, as well; the capacity of this nation to accommodate diversity—genuine diversity—is as much a blessing as its continuing racism is a scandal.

To accommodate diversity: Pluralism has multiple definitions and elusive connotations; diversity alone does not begin to capture the richness of its core meaning. Pluralism means not only that the detached observer perceives differences; it means that the involved participant sees those same differences, and lives with them. It means, as well, that the system itself protects the integrity of groups smaller than the whole and that it does not merely accommodate such groups but cherishes them.

To that end, pluralism implies an understanding that the process by which a free nation (or a group, or a people, or a community) arrives at a usable truth is more important than the truth itself. In a complex modern society, process *is* substance; we will not live to see the end of the game, to learn the final truth, so all there is for us is the way in which the game is played. *The ends of democracy are its means;* that is the central insight of pluralism as a sociopolitical principle.

Does that mean that this grand experiment in freedom and democracy reduces to nothing more than the narrow notion of "process"? But consider: It is not very helpful to speak of "subcultures" in America, since the word "subculture" implies that there is some "super" culture to which the subcultures are subordinate. A generation and more back, it was possible to speak comfortably (or with discomfort) about the regnant WASP culture, but that makes little sense today. What we have instead is a collection of overlapping cultures that co-exist more or less peaceably, and that together add up to a whole—America—that is greater than the sum of its component cultural parts—for the whole includes, along with the parts, the rules and habits of interaction that govern their relationship.

Back in 1775, Robert Beverly of Virginia warned that the already heterogeneous continent could not be molded into a united nation:

> We are an infant Country, unconnected in Interest and naturally disunited by Inclination. Our Forms of Government differ egregiously, but our religious Tenets still more so. Our modes of Life vary, and our Articles of Commerce interfere prodigiously. Nor are we naturally more disjointed in Situation than in Temper. It is true indeed there seems to be a Sort of Union at present, but I am afraid it is only in Appearance. Ambition, Resentment, and Interest may have united us for a Moment, but be assured, when Interests shall interfere and a Dispute shall arise concerning Superiority, a Code of Laws, and all the Concomitants of a new Government, that the Union will soon be converted into Envy, Malevolence, and Faction, and most probably will introduce a greater degree of Opposition than even now prevails against the Mother Country.

The question of how much sameness the Union required and how much diversity it could accommodate has been with us since before the nation's beginnings and is not yet settled. In the political realm, it is expressed in the debate over federalism, Beverly's concern. In the social realm, it has been raised in debates over religious freedom and immigration policy and a dozen other issues that have challenged the nation to clarify its assumptions and its purposes. This challenge, too, antedates the Union. We have, for example, the remarkable letter from the directors of the West India Company, written to Peter Stuyvesant, Governor of New Amsterdam, in 1655:

> Your last letter informed us that you had banished from the Province ... a certain Quaker.... Although we heartily desire, that these and other sectarians remain away from there, yet as they do not, we doubt very much, whether we can proceed against them rigorously without diminishing the population and stopping immigration, which must be favoured at a so tender stage of the country's existence. You may therefore shut your eyes, at least not force people's consciences, but allow everyone to have his own belief, as long as

he behaves quietly and legally, gives no offense to his neighbors and does not oppose the government.

(The company directors sent a similar letter to Stuyvesant in the same year, dealing with the Jews. Its key sentence reads, "Therefore after many deliberations we have finally decided and resolved to apostille upon a certain petition presented by said Portuguese Jews that these people may travel and trade to and in New Netherland and live and remain there, provided the poor among them shall not become a burden to the company or the community, but be supported by their own nation.")

In the first chapter, I sketched the history of America's ambivalence, both in theory and in practice, toward diversity, and told of how, in recent years, this nation has come to be considerably more comfortable with the doctrine expressed in the directors' letter to Stuyvesant: not to force people's consciences, to allow everyone to have his or her own belief. On that doctrine, the house of pluralism, with all its rules and habits, is built.

Surely no American fact has had greater bearing than pluralism on the character and commitments of the emergent American Jew. America's Jews have not only and obviously benefited from pluralism; they have also learned from it and been changed by it. More still: they have not only "learned" pluralism; they have become its devoted teachers as well. Out of their own experience, Jews have understood that pluralism can never be taken for granted; it is a bold principle, and many are inclined to a more ethnocentric or monolithic way. The path to pluralism is an exhausting obstacle course, the temptations to take some other road are endless. Hence the defense of pluralism requires continuing effort. It should come as no surprise that Jews, who are among pluralism's most obvious beneficiaries, should also be among its most ardent advocates.

Pluralism is not only a principle; it is also a descriptive term, designating a particular form of group organization and life. In a pluralistic social system, there is a multiplicity of groups that are both autonomous and interdependent, characterized both by their internal cohesion and by their interaction with one another. Imagine, by way of contrast, a society in which the diverse groups are all highly cohesive, but in which there is little interaction (or only formal interaction) among them. Feudal and tribal and caste societies illustrate that social form. At the other extreme we encounter societies in which there is a very high level of interaction, but in which the interaction is unstructured, not mediated by a stable group life. That is the form (actually, the formlessness) we know as mass society.

Pluralism contrasts with these, but there is no "pure" pluralistic system. Even in America, where pluralism has been so carefully nurtured, where pluralism as a social form is mirrored in the governmental structure and in the marketplace, there are still groups that are locked out, on the one hand, and there are individuals who live anomic lives, displaced and alienated, on the other. Each has its own particular etiology; together, they are affected by the fact that pluralism is inherently an unstable state. Both its essential elements, cohesion and interaction, can easily slide into excess: the group may become a trap rather than, as pluralist theory contemplates, a base; interaction without structure to give it form may make of us a lonely crowd.

We are dealing here with a variant of the classic tension between liberty and community. Since the time of the French Revolution, no problem in social theory has received more attention, and none remains more perplexing. Disraeli complained that "modern society acknowledges no neighbour," and that sentiment has been echoed by a host of critics who have lamented the loss of community that seems an inevitable consequence of modernization. At the same time, freedom has been widely held to require that the individual be released from all the inherited ties to traditional communities.

The social scientists and philosophers of an earlier day, in the guise of dispassionate analysts, frequently became advocates for the one side or the other, now celebrating the virtues of community, now condemning its non-rational foundations, now celebrating the benefits of the secular city, now disparaging its inherent rootlessness. Mostly, those who defended community were charged with being both anti-modern and anti-empirical, since it was "obvious" that history was decisively on the side of secularization. (Secularization, in this sense, means not only the abandonment of religion, but the displacement of *all* traditional attachments by rational and utilitarian considerations.) As Max Weber observed, "secularization may be good, or it may be bad, but it is our destiny."

Lately, and for some of the same reasons that have led to the end of WASP dominance, rather more attention has been devoted to the question of balance. We have moved toward a more sensitive recognition that we are best served by "mixed societies" that seek to maximize both liberty and community. We have abandoned, at least for now, the melting pot in favor of such bold endorsements of pluralism as bilingual education.

I sketch these issues here because of their importance for understanding America's Jews. It is pluralism that has permitted us both to be a part of the larger society and to stand apart from it. And it is precisely the tension between liberty (read: individualism) and community that has been the preoccupying dilemma of the American Jewish community. How intimately a part of the society can the Jew be without losing his/her Jewish identity? How separate can the Jewish community remain without cutting itself off? If, in the name of cohesion, of Jewish identity and continuity, we choose to send our children to Jewish day schools, where will they learn to interact with other Americans? If, for the sake of interaction, we seek to immerse ourselves in the larger society, how will we resist our final assimilation by it?

The precarious resolution most favored by Jews has been a society in which the component groups themselves decide where the boundaries shall be drawn. We claim the right to live wherever we choose, and we do battle with those who would exclude us because we are Jews—but most of the time, we choose to live in Jewish neighborhoods. We are offended when Christian parents oppose their child's betrothal to a Jew—but we do not want our children to marry Christians. We want, in short, the right to determine for ourselves when and how our Jewishness shall matter. And it is the vigor and strength of American pluralism that permits us, most of the time, to get what we want. That is what makes of our experience in this land a genuinely new chapter in Jewish history; here, the occasional jolt notwithstanding, we are at liberty to assert our own boundaries.

Yet for all the delight of this new chapter, there comes with it, as I have said, a dilemma. That dilemma derives from the confusions of a pluralistic social structure, for there are still other things we want: We want that Jews shall not be barred from membership in any country club they wish to join—and we want them not to wish to join country clubs that have few Jewish members. We praise those Jews who are fluent in one or another of the universal languages, such as science and music, but we condemn them if they have forgotten their native tongue. We want, that is, not only the right to determine when the fact of Jewishness shall matter (to our neighbors), but also the right to insist that it shall (to the Jews). We want, with Shylock, the right to walk, talk, buy, and sell with Christians, and the right to eat, drink, and pray alone, but we want more than Shylock did: We want to ensure that Jews will in fact exercise those rights. We want no barriers, but we do want boundaries, and the distinction between the two is not at all an obvious distinction. We want to be able to preach universalism but to practice particularism.

That is our dilemma, and by naming it we begin to get a better hold on it, and to that extent on ourselves. I have used the words before: particularism and universalism. There is no more powerful key to an understanding of both Jewish possibilities and Jewish paradoxes than these words provide. It is time to bring them front and center, to explore the meaning of each and the manner of their relationship.

Traditionally and even today, Jewish universalists have seen Jewish particularism as an embarrassment, while Jewish particularists have seen Jewish universalism as a threat. But these two orientations, which have co-existed in uneasy competition since our beginnings as a people, take on new meaning and present new opportunities in pluralistic America. I will presently argue that here in America we are not required to choose between them, that the tension between the two is not, as is so generally believed, a dilemma to be resolved but an existential condition to be lived and even savored. Alone, each is precarious; together, as the poet John

Ciardi put it in describing marriage, they are an arch, two weaknesses leaning into a strength.

In the Jewish communities of pre-Enlightenment times, intellectual leadership and religious leadership coincided. With the Enlightenment, a gap opened between the two, and then a gulf. By the middle years of this century, it had become unfashionable for serious intellectuals to confess to religious belief or to assert a religious identity. The fracture was not restricted to the Jews, but it was far more extensive in the Jewish community than in others, and it was also of greater consequence. As most Jewish intellectuals saw it, there were two worlds: the world of liberal universalism, secular and seductive, and the world of Jewish particularism, religious and regressive. Secularism was more than an opportunity; it was a conviction, too. Its constricted alternative was, accordingly, relegated to a corner of the mind, became a vestigial category.

Nor was the vestige permitted to rest undisturbed in a lonely corner of our memory; it was ideologically besieged. At issue was not merely the scope of religion's reach, which secularism sought to narrow. (That in itself represented a major problem for the Jews, since classical Judaism defined the area of the sacred as virtually all-encompassing.) Secularism had as well an ideological underpinning that very many Jews found enticing. As it became fashionable for intellectuals, following in the footsteps of Marx, or of Freud, or of Durkheim (among very many others), to dismiss religion as an atavistic social construct, the wave of the informed future was identified as universalism. The secular world was a world, so it was claimed, where rationalism and utilitarianism would replace traditional loyalties (and antipathies), reverence, and mystery. Particularism in general, and especially religious particularism, was dismissed as parochial; ethnic loyalties were classified as necessarily ethnocentric, hence debilitating, malignant, a barrier to the brave new and universal world aborning. Human history was defined as linear, moving from clans to tribes to nations to a future without any boundaries. True freedom—and for that matter peace, which depended, did it not, on an end to religious and ethnic tribalism?—could happen only in a world of universalistic temper.

What a blessing for the Jews! Since anti-Semitism was a monstrous irrationality, the secular (i.e., rational, modern) society would excise it. The inevitable triumph of secularism meant that Jews would at last be viewed and treated as people, not as Jews, that the standards according to which Jews would be measured and judged would be universalistic rather than particularistic standards. And since the most compelling claims of the Jewish religious tradition were, in any case, ethical claims, which could readily be transferred to the secular domain and there pursued to more substantial effect, why not? No betrayal was involved; on the contrary, universalism promised a fulfillment of prophetic hopes.

In this form, the universalist argument could be used as an exit visa from the Jewish community. In a different version—by simply bringing Judaism into line with universalist principles—the universalist could comfortably remain within the community. So the Reform rabbis of America, in 1885, adopted as the platform for their movement a document that included both an endorsement of universalism and a denunciation of particularism.

> We recognize in every religion an attempt to grasp the Infinite One, and in every mode, source or book of revelation held sacred in any religious system the consciousness of the indwelling of God in man. . . . We recognize in the modern era of universal culture of heart and intellect the approach of the realization of Israel's great Messianic hope for the establishment of the kingdom of truth, justice and peace among all men. . . . We recognize in Judaism a progressive religion, ever striving to be in accord with the postulates of reason. . . . We recognize in the Mosaic legislation a system of training of the Jewish people for its mission during its national life in Palestine, and today we accept as binding only the moral laws and maintain only such ceremonies as elevate and sanctify our lives, but reject all such as are not adapted to the views and habits of modern civilization. . . . We consider ourselves no longer a nation but a religious community.

(It was not until 1937 that this document, known as the Pittsburgh Platform, was supplanted.)

There were also more straightforward tactical attractions to universalism. If the Jews could preach universalism, they would be less likely to be seen as cultic, eccentric, subversive—different. Jews and their Judaism would be seen at worst as an innocuous sect, no threat at all to the general secular-humanistic consensus. Moreover, if they could actually manage to convert others to universalism, the prospect of anti-Semitism would diminish still more. And the language of universalism was not, after all, an alien language. There were ample passages from classical Jewish texts that could appropriately be cited as evidence of Judaism's universalistic orientation.

In time, the universalist passion of the intellectuals became also the popular persuasion of the people. In their landmark study of the 1950s, Marshall Sklare and Joseph Greenblum asked a sample of Jewish respondents in Lakeville—their name for a suburb north of Chicago—to assess the importance of a number of attributes. How essential was each, they asked, to a person who would be a "good Jew"?

The attribute deemed more essential than any other—by 93 percent of the respondents, with another 6 percent saying it was "desirable"—was leading "an ethical and moral life." The next most endorsed "essential" (85 percent held it was that) was "to accept being a Jew and not try to hide it." And then, in quick succession, we get "support all humanitarian causes" and "promote civil betterment and improvement in the community" (tied at 67 percent, with 29 percent more terming these "desirable"), and then "gain the respect of one's Christian neighbors" (59 percent) and "help the underprivileged improve their lot" (58 percent). These all far outranked such items as belonging to a synagogue (31 percent) or other Jewish organization (17 percent), marrying within the Jewish faith (23 percent), and observing the dietary laws (1 percent).

It may be argued, of course, that this was an affluent suburb, and the time was the 1950s, the heyday of Jewish universalism, that today's answers would be very different. And, in fact, subsequent studies that have asked the Sklare/Greenblum question have found considerable variation in the responses. But over and over, it is the broadly ethical questions that elicit the greatest positive consensus; there is invariably much less agreement to the more explicitly Jewish items. So, for example, we have a survey in 1986, three decades after the Sklare/Greenblum study, well into a period that has been

widely characterized as one of resurgent particularism, that finds
that 96 percent of all American Jews agree that "As Jews we should
be concerned about all people, not just Jews"; 71 percent agree that
"as Jews, we have special moral and ethical obligations"; and 89
percent agree that "I get just as upset by terrorist attacks on non-
Jews as I do when terrorists attack Jews."

Commitment to universalism, it appears, is understood by very
many American Jews as an essential element in being a "good" Jew.
Indeed, we may go further. For a significant number of Jews, "support for all humanitarian causes" and concern for "all people" are
not merely essential elements; they are the very purpose of Judaism.

Why should this be so? Jonathan Woocher, in his *Sacred Survival,*
carefully argues a critical interpretation: "Civil Judaism focuses on
the unobjectionable, primarily ethical dimensions of the tradition.
Of necessity, its 'Jewish tradition' represents a kind of religious
common denominator, general principles of moral behavior, generalized affirmation of a modicum of ritual." Arnold Eisen pushes still
harder in his *The Chosen People in America:*

> A fragmented community, unsure of its proper distinctiveness from
> the outer world, turned [from *halachah*] to ideology. . . . If religion
> seeks to assure a person that the binding core of authority ties the
> acts of his or her daily life to the God who gives life, the acts must
> be there to be sanctified. Except for Orthodoxy, and from some
> among the other movements, those acts had been reduced to philan-
> thropy and pursuit of social justice.

These observations might easily be restated to fit my own argument in earlier chapters: In searching for a content that will justify
the whole of the Jewish saga, for a difference that will make of the
fact of Jewishness something more than a bitter accident, yet will
not lead to a subversive parochialism—un-modern and un-Ameri-
can—why not focus on those elements in the tradition, its ethical
elements, that are most nobly universal? If our sermons are heard
by others, they will think us less subversive; if our sermons persuade them, they will be more tolerant.

But the idea of a Jewish mission offers more than a sermonic
theme, does more even than sustain the morale and cohesion of an

otherwise fragmented community. It comes not principally as a calculation, designed to impress others, but as a consolation, designed to comfort the Jews themselves. It is vintage Jewish theodicy, our very specific response to the question that has haunted the Jews: Why do we, God's delight, suffer so? And now we take the traditional response and use it to answer our new and more urgent question: Who are the Jews? The Jews are manifestly a people apart, separated from others both by their own choice and by their neighbors' preference. How is that apartness commonly explained, rationalized, justified?

Try this: "When your ancestors were still worshipping thunder and livestock, ours were announcing the universal Word of God." Or, more directly, with words such as these: "The election of the Jews—whether by God, or by themselves, or by their enemies—cannot be just an accident. A history so crammed with consequence must have a point, a purpose. What meaning can there be to match the madness of it all? The largest meaning of all: the Jews as Jonah, the particular messengers of universal repentance to a world that is evil." As Arthur Hertzberg puts it, "The very devotion with which the Jew continues to affirm the universal values of liberalism has become the brand-mark of his own particularism, the sign of the uniqueness of his own position."

So it is that many Jews devoutly (some might say smugly) believe that when it comes to ethics, we are beyond criticism—at least beyond criticism by others. No need, most of the time, to examine whether our ethical assertions are any more than that, the understandable conceit of a people that so craves consolation, compensation, and, most of all, assurance that its feverish history *means* something.

Presently, we will get to the relationship between these perceptions and the behavior of the Jews, between code and conduct. What I am arguing here is that very many—perhaps, indeed, most— American Jews understand the Jewish moral mission as the essential meaning of Judaism. That is how Judaism is universalized, made to accord with modernity.

Who are the Jews? Here is a passage from a children's text, published in 1986, entitled *Why Be Different? A Look into Judaism:*

The Jews were chosen by God to play a special role in the world. Their task is to teach people about God and to make the world a better place. There are two ways that Jews are to work at this task:

1. By spreading the idea of ethical monotheism throughout the world.

2. By living according to the Torah. By doing this, Jews will become an example to the rest of the world. As the great Jewish prophet Isaiah said, the Jews must become "a light unto the nations."

"Jews," the authors continue, "are required to fight evil, even though it often happens to people they do not know and even when they do not actually see the evil taking place." And, "The most important thing that God expects from people is to do good things for fellow human beings."

I have purposely chosen to cite a text that has no overt political intention and that is quite traditional and particularistic in its orientation, a book that rejects ethical relativism and that within the context of Jewish discussion can scarcely be thought a liberal text. Yet even here, the substance of Jewish particularism is defined as universalism.

As it is virtually everywhere. Who are the Jews? Read the texts, read the letters to the editor; hear the lectures, hear the sermons. Recall Albert Einstein: "The bond which unites the Jews in the course of thousands of years, and unites them also today, is, first of all, the democratic ideal of social justice, with the addition of the idea of mutual help and tolerance among all human beings."

Or take the words of Y. L. Peretz, writing at the turn of the century in Poland on "The Jewish Way":

Nomadic blood. A wandering clan in the desert. Implanted in its blood—honesty and justice. Of these qualities does it fashion its God, a God who accompanies it on all its wanderings and is therefore not formed of wood or stone, a God who moves and lives. . . . The flag of a Jewish renaissance must be raised again, the banner of Messiah, world-judgment, and world-liberation, the symbol of a future free humanity. This is the mission of the eternal people.

Or read the contemporary French writer, Olivier Revault D'Allonnes:

[Judaism] gives priority to what *must be* over what *is,* because it implies turning reality inside out, and already begins to accomplish this by turning its attention and its heart toward those who are forgotten and scorned, the poor, the oppressed, the *anavim,* the humble friends of God. In the ancient pagan world, this Jewish lesson is scandalous, it is scandal itself, because it attacks the most profound structures of societies and empires. Is it really otherwise today?

Plainly, very many Jews, secular and religious alike, have in this century, more even than in centuries past, shared the sentiments I have cited. And even if there is a utilitarian purpose to Jewish universalism, its message is powerful in its own terms: Whether it is God who commands the commitment to justice—which is, given the state of our world, a command to repair—or our historical experience, as it has come to be understood, the conclusion is the same. He, too, was created by God, and you, too, were a stranger in Egypt, therefore you are to know the heart of the stranger; justice, justice shalt thou pursue. The fact that we may *need* to believe that does not derogate from the sincerity of our conviction; public commitments are not tarnished by their derivation from private motives.

And what of particularism? Jewish particularism, save as it is rooted in the doctrine of Jewish chosenness, begins less as an ideological commitment than as a sociological condition. Cohen (1986) reports that when asked how many of their three closest friends are Jewish, half of America's Jews report that all three are, and another quarter report that two out of the three are. Nearly four out of five say that being Jewish is important to them because it provides them with ties to other Jews, and three out of five view the Jewish people as "an extension of my family."

The late author Maurice Samuel once observed that "If somewhere in China today an individual [not Jewish] were to work out for himself all the ethical and theological principles of Judaism, and live up to them, would that make of him a Jew? My answer is no. He would be as good a person as any Jew, and better than most Jews; but he would not be a Jew." What is missing, according to Samuel,

is an association with the fellowship of Jews, and an acceptance of
the responsibilities and instrumentalities of that fellowship.

Samuel is right: the core method of Judaism is community. Ours
is not a personal testament, but a collective and public commitment.
That is the method we have preached and practiced, and it is at the
very heart of our understanding. We are the tribe that proclaimed
the universality of God, but insisted on remaining a tribe. Others,
not understanding why we have felt such urgency about remaining
apart, have asked—and sometimes demanded—that we follow our
universalist insight to its logical conclusion and ourselves become
universal. We have steadfastly refused.

Midrash: God began with one man. That didn't work, so he destroyed everything and started over again with one family. And
when that didn't work, he turned to a people, a people that requires
a quorum for prayer, a people whose most solemn confessional—
the Yom Kippur liturgy—is a public event, and is spoken in the first
person plural (*ashamnu,* we have sinned; *bagadnu,* we have betrayed).

I have called community a method, a means, and we will return
to that in a while. But community is often viewed as an end, and
the confusion of ends and means raises a serious problem. As end,
community comes to provide us with identity, and requires no other
justification. People need some sense of location, and, as I observed
in the last chapter, Jewish is what Jews are. When Cohen (1986)
asked his respondents why "being Jewish" is important to them, 94
percent chose "I was born Jewish" as one of their answers; the same
number selected "It is my culture." All the talk of distinctive values,
of mission and purpose, fades; one is Jewish because one is Jewish,
and because being Jewish is a way of connecting with the past and
with other Jews in the present. On this reading, the values of the
Jews may not be distinctive at all, may be the same generalized
values that are shared by almost all Americans, the universalistic
values of the civic culture or the materialistic values of the bourgeois culture. It doesn't matter, for what defines the Jews *as Jews* is
community; not values, not ideology.

A recent book by Calvin Goldscheider and Alan S. Zuckerman,
intriguingly entitled *The Transformation of the Jews,* makes this case in
considerable detail. The title summarizes the authors' belief that

what others have mistaken as an inevitable erosion of Jewish identity and commitment is, in truth, a "transformation" of Jewish
identity, an adaptation to Jewry's new circumstances. In order to
understand this transformation, Goldscheider and Zuckerman
claim, we must set aside our traditional interest in Jewish values and
focus instead on patterns of Jewish interaction. "Those scholars
who equate the beliefs of Jews with the ideas and values espoused
by their intellectuals replace the analysis of Jewish society and
politics with intellectual history. There is no reason to assume that
the cohesion of Jewish communities, for example, varies with the
kinds of ideas set forward by Jewish intellectuals."

Instead, the analyst should recognize that "For most Jews, most
of the time, ideologies and beliefs justif[y] decisions reached on
other grounds. . . . For most Jews, most of the time, the constraints
of economic position and opportunity, place of residence, educational skills, political limitations and rights, and tugs of family and
friends have outweighed personal convictions." (In any case, "We
know very little about the values held by contemporary Jews. Few
surveys exist to shed light on their beliefs and attitudes.")

What it comes down to, in this view, is that "Even for Jews who
do not actively seek to be Jews, their ties, networks, and connections
to other Jews through family, friends, neighbors, jobs, schools, and
leisure activities are important sources of Jewish communal
strength."

All the concern over Jewish identity and Jewish survival has thus
been misdirected. Kinship and friendship and the other forces that
Goldscheider and Zuckerman specify are in fact more powerful than
we had supposed; modernization does not necessarily destroy the
ethnic bond. For here are the Jews, after all; believers or not, they
cluster together, they stay Jews. Best, then, to set aside culture and
values, ideologies and beliefs, none of which we know much about,
and to focus, as Goldscheider and Zuckerman do, on a "detailed
examination of family, marriage, childbearing, social class, residence, occupation, and education." These, not values, are the arenas
of interaction that define Jewish cohesion and solidarity, hence
Jewish survival.

The Jewish community, on the Goldscheider/Zuckerman reading, is a community of limited liability, based on shared tastes and on shared interests, but not on shared values. It is a light-year distant from the community the Jews have supposed themselves to be, the community that has chosen to be bound together in mission.

I do not deprecate the significance of kinship, of networks of association, of community-as-end. Insofar as such community offers its members a surrogate extended family, and thereby a support system, it is not merely a haphazard agglomeration of affiliations; it has moral force as well. It provides its participants with elements of predictability and of fraternity, and even acts as a source of values. It helps make order out of chaos, it is a comfort. And, as Goldscheider and Zuckerman emphasize, it has the considerable advantage that our understanding of it does not rest, as an examination of culture and values must, on speculation.

But even if we accept the Goldscheider-Zuckerman thesis—and it is very far from the accepted sociological wisdom—ethnicity and propinquity do not exhaust the possibilities.* Something is missing: To say that a community is adequately described only by those aspects of its life that can be accurately measured is to confuse the method of inquiry with its purpose. (Remember the writer Peretz, who was not satisfied to count calories, who insisted on hearing stories?)

Earlier, I wrote of the fodder and the crib and of their importance to an understanding of what Jews and Judaism are about. But to go beyond the texts does not require that we omit the texts, and also the ideas. It seems to me the case—and, I think, to very many Jews as well—that a Judaism transformed from the self-conscious possession of a religious civilization to the instinctive response of a hereditary grouping cannot inspire the effort, the devotion, and the dedication that have traditionally characterized the Jews. Sooner or later, no matter how Judaism—or Jewishness—is justified, whether as a system that is divinely ordained or as an affiliation that helps

---

*I should add that there is considerable evidence that as new generations, increasingly remote from the immigrant experience, come of age, they care less and cluster less, their eagerness for Jewishness through propinquity diminishes. One recent survey, for example, finds that among first-generation Jews, 88 percent claim that all their close friends are Jewish; in the second generation, the figure drops to 77 percent, and in the third to 52 percent; by the fourth generation, it is 34 percent. (Cohen, 1986.)

people feel located, its practitioners must and will insist on more. They will not accept that all that they have been taught and profess to believe is merely a convenient rationalization, a way of dignifying our need for identity and human warmth. Nor will they concede that the need for warmth is necessarily prior to the need for a compelling ideology. They will not be satisfied to think of themselves as blind actors, be it in God's plan or in their parents' tradition or in an impersonal sociological unfolding. We have been taught from our beginning that we are members of a faith community, not merely inert particles that are moved by sociological forces we do not comprehend and cannot resist. Are we now to accept that we have tumbled from thundering prophecy to timorous propinquity, that our ideas are merely a flimsy costume, and that we talk the old-fashioned way merely to hide the disconcerting truth from ourselves? That is a transformation devoutly to be shunned.

There is no doubt that some, perhaps even most, Jews might be classified as "inertial Jews," for whom being Jewish is essentially about patterns of affiliation and association rather than values and beliefs and ideas. These are people who may even perceive themselves as deeply devoted to Jewish continuity, who are aware, of course—no Jew is not—that they are heirs to a received tradition, but for whom the purpose of the tradition is only to lend dignity to the current social forces that prompt Jews to cluster together; its content is irrelevant, is indeed merely a rationalization. The tradition becomes the means, community the end.

But such an inertial Judaism must one day wear thin and then out. A Judaism that knows neither denial nor affirmation, that is exclusively about togetherness, must become a vestigial category. Our values—as also our effort to clarify them—cannot be reduced to rationalizations; they have too much weight behind them, and too much purpose. They add dignity and zest to our lives as individuals, to our life as a people. And they thereby elevate our morale. Whether they originate in virginal conviction or in post-hoc rationalization, we want and need and will not let go our values. They enable us to take ourselves seriously. Whether we are eager or reluctant to translate them into behavior, we want and expect and insist that they be regularly articulated. It is our values that connect the mundane to the majestic. That connection may be no more than a vainglorious illusion, or it may be what saves Jewish history from the absurd. Either way, we will not let go of it.

Values? In America? Can we usefully speak here of Jewish values, or is such talk merely sentimental blather? Values arise out of a culture; they are the internalized monitors of what is proper and improper. America's Jews participate fully in American culture. Given the sheer scope of that culture, does it not overwhelm everything else, leaving little or no room for a distinctive Jewish culture, hence for distinctive Jewish values?

One reading: A lament for the "Americanization" of the Jew, whose story is of how a noble ancient culture has succumbed to the seductive temptations of the fleshpot, the People of the Book become the people of the buck, doomed to decline, then fail. Perhaps the Jews will survive, perhaps not; little matter, for they have abandoned their mission and their message.

This reading derives from a caricature of America, as also of its Jews; it is a parodic reading. It focuses on the America of privatism, alienation, moral vacuity, materialism, and such, on Ivan Boesky's greed, the Jewish American Princess (and Prince), Sammy Glick, and the safari bar mitzvah party. (It is, incidentally, not clear at all that the values these represent are more characteristic of New York or Los Angeles today than of Minsk or Warsaw or Berlin yesterday. The model of the immigrant as a paragon of virtue who was here corrupted by shallow American values is without historic foundation.) Yet along with the American dross, there is American gold. There is America's unprecedented (if still differentially available) freedom, its uncommon investment in higher education, its remarkable institutional stability, its impressive mechanisms for self-correction, the genius of its pluralism. And, plainly, along with all the spoiled and shallow and greedy Jews, there are thoughtful and modest and honest Jews. To say that we have been "Americanized," therefore, is not to say nearly enough: We need to know not only how much Jews have been affected by America, but what aspects of the endlessly complex American culture they have internalized, and how.

I have already observed that American culture is highly permissive. In America, the only consensus required of us is on the rules of the game; those rules are the principal source of American values, all that America demands its diverse cultural groups accept. The procedural values—tolerance, fair play, freedom of speech, minority rights, and so on—are what we call, loosely, "the American way." As to the rest, America not only allows, it *expects* its members to turn to more limited entities. And, by virtue of its rules, America can accommodate a startlingly high level of dissensus. This nation is so vast that no single symbol can adequately capture its diversity nor any one source account for our values in all their variety; even television is no more than an especially powerful one among many and often competing sources of values.

A particular culture "succeeds"—indeed, may be said to exist— insofar as its institutions and patterns of communication (including its language) implant in its members a set of standards—moral, aesthetic, and even cognitive—that define the right and the good, that are felt to be shared by all, and that can be and are invoked as guides to behavior. These we call values, and in a permissive America, it is possible for Jews, if they are so disposed, to turn to the Jewish community as a source of substantive values.* Because of the compatibility between classic Jewish conceptions and historic American conceptions, we are here invited to take the Hebrew prophets seriously, to make of their injunctions regarding freedom, law, justice, compassion, and so forth a political agenda for our own time. There is room here for our indignation, our outrage, our readiness to say yes to life and therefore to say no to injustice in all its forms—*and* to feel ourselves at home. There is room also for those things we have learned not only from our texts but also from our

---

*The literature on values is both vast and confusing. I use the term to suggest internalized standards of propriety—in particular, of moral propriety. Values are not the same as norms, even though both prescribe behavior. (The difference is captured by two Yiddish phrases: *men tor nit* and *es past nit*. The first means, more or less, it is forbidden, one mustn't; the second means, more or less, it is improper, one shouldn't.) The dictionary is helpful here: a norm is "a rule or an authoritative standard"; a value is "that which is worthy of esteem for its own sake; that which has intrinsic worth."

And values are not the same as interests, even though both affect behavior. Interests go to the expedient, the wise; they are calculated. Values, as I have suggested, go to the right, the good; they are, typically, implicit, even pre-conscious. The relationship between Jewish values and Jewish interests is a matter of pressing concern, which I come to in a later chapter.

experience—chief among them mutual responsibility and concern for the welfare of the community.*

On this reading, the fear of Americanization is mistaken; the threads of the two cultures are readily woven into a new and substantial fabric.

But we are left with a major problem. One does not, in fact, "turn to" a particular community in order to glean one's values. The process of value acquisition is too subtle; it is the consequence of being *of*, not of turning *to*, a community. If we want to ascertain the degree to which the American Jew derives his or her values from the Jewish community, we therefore have first to inquire into the nature of that community. And the problem is that the Jewish community does not provide for most of its members the intimacy of association that is required if it is to be a central source of their values. The American Jewish community seems entirely too loose an aggregation to be capable of implanting in its members a set of standards that "define the right, the good, that are felt to be shared by all and are invoked as guides to behavior," as I earlier suggested a "successful" culture must.

It is true that Jews are taught to regard the Jewish people as a kind of extended family, and that some aspects of Jewish relationships are best understood as family-like. (We speak, often, of our "brothers and sisters" in the Soviet Union, of our "kinfolk" in Israel, and so forth. In fact, Cohen [1980] finds that 60 percent of us agree that "I see the Jewish people as an extension of my family"; only 23 percent disagree.) But for all its residual pull, the Jewish "family" is dispersed and fragmented. It lacks, by and large, the mechanisms and institutions through which it might confidently transmit Jewish values, however defined. The biological family, the homogeneous neighborhood, the traditional afternoon school—all the elements that characterized the community in the first generations after the mass immigration to America, up until the end of World War II— have been radically transformed, their grip dramatically attenuated.

---

*The distinction between our texts and our experience is really quite artificial. There was, after all, a time when the prophets were part of our experience. And perhaps the day will come when our own experience will be inscribed as our descendants' text.

For most Jews, the very notion of community is a euphemism; their actual experience is one of *association* rather than *community*.* An association is something one *joins;* it is segmented rather than comprehensive, mechanical rather than organic, specific rather than diffuse. And its ability to serve as a source of values is inherently limited. It cannot be, for example, midwife to the indignation of which I earlier wrote.

Nor can the network of Jewish organizations function as a surrogate for the traditional community. Very many Jews are outside its scope altogether; only about half—some say two thirds—of all American Jews belong to any Jewish organization.†

Must we, then, accept the Goldscheider/Zuckerman thesis that here in America it is no longer our values that connect us, but other things: some shared interests, some old school ties, the usual pulls of ethnicity? If it is true that Jewish culture in America is a culture of organization and affiliation rather than a culture of community and belonging, how can it be a source of values? Perhaps we have made too much of the other stuff, the stuff about God and justice and such, and should settle for folk festivals, knishes, and the Anti-Defamation League. In any case, we are people, not prophets. When we go to our jobs in the morning and to our PTA meetings at night, we do not have "to break the oppressors' yoke" furrowed on our brows, nor do we say, "Let us defend pluralism today." We are rather more likely to smile agreeably, say, "Have a nice day," and let it go at that. Ought the honest search for Jewish meaning to look, therefore, to the ordinary lives Jews live rather than to the extraordinary messages their tradition contains? If it does, perhaps we will find that ethnicity is all there needs to be; in view of the surprising resurgence of ethnicity in the 1960s and since, why dispute that possibility? Instead, relax, harken to Goldscheider and Zuckerman, go with the flow, accept our ethnicity for what it is—an expression

---

*The reader familiar with the sociological literature will note the relevance here of diverse conventional sociological dichotomies, including Tonnies' *Gemeinschaft* and *Gesellschaft,* Weber's traditional and rational, Becker's sacred and secular.

†Half belong to a synagogue, 40 percent to some other Jewish organization. At the same time, and contrary to the conventional wisdom, there does not seem to be much attrition in affiliation; during the years of child rearing, for example, and especially around the time of bar and bat mitzvah, there is nearly universal synagogue affiliation.

of the universal human need for solidarity, a concern for protection of the group, a comforting source of stability in a reeling world—and put an end to the chronic fretting about Jewish survival—and about Jewish values. Just *be*. Who knows? Perhaps the real American Jewish synthesis is the abandonment of Jewish values and the retention of ethnic ties. Keep your Jewish friends, for warmth's sake, but do not confuse the blessings of propinquity with the burden of principle, of purpose.

I reject that view, of course. It describes not a synthesis, but a surrender. It seems to me a peculiar, even perverse, and surely disappointing conclusion to the saga of a religious civilization, a community whose very raison d'etre has so widely been thought to be the preservation and transmission of values. I reject it because, as inadequate as American Jewish culture may be as a source of values, and as inarticulate as most of us remain when challenged to name distinctive Jewish values, the very fact of our belief that it is for the sake of our values that we persist is a crucial ingredient in our will to persist. Without the overlay of values, the community itself would soon collapse. I reject it, finally, because it seems to me both more honest and more useful, after acknowledging the benefits of community, to regard the Jewish community principally as a means rather than as an end in itself. Save as the highest purpose of community is the realization of values, its capacity to command the loyalties of its members will shrivel, and they will wander elsewhere in search of identity and warmth. That is why community as an end in itself is self-defeating. That is why community must be *about* something, why, at least in a pluralistic society, its own particularity is not sufficient to sustain it.

Community, then, as method: We are a people particular in structure, universal in belief. But how can these apparent antinomic orientations lean into and reinforce each other?

9

Particularism and Universalism:
The Synthesis

EACH GENERATION finds its own formulas for the expression of Jewish particularism. Landsmanschaft and lobby, language and cuisine, neighborhood and synagogue: all these and more offer opportunity and reinforcement for the expression of the distinctive mores that define the community. They are among the ways in which boundaries are drawn, among the devices that enable us to know who stands within the community, who outside it.*

But the Jews are a community in history, not only in geography. Together with the unique expressions that each generation develops to suit its own place and time, there are also the common elements of Jewish expression that link the Jews of this place and this time to the Jews of other places, other times. Of these, none provides as

*In a pluralistic society, very few people live entirely within the boundaries of a single community. Boundaries blur, overlap, are permeable. For American Jews, living within the boundaries of the Jewish community rarely if ever means living wholly within those boundaries. One of the more remarkable stories of the Jewish experience in America is of those emphatically particularistic Hasidic subcommunities, separated both from America and from other Jews by dress and by language and by dozens of other elements of style and substance, who have brilliantly incorporated into their traditional ways some of the most advanced elements of American technology and commerce.

precise a link as religious ritual. Such ritual can be a useful window on the dilemma I have been discussing, so it is there that I begin this examination of the interaction between structure and belief, between particularism and universalism.

The tenacity of ritual, even in the face of modernity, is by now well established. Survey research among Jews often uses ritual religious observance as a way of measuring Jewish identity, and though it is a remarkably peripheral way to get at what it purports to measure, the data do tell us that such observance is alive and in fair health. More precisely, where it was once supposed that each generation would be but a mere shadow of its predecessor, it turns out instead that the marked atrophy in observance as between first-generation and native-born American Jews was largely a one-generation phenomenon. Some key elements of the tradition have, indeed, fallen into disuse, unable to withstand American social and economic patterns (or the sloth of the people, depending on one's point of view). But while fewer people in this generation than in the last observe, say, the dietary code, more people light Sabbath candles.

I am not here interested in which religious customs are still observed, or by how many people. My concern is with ritual observance in general and with the problems it raises for would-be modern people rather than with any specific tradition or commandment. Modernity insists on rationality; while the purpose of ritual may be rational, its content is not.

In order to deal with the apparent conflict between the claims of modern rationalism and the claims of traditional ritual, it was, for a time, thought useful to propose rational justifications for the tradition. It was common, for example, to teach Jewish children of the wisdom of Jewish dietary laws by pointing out that if you stayed away from eating pork, you wouldn't contract trichinosis. See how clever the Bible is?

But the point of not eating pork is not to avoid disease; if that were its point, we'd these days more likely permit pork and, if recent newspaper reports are to be believed, prohibit chicken. The point of not eating pork, or of observing any other commandment or tradition, has nothing to do with its rationality (or lack thereof), since we may assume that as rational people, we don't need the tradition to tell us to behave rationally.

What then is the point? That is, why do (or should) modern people observe customs, commandments, traditions that make no rational sense, that we may even have come to understand as vestiges of primitive understandings?

Take, for example, the matter of affixing a *mezuzah* to the "doorposts"—we call them jambs—of the rooms of our homes.

The formal origins of this tradition are clear: In Deuteronomy (6:9 and 11:20), we are enjoined to "write them [the words of God] on the *mezuzot* of your house and in your gates." (The meaning of the word itself has changed. It began as doorposts, but came to mean the passages that are affixed to the doorposts in accordance with the injunction, and today is understood by most people as the case in which the parchment containing the passages is inserted.)

Now, if one were to ask most American Jews whether they believe in the protective power of amulets, they would, I presume—no one to my knowledge has bothered to ask—answer in the negative. Yet a majority of Jewish households have a *mezuzah* affixed at least to the main entrance of their homes. And there is little question that the origins of the practice, in pagan antiquity, have to do precisely with providing "protection" for the home.

What is an astrophysicist doing with an amulet?

More: We are instructed that the *mezuzah* is to be affixed to the right-hand doorpost of the room in the top third of the doorpost and slanting inward, and that the writing inside it is to be inspected at least twice every seven years.

Quite plainly, most Jews who have *mezuzot* in their homes do not know the derivation of the custom. They do not know what the words inscribed therein are, nor what they mean. If they happen to know that the *mezuzah* is supposed to slant inward, they surely do not know that the reason for the angle is that the commentator Rashi and his grandson, Rabeinu Tam, could not agree, the one holding that it was to be affixed vertically, the other horizontally. The angle, in other words, is a compromise. What is a clinical psychologist doing with an angled amulet?

Old forms may be invested with new meanings. No, we do not

believe in amulets. (In Israel, there was shock when, several years back, the Lubavitcher Rebbe asserted that the reason so many PLO rockets were directed against the town of Kiryat Shmoneh was that the *mezuzot* of the town had not been inspected in timely fashion, and that many were faulty.) But we do, it seems, believe in announcing that ours is a Jewish home. Perhaps we even mean to announce that ours is a home in which God is revered, although I think that less likely our popular purpose. And some of us are simply following a commandment, no more, no less. What joins the divergent purposes is a rudimentary and benign perspective: This is something Jews do.

All peoples and all groups do things that make no particular sense in themselves, but reinforce and sometimes celebrate their particularity. Such things may be unnerving to those who seek to be wholly modern, but they can be exciting, too. So, for another example, there is a tiny element of *halachah,* the body of Jewish law, that deals, of all things, with how we are enjoined to put on and tie our shoes each day. (I quote it in its entirety in order to convey the flavor of Talmudic discourse.)

> R. Johanan said: Like *tefillin* [phylacteries] so are shoes: just as *tefillin* [are donned] on the left [hand], so are shoes [put on] the left [foot first]. An objection is raised: When one puts on his shoes, he must put on the right first and then the left?—Said R. Joseph: Now that it was taught thus, while R. Johanan said the reverse, he who acts either way acts [well]. Said Abaye to him: But perhaps R. Johanan did not hear this . . . but if he had heard it he would have retracted? Or perhaps he heard it and held that the *halachah* is not as that *Mishnah?* R. Nahman b. Isaac said: A God-fearing person satisfies both views. And who is that? Mar, the son of Rabina. What did he do? He put on the right foot [sandal] but did not tie it. Then he put on the left, tied it, and then tied the right [sandal]. . . . Our Rabbis taught: When one puts on his shoes, he must put on the right first and then the left; when he removes [them], he must remove the left [first] and then the right.

I say this can be exciting, even in an era of penny-loafers, because without attention to detail we are left merely with broad principles, and while broad principles are pretty, and may on occasion be more than that, life is lived in its details. As the Israeli scholar Natan

Rotenstreich has observed, "Principles as such cannot be observed; they can only be formulated." Behavior depends on habit more than on principle.

I am not suggesting that the life of a mature Jew must conform to the details of the *halachah;* that is scarcely my position. I mean instead to propose that details, whether derived from reason or from revelation or simply from tradition ("this is something Jews do"), are essential. They are the nutrients of particularity.

From the purist's standpoint, my argument is at best superfluous: the *halachah* is self-validating. It is God's word, as handed down in an unbroken succession that began with Moses at Sinai, who received both the written and unwritten law, and it was handed over by Moses to Joshua, and then in succession to the prophets, the scribes, the sages, and the rabbis. Only those who have devoted their lives to its study and who accept it as normative may legitimately interpret it. But in so self-contained a system, though it may retain its purity, the *halachah* cannot retain its power. For it ignores the circumstances, the culture, the consciousness of each generation. It ignores the inevitable fact that the "legislation" one generation takes as the appropriate translation of principle will come to be seen as irrelevant, or downright wrong, by the next. (There will be seasons when it comes time to re-examine even the principles themselves.) More: It is scarcely conceivable that we will willingly abandon all the lessons of secular modernity, that we will take for ourselves the entirety of a system that was devised in and for other times and other places. If we seek now to reclaim human dignity, the path from the excesses of modernity cannot take us to the excesses of the pre-modern. If we have learned the limits of pure reason, we have also learned its delights; we need not willingly suspend our will, place ourselves in a cultic embrace and forgo entirely our anxiety-provoking autonomy. It is not necessary, and it is not possible, not even for the sake of Jewish particularity.

What a modern particularism (or a communitarian universalism) requires instead is the discovery of a place somewhere between deracinated modernity and mindless tradition, a way, as I have said, of investing old forms with new meaning.

*   *   *

The *Aleinu* prayer, recited at the close of all congregational worship services—weekdays, Sabbaths, and Festivals—provides an interesting illustration of both the tension between particularism and universalism and the struggle toward new meaning. Upon hearing it, one is initially startled by its celebration of particularism: "It is incumbent upon us to praise the Master of all, to attribute greatness to the Creator of the Beginning, who did not make us like the nations of other lands, and did not place us like the families of the earth; who did not design our destiny to be like theirs, nor our lot like that of all their multitude." (The translation of the Hebrew of the *Aleinu* prayer is exceedingly difficult; I have here chosen a literal version.) In brief, we thank God for having singled us out. And if that were all there were, the prayer would be an insular particularist's delight.

But there's another paragraph, and then a coda. In the second paragraph, we express our imminent hope for the day "when the abominations shall be removed from the earth, and the false gods exterminated; when the world will be repaired under the reign of the Almighty, and all mankind will call upon your name, all the wicked of the earth will be turned to you. May all the inhabitants of the world know that to you every knee must bend and every tongue swear allegiance."

Those who insist will find in that paragraph, too, a radically ethnocentric statement. After all, the language insists that all people must worship *our* God. But that distorts Jewish theology beyond recognition. From our early days, we have said to the world, "You can have our God; it's us you can't have. Our God is a universal God, we a particular people." There's no need for "the synagogue universal"; on the appointed day,

> He will judge among the many peoples, and arbitrate for the multitude of nations, however distant; and they shall beat their swords into plowshares and their spears into pruning hooks. Nation shall not take up sword against nation,; they shall never again know war; *but every man shall sit under his grapevine or fig tree* with no one to disturb him. For it was the Lord of Hosts who spoke. Though all the peoples walk each in the names of its gods, we will walk in the name of the Lord our God forever and ever. (Micah, 4:3–5; emphasis added)

Zion is accessible to all. It is not Jewish dominion we seek, but God's. "All mankind will call upon your Name."

The coda? "On *that* day"—the day, that is, when God's sovereignty will at last be universally established and accepted—God "will be King over all the earth; on *that* day, the Lord will be One, and his name will be One."

What can it possibly mean for a people whose central prayer asserts that God is already One ("Hear O Israel, the Lord is our God, the Lord is One") here to propose that only on *that* day will God be One? It means, first, that there is a reciprocal relationship between humankind and God; only when God's universality is accepted does God become One. And then God's name, too, becomes One, for universality is at last perceived as God's most significant attribute. It means, as well, that we are urged to move beyond our particularity, to acknowledge that for all that we may celebrate our special relationship with God, God's work is not done—and therefore neither is ours.

Reading—more accurately, studying—the liturgy offers interesting and sometimes important insight into the ambiguous dispositions of a people. The "On that day" coda in the *Aleinu* is from the Book of Zachariah, where its context is scarcely universal. Three verses later, we read, for example: "As for those people that warred against Jerusalem, the Lord will smite them with this plague: their flesh shall rot away while they stand on their feet; their eyes shall rot away in their sockets; and their tongues shall rot away in their mouths."

These days, we're far more likely to cite the swords become plowshares than the rotting eyes. How far our intentions have shifted—and how unsettled they remain—can be judged from the current renderings, in the standard prayerbook of the Reform movement, of the first paragraph of the *Aleinu.* I say "renderings" because *Gates of Prayer* offers several different versions of both the Hebrew and the English. Recall the literal translation of the key words of the opening verse: "who did not make us like the nations of other lands, and did not place us like the families of the earth; who did not design our destiny to be like theirs, nor our lot like that of all their multitude." One version in the Reform prayerbook pre-

serves the original Hebrew, and offers the following softened English: "who has set us apart from the other families of the earth,
giving us a destiny unique among the nations." A second simply
skips the language about difference and provides this in English:
"who spread out the heavens and established the earth, whose glory
is revealed in the heavens above, and whose greatness is manifest
throughout the world." The third version, with the same Hebrew
as the second, gives us, "Let us revere the God of life, and sing the
praise of Nature's Lord, who spread out the heavens and established
the earth, whose glory is proclaimed by the starry skies, and whose
wonders are revealed in the human heart." Finally, we get a Hebrew
version that means, in fact, "We are obliged to praise the Lord of
all, to attribute greatness to the Creator of the Beginning, who has
assigned us the task of unifying His name, and the destiny of
crowning His Kingship." And, just to confuse the issue still more,
the parallel English for these verses reads, "We praise Him who gave
us life. In our rejoicing He is God; He is God in our grief. In anguish
and deliverance alike, we praise; in darkness and light we affirm our
faith. Therefore we bow our heads in reverence, before the Eternal
God of life, the Holy One, blessed be He."

All this suggests that what we make of the original text, of the
"old forms," reflects our confusions as well as our insights; we are
rich in both. It derives from what those before have made of it, and
from our own situation. We take the prayers we were given, and we
make up new prayers, and most of the prayers we compose will
quickly and deservedly be forgotten, but now and again one of them
will capture an enduring truth and become a prayer for the next
generations to take. That is the way a generation becomes something more than a vessel through which the tradition is poured; that
is how we leave our own thumbprint on the tradition. Our recitation of the *Aleinu,* a prayer first uttered by Jews at least as far back
as the third century and quite possibly several hundred years earlier,
places us squarely within the tradition. Our renderings of it, reflecting as they do the unresolved tension between our particularism and
our universalism, illustrate the specific situation of this generation
of America's Jews; its thumbprint is still blurred.

That is why, as I wrote earlier, we must know what Jews wrestle with if we seek to understand them. They—we—are different from all other Jews precisely because we are in America. And they—we—are different from all other Americans precisely because we are Jews. It is not at all clear to me that we will stay Jews, since, as I have argued, the particularity we celebrate is often devoid of content, contingent on crisis, and the universality that beckons us is so very seductive. But the themes are there, available to us if we will make ourselves accessible to them and invest our insights into them. And the substance of the distinctiveness—the continuing struggle to combine particularism and universalism—is surely worth protecting, for it offers a useful paradigm for general application. It is a way of making the crowd less lonely and the enclave less insular.

Ethically neutral rituals are not without function; they provide the particular rhythm for a people's life. Given the preoccupation of Jewish (as of much religious) ritual with time, with marking off the hours of the day and the days of the week and the months and the years, we may think of ritual as a kind of metronome, a way for us to keep time. And then come the ethical commandments and rituals, a way to move beyond the keeping of time to its sanctification. (The *halachah* itself makes no distinction between those rituals that have ethical content and those that are devoid of it.)

It is possible to be hypnotized by the steady beat of the metronome, and to forget that it is there to provide the framework for melody. (The opposite error, of course, is to suppose that the idiosyncratic drumbeat each of us hears is enough to go with.) Writing in the Orthodox publication *Jewish Action,* Rabbi Emanuel Feldman makes the point: "The two terms—an observant Jew and a religious Jew—are not necessarily synonymous." Metronomes have their uses, and their abuses.

For the Jew who feels himself, herself, commanded—I mean really commanded, not merely urged—to observe and obey, the rules and the rituals are self-justifying. For most of us, they are not. We may observe them, more or less, out of habit or deference or, as I have suggested, out of a sense that if the Jews are to maintain their apartness, their particularity, the rules and rituals are important. We may observe them because in moments of trauma, they can be a sustaining resource. But in the last analysis, their importance is derivative; they come to make other things possible. They are among the means of a people, but not its meaning; they are devices by which a people seeks to assure its continuity. In the case of the Jews, they are doubly important, since the success of Jewish universalism might otherwise lead inexorably to the disappearance of the Jews, content defeating continuity, ends defeating means, the logic of our universalist conviction finally leading us to abandon our particularism.

Just a few years back, that seemed to be the direction in which we were headed, and the echo of that time is still with us. Not so long ago, it was a common experience of American Jews to seek to hide their particularity. On the way to Hebrew school, we'd turn our books over so no one would see the peculiar writing. Back then, "Is it good for the Jews?" was a grandmother's question. It captured the peculiar sensibility of a generation (or was it generations?) for whom the only lens that mattered was the Jewish lens. A plane crash, a precinct election, a scandal, a success: Is it good (or bad) for the Jews?

When it was our grandmothers who asked the question, we indulged them. They were immigrants; how were they to know that here in America, we were invited to other questions, offered twenty-twenty lenses? But when it was our peers, we winced; how could they be so constricted, so utterly parochial? Judaism, we thought, was a launching pad—and they obstinately made of it a tether.

Or: The question of how much Jews "owe" the outside world was, until recently, a hypothetical question. It presumes that in the wall of separation that is the boundary between Jews and others, there is a gate that Jews can enter and exit at will. But for most of Jewish history, there was no such gate.

Then, one day, we awoke in a country where the gate swings freely, lubricated by a pluralism more fluid than we have ever known before. So the question has shifted: beyond nostalgia, what is there to draw us back to our side of the wall?

Before the 1950s, when we were still largely a community of immigrants and their children, and when American nativism was still a potent force, we were satisfied with the occasional exploratory expedition to the "other side." But generational and cultural change led, during the fifties, to a headlong rush to explore the new territory that had opened to us. For the individual Jew, the experience was often heady. For the Jewish community, it was a time of anxiety: once exposed to America's seductions, what would induce the Jew to return to the fold?

And many, at least for a time, did not. It was the old story, the story of the melting pot, this time played out not in scholarly debates or in a Broadway theater but in the lives of real people. We had recently won a war for the soul (as well as the body) of the West, a war that was fought, inter alia, against racism, that was fought in the name of the brotherhood of man. We'd all thrilled to the photographs in Steichen's *The Family of Man,* we'd all taken Carl Sandburg to heart, we'd finally been invited not only to enroll in the universities but to teach in the best of them. What any longer justified our need/desire to stay on our side of the wall? Why not just take all those nice ethics and move on, and out? And we knew one other thing: in the aftermath of the war, anti-Semitism had become utterly disreputable. That new fact of Jewish life was the protective lotion that would permit us to wander freely into fields we'd not had the courage to explore before. So: our own logic no longer supported separation, community; others no longer imposed it upon us.

If, until now, Judaism had been both an imposition and an act of defiance, a stubborn and stiff-necked insistence on our right to stay Jews, what passion would fuel it now that no one disputed our claim? (Philip Roth, in 1961: "Our rejection, our abhorrence, finally, of Christian fantasy leads us to proclaim to the world that we are Jews still—alone, however, what have we to proclaim to one another?") Look before you: Endless vistas, challenge galore, life in all its parts. Now look back: A cryptic and constricted and even mildly subversive anachronism, committed to boundaries that have no rational foundation. The world of our fathers, to be refuted or respected, but surely not to be projected onto our children. (As Irving Howe, author of the hugely successful *World of Our Fathers,* himself explained, "Jews hurried out to buy" his book from "a readiness to say farewell in a last fond gesture . . . an affectionate glance at the world of their fathers before turning their backs forever and moving on, as they had to.") The world of our fathers, and of our grandmothers and their stingy question.

So, off to take our place, and a good place it is. You want the bourgeoisie? It's yours. So, if you prefer, is the movement, or the laboratory; take your pick—the fleshpot, the sheltered grove, the barricade, whatever suits your style. No betrayal required, nor even any need to abandon (as if it were possible) your Jewish sensibility, that special, somewhat skewed way of seeing things. Just an indulgent glance backward, an occasional visit to the old neighborhood, a lingering sense of kinship with the other Jews moving out, moving on, off to fight the good fight, for freedom, for democracy, for brotherhood, or just for personal success.

You're an intellectual? Pack up your *tzuris* and trade them in for angst; your troubles are no longer parochial Jewish troubles, they are universal existential troubles, yours as a human being rather than as a Jew. (Same troubles, of course, but the new ones don't smell of herring.) You can view the Jewish bourgeoisie with appropriate contempt, and still drop the occasional Yiddishism into your discourse.

And the test of your readiness, be you middle class or intellectual, is simple: Have you outgrown your grandmother's way of seeing the world, have you stopped asking and stopped feeling the question of whether it's good for the Jews? For to insist on the question is to raise Judaism from an exotic ethnic background to a behavioral imperative, and it is therefore forbidden.

One can poke gentle fun at it all from this distance, but it was hardly laughable at the time. Those of the middle class who fell away were sorrow enough. But they, at least, were quiet in their going. Not so the intellectuals, ever seeking the last and often nasty word. The immigrants' children who had made it to conventional respectability did not appreciate the derision to which they were subjected by the intellectuals. They had conceived a new life for themselves, and they did not want it mocked by Philip Roth or, later, Woody Allen. Nor, for their part, did the intellectuals welcome their depiction as traitors.

The words were very sharp indeed. In 1944, in a symposium in the *Contemporary Jewish Record*—predecessor to *Commentary* magazine—Alfred Kazin, later to write the deeply moving and evocative *A Walker in the City* and later still *New York Jew*, sought to answer the question, "Who is the American Jew?" "What," he wrote, "is Jewish in him? What does he believe, especially in these terrible years, that separates him at all from our national habits of acquisitiveness, showiness and ignorant brag? . . . What a pity that he should feel 'different,' when he believes so little; what a stupendous moral pity, historically, that the Fascist cutthroats should have their eyes on him, too, when he asks for so little—only to be safe, in all the Babbitt warrens."

The attitudes of the intellectuals toward the fact of their Jewishness were nowhere more revealingly recorded than in a 1961 *Commentary* symposium entitled "Jewishness and the Younger Intellectuals." There were thirty-one participants, and with just a few exceptions, their theme was alienation, rooted in an assortment of reasons. Raziel Abelson, for example, linked herself to Spinoza, Marx, Freud, and Einstein, and dismissed the Jewish community:

> the Orthodox Jew, steeped in the medieval traditions of the ghetto, the Reform Jew who, unconcerned about the contradiction involved, tries to bring ancient traditions "up to date," and the dedicated Zionist who sees the fulfillment of the Biblical covenant in the advancement of the State of Israel, all seem to me to ignore the role that the modern Jew is best qualified to perform—namely, that of spokesman for a rationally organized, democratic world society, unfettered by parochial traditions and superstitions.

Jason Epstein had "the impression that the traditional human groupings are on the way out." Herbert Gold believed that the "history of the Jew will be one with the history of everybody else." Ned Polsky saw "no virtues unique to the Jewish tradition, and some evils." And Philip Roth asked the ultimate perplexing question: he can connect to the Jews only as he apprehends their God, and until that time comes, "there will continue to exist between myself and those others who seek his presence, a question, sometimes spoken, sometimes not, which for all the pain it may engender, for all the disappointment and bewilderment it may produce, cannot be swept away by nostalgia or sentimentality or even by a blind and valiant effort of the will: how are you connected to me as another man is not?"

The symposium sample was skewed. It included only people under the age of forty, and excluded anyone with a "definite religious commitment." But these were the prodigals, and their criticism—a perfunctory acknowledgment of the erstwhile Jewish qualities of intellect and compassion, followed by a declaration of independence from the organized Jewish community, perceived as unbearably middle class—stung the community. Norman Podhoretz, *Commentary*'s editor, summarized the symposium: The "overwhelming majority" of the participants feel that "they properly belong to a much wider world than is encompassed by the Jewish community"; most "assume easily . . . that the American Jewish community is indistinguishable from the middle-class community in general and bears no sign of the former attributes of the Jewish people." How could so blunt a verdict not sting and provoke angry resentment?

From a letter in response to the *Commentary* symposium:

> The many contributors who are involved in the academic life seem to be living in an America I don't know. It is an America with hardly any anti-Semitism, where Jews are just like everybody else. . . . It just isn't my world. No synagogue markings, no job discrimination, no exclusive country clubs, no social exclusion, and no special contributions to America . . . no holidays and family gatherings and feasts, no group dinners and charity theater parties and fundraising dinners, no pride in Israeli accomplishments, no horror at the greatest and most incredible inhumanity against Jews in our lifetime. . . . How about a symposium of your non-intellectual readers?

Yet who knows what a symposium of non-intellectuals would have revealed? Intellectual achievement was by no means a precondition for assimilation; large segments of the middle class had moved in that direction. Those who, whether out of commitment or inertia, remained within the community were often unable to articulate the rationale for their attachment to it. Take, for example, the matter of intermarriage. A Jewish youngster announces his or her intentions of marrying "out of the faith." The parents are distraught, but cannot explain, beyond their own hurt, what is at stake in the matter, why they take it so very seriously. And the children are confused; all their lives, they've heard their parents roar universalism, and now, suddenly, they whimper particularism. All their lives, their parents have insisted that each person is to be judged according to personal merit; now it is the categories of belonging that control. An articulate parental explanation would have to go something like this: "We understand that she [he] is a lovely person, and that you have many values in common. In fact, we congratulate you on your good taste, and if your private act had no public consequences, we'd be overjoyed. But it does have public consequences; there are boundaries you may not cross without damaging the structure, the fragile structure, we call the Jewish community. Why care about that structure? Because it is a principal source of your values. Your intended may have the same values, but she [he] came to them from a different direction, out of a different structure. (Ours is not the only one with those values.) But the halfway point between our structure and your proposed mate's is just that—a point, not a structure. You can't live on a point. So we're worried about us, about our community, and we're also worried about your children, and what they will be able to turn to. Our people, with all its hazards, offers you a scaffolding. Don't take that lightly."

Do we really expect that people will have the capacity to parse their lives in that fashion? Living simultaneously as particularists and universalists, as we try to, means that we are in search of a way to make one world out of two, two that are usually perceived as irreconcilable. But it does not mean that we know how to explain ourselves. We are not social theorists; we are a people, trying to make it through unsettled times. Try explaining that. So instead of analysis we get weeping and wailing and gnashing of teeth, and children who cannot quite figure out why all the fuss.

The community was caught: on the one hand, it was deeply hurt by the rebellion; on the other, it took great pride in the achievements of its prodigal sons and daughters, and it presumed to know, obviously better than they, how much their achievements were connected to the fact of their Jewishness. But it was unable to provide a defense commensurate to the attack. Its choices had taken on a dynamic of their own, become largely self-sustaining, even self-justifying. Too often, its rationale boiled down to anti-Semitism, Israel, and family gatherings. Sometimes, it was no more than "Because," or, "That's how Jews do things." None of these can be thought a beguiling invitation to the world of custom, to the world of transgenerational continuity, to the world of community.

So the community held its breath, convened conferences on such topics as "The College Campus: A Jewish Disaster Area?"—and awaited the return of its intellectuals.

Today, walking through the buildings of MIT, one sees scores of yarmulkes. Today, on dozens of college campuses around the country, High Holiday services are packed—and they are packed not only with freshmen who have yet to learn that religion is an anachronism; they are packed as well with professors who once knew that, and have since come to a different view.

Once, universalism was so much the Jewish rage that it seemed the only thing that held us back from going all the way was that the world wouldn't let us. Too often, our neighbors found ways, mostly ugly, to remind us of that which we sought so energetically to forget. Today, we revel, without evident penalty, in our particularity.

The tension between particularism and universalism is hardly unique to the Jews; it has long been remarked by sociologists. Their general view has been that traditional societies are characterized by high levels of particularism, while the process of modernization induces a growing universalism.

Which side are you on? Forced to choose, most of us would surely prefer the modern society to the traditional. The one suggests sophistication, rationality, cosmopolitanism; the other implies superstition, ignorance, the tyranny of irrational custom. For all the popular criticism of modern urban culture—criticism that dates back to Cicero,* and earlier—who would really choose to turn back the clock?

*In his *Republic,* Cicero wrote that "Maritime cities are . . . exposed to corrupt influences, and revolutions of manners. Their civilization is more or less adulterated by new language and customs, and they import not only foreign merchandise, but also foreign fashions, which allow not fixation or consolidation of the institutions of such cities."

But the key words in the preceding paragraph are "Forced to choose." Who forces? If we have come to understand anything at all about the ways of humankind, it is that we cannot safely ignore what Pareto called the "non-logical" aspects of human behavior: the centrality of family and friendship networks, the power of ethnic and geographic loyalties, the pervasiveness of the religious instinct, the uses of sentiment. We cannot safely ignore them, and we ought not to smugly deprecate them—nor are we required to choose against them as once we thought we were. The war for radical secularization has been reduced to a set of isolated skirmishes. Its erstwhile champions have mostly quit, recognizing not only that they have lost the war, but that they were fighting for a worthless cause. They stood for pure reason as against imagination; we have learned that we cannot and need not and will not give up on imagination. Surely no religious culture can, for religion rests, finally, on a shared imagination. The mythless society, as Rollo May observed, is a myth. That is the fundamental insight of the post-modern period.

The social pendulum is poorly calibrated; the post-modern impulse may lead as easily to punk as to an enriched rationalism, a renewed and mature spirituality. We have all seen—and see daily—the ugly uses to which myth may be put, and it is not easy to persuade people that there is no need to choose between myth and reason, that the two can nestle comfortably together.

So, too, with respect to the "choice" between particularism and universalism. We must speak, then, of a "both-and" understanding, of an arch: the tension between the two is not an either-or problem in search of resolution; it is an existential condition, a condition to be lived with, possibly even enjoyed, as we move back and forth between the two. *And in America, it can be enjoyed.* Here (and now, at last), we can be both universalistic and particularistic, both rational and traditional, both sentimental and utilitarian.

An earlier generation may have felt it necessary, in order to demonstrate its freedom from superstition and its universalistic values, to cast off every vestige of the tradition, every tie to the community. (The legends of radical Jews in turn-of-the-century New York making a point of eating pork near a synagogue on Yom Kippur are not legends; there were such Jews and, at the time, their rebellion was terribly important to them.) Today, there is no longer the need to apologize for a commitment to (as distinguished from an obsession with) tradition and ritual, even where the intrinsic merits of the practice are obscure. And "the community," it turns out, is a collection of communities; almost no matter one's ideology, there's a niche that will suit.

Is it really so neat as that? Does not our resurgent particularism threaten our continuing commitment to liberal universalism?

It is misleading and too facile simply to say that some Jews are universalists, others particularists. While at the bases of the arch there are, indeed, those who are definitively the one or the other, very many live near where the halves lean into each other. The excesses of both particularism and universalism are only a danger, not a destiny. Let us, for example, return to the 1986 Cohen survey where we found that 96(!) percent of the respondents agreed that *"As Jews,* we should be concerned about all people, and not just Jews" (emphasis added). Fifty-three percent of the respondents in that same survey rejected the statement that "I feel more concerned about oppression of Jews in certain countries than I do about most instances of oppression of other peoples." And 89 percent, as I have already noted, agreed that "I get just as upset by terrorist attacks upon non-Jews as I do when terrorists attack Jews."

The answers to the last two items are at sharp variance with my own impressions, as well as with those of virtually every observer— including the author of the survey from which they are drawn— who has commented on them. (Indeed, they explicitly contradict a point I made in Chapter 5, where I described how most Jews feel a measure of relief when they learn that today's terrorist depredation was visited upon "others.") It is always dangerous to allow impression to overrule data, but I do not believe these data accurately reflect the real dispositions of the respondents; instead, they reflect what the respondents take to be the "acceptable" answer. There is, in other words, an apparent break between our instincts and our ideology, for despite our answers, we do, indeed, feel more keenly the oppression of other Jews, the attacks against them. It would be perverse if we did not: after all, 85 percent of the respondents in the survey assert that they feel close to other Jews, 74 percent agree that "as a Jew, I have a special responsibility to help other Jews," and again, 60 percent agree that "I see the Jewish people as an extension of my family."

The surprise is not that people feel more concerned or more upset when it is other Jews who are in trouble; that is what being close, being family, means. The surprise is that so many who feel that way are at the same time constrained to announce their universalism.

Other data reveal the same apparent discrepancy. Some years back, in the course of a survey of Boston's Jews, I posited four summer camps to our respondents and asked them to choose the one they'd prefer for their children. The four were "Camp Lincoln," described as "a camp attended by children of many different religions, races, and nationalities; emphasis is put on all the various cultures and religions represented by the children"; "Camp Beaver, a 'regular' overnight camp where a majority of the campers are Jewish—no particular emphasis is placed on things Jewish"; "Camp Maccabee, an all-Jewish camp in which Jewish culture and history are stressed, but not religion"; and "Camp Judah, an all-Jewish camp in which Jewish religion and culture are stressed." Over half the respondents named Camp Lincoln as their first choice—but over half in fact sent their children to summer camps that were exclusively Jewish.

Is Jewish universalism, then, merely a sham, a rationalization, a cosmetic rhetorical cover for Jewish particularism? But if that is so, then how do we explain Jewish voting behavior—to take just one example—which, as we will soon see, consistently endorses welfare programs that will bring no direct benefit to Jewish voters, that will, in fact, cost them money in the form of higher taxes? A puzzle. And, I think, an important puzzle, for the solution that seems to me best to fit both the available data and the impressionistic evidence provides a critical clue to the character of the American Jew—to the extent one can assign a "character" to nearly 6 million individuals.

People abandoned religion in favor of secularity because rationalism and science promised so much. The world had been perceived as theocentric; with the conquest of science, it promised to become homocentric; man was at last to be the measure of things. But the

very world that had promised man first autonomy, then sovereignty, produced radical alienation as its debilitating side effect. Its
blessings were manifold; so, too, its curses. (There is no need to
deny its blessings in order to acknowledge its curses.) The experience of human dignity has been vastly expanded, but modernity has
yet to deliver us from evil. And even where it is not evil that
degrades us, even in lands of freedom and abundance and relative
peace, people are often reduced to commodities.

Irony of ironies, now we turn to religious communities to *restore*
the dignity of the person, to accomplish precisely that which the
abandonment of religion was meant to make possible and did not.
Again: we want—we need—to feel both rooted and modern, we do
not want to have to choose the one or the other. And if there is any
one thing that the saga of America's Jews illustrates—with all its
meandering, with all its missed opportunities and its mixed directions, with all its limitations—it is the possibility of living, not
comfortably but creatively, in two worlds: the world of roots, of
tradition, of sentiment, of kinship, and the world of the laboratory
and the marketplace. Both the world of covenant and the world of
contract: the post-modern world.

Jewish particularism, on this reading, is not merely a defense
against loneliness, a self-indulgent retreat to the ethnic enclave. It
is not a regression to an unenlightened past; we have come to
understand and believe what Mordecai M. Kaplan taught: "The
past has a vote, not a veto," and our rejection of its veto power has
made it easier for us to count its vote. Nor, finally, is Jewish particularism merely an example of a primitive need for human sociability. It is an assertion of the dignity of sociability, hence of human
dignity: In the image of God created He us.

And so it should come after all as no surprise that Jews express
at one and the same time a concern for the particular along with
their commitment to the universal. For many years, it was an accepted sociological axiom that to license the group would encourage
people to turn their backs on the larger human family—or even,
often enough, to take up arms against it. The Jews stand (unsteadily,
to be sure) as witnesses to a different vision, a different version. This
witness, rather than cosmetic hypocrisy, best explains how Jews can

at one and the same time declare their loyalties to other Jews and to all of humankind. Enthusiastically modern before, we now grope toward a richer post-modern understanding.

Another way of saying all this, as literate Jews may well have realized by now, is that to live with the tension intact means to stand at the intersection of Hillel's two classic questions: *If I am not for myself, who will be for me?* And, *If I am only for myself, what am I?* It is precisely there, at that intersection, that we can discern a Jewish meaning waiting to be formulated.

10

Intersections:
A Formulated Meaning

A FORMULATED MEANING for American Jews: *tikun olam*—the repair of the world. This is (we say, and mean) God's world, but it does not work as it was meant to. The story begins with Eden, and goes on through the trials and errors of all the generations since. This exquisitely organic whole, this ecological masterpiece, has been fractured a thousand times, has been scarred and marred and blighted and polluted and bloodied, its beauty transformed, become hideous; it does not work, not as it was meant to, *not as it might.*

We are called to see the beauty through the blemishes, to believe it can be restored, and to feel ourselves implicated in its restoration. We are called to be fixers. We are so called whether Eden is fable or fact, whether Sinai is law or lore. And all the rest, as it is said, is commentary.

A commentary: *Tikun olam* is a meaning that carried us throughout much of Jewish history. The shattering of the old ways, of the traditional culture with its implicit understandings and connections, requires that in our time it be formulated anew, explicitly. As we have seen, many American Jews have come to view ethics as the very essence of Judaism. It is the thread in Judaism's tapestry that weaves most neatly into America's own moral claims, and it can more readily be explained to our neighbors and to our children than Judaism's sometimes esoteric ritual. But a general ethical sensibility is not yet an active ethical commitment. American Jewry is distinguished not only by its understanding of pluralism, by the fact that it lives where particularism and universalism meet, but also by the opportunity it is offered, as an empowered community, to move from ethics to justice, to define itself as a partnership in *tikun olam.* In America, in our time, such a partnership can serve as our preeminent motive, the path through which our past is vindicated, our present warranted, and our future affirmed.

Is there not an element of grandiosity here? A tiny people, preoccupied with its own survival, not immune to venality and small-mindedness, not without hunters and hustlers, purports to be about nothing less than the repair of the world. Does that not announce as an achievement what is at best an ambition? Is such an announcement not a case of moral posturing rather than a serious description of America's Jews?

Our claims *are* exaggerated, though they are not entirely without foundation. Their inflation not only irritates and sometimes infuriates our neighbors; it induces in us a smugness that may have been appropriate (or, at any rate, understandable) back in the days of Berl and his friends in Pinsk, before we came to power, but that has no place in Jewish life any longer. Ethics as explanation of what Judaism is and as consolation for what Jews have been through are not yet ethics as informing purpose, as culture, as description of what the Jewish community is about. *Tikun olam* as a slogan is not yet *tikun olam* as a passion. An empowered people must sooner rather than later make the transition from promise to fulfillment, lest its claims be rendered incredible.

But there, in the space between the claim and the commitment, stands a golden calf, and yet another. So it is for all humankind; who is there that does not know the temptations that fall between the celebration of the ethical heritage that has been offered and its implementation, between the experienced "is" and the idealized "ought"? For Jews, whose ethical claims tend to the extravagant and whose very definition of self depends so heavily on them, the gap raises a problem of special urgency.

The problem is not new. In 1898, the essayist Ahad Ha'Am wrote, in a tone suggesting that the proposition was beyond dispute, that "It is almost universally admitted that the Jews have a genius for morality, and in this respect are superior to all other nations." And almost immediately added:

> the profound tragedy of our spiritual life in the present day is perhaps only a result of our failure to justify in practice the potentialities of our election. On the one hand, there still lives within us, though it be only in the form of an instinctive feeling, a belief in that moral fitness for which we were chosen from all the nations, and in that national mission which consists in living the highest type of moral life. . . . But, on the other hand, since the day when we left the Ghetto, and started to partake of the world's life and its civilization, we cannot help seeing that our superiority is potential merely.

It was only potential then, and a hundred years later the gap is still too wide, and the work that awaits is not less. In Ahad Ha'Am's time, there were handy excuses: We're new to civil society, or the affliction of anti-Semitism continues to disable us. But in a time of Jewish empowerment, in this time, the more so in this place, the excuses are lame. A community that asserts its devotion to *tikun olam,* as ours so often does, cannot simply call attention to the disproportionately large number of its members who have heard the call and responded to it. That is important evidence, but it is not conclusive. For if they are to be counted, so are the indifferent and the complacent and all the others who have not heard the call, or who, on hearing it, have turned away. And there are too many of those. There always are.

Yet this critical view, unmoderated, is a distortion, only half a truth. There is a corollary perspective that nests alongside it and completes the truth: Our claims, as I have said, are not without foundation. The gap is there, but there are countless Jews who strain to narrow it. One measure: Try writing the story of the battle for justice in America as if no Jews had ever come to this land; the story that results is very different from the one we've known. *Tikun olam?*

Then count the scientists and the teachers, the musicians and the writers, the philanthropists and the union organizers. Include the city planners and the social workers, the therapists and jurists. Add in the scholars and physicians and the volunteers who help bring food to the hungry.

No report card, no balance sheet. If there's a purpose to these reflections, it's not to provide a summary tally, but to engage in a timeless Jewish ritual. We chastise each other for not doing enough and for claiming too much; we urge ourselves on by remembering in whose footsteps we walk and what we've been taught. Such exhortations are not idle mouthings; they are among the ways we have for narrowing the inevitable distance between our idealized image of ourselves and our actual selves. And at the end of the ritual comes a caution, a reminder of the companion danger: A people that speaks of *tikun olam* can easily move from sanctity to sanctimony, its claims of virtue themselves become a vice.

A commentary: Happily, for our sake and for theirs, for the world's and for God's, the work of repair provides an agenda we share with many activist religious and other communities. Why, then, the Jews? More precisely, if all that Judaism comes down (or rises up) to is decency and justice and such, commitments that hardly distinguish us from very many others, why be Jewish?

I call this the "Why not ethical culture?" problem and, in one version or another, it is raised more often than any other single question when I encounter Jewish audiences and speak with them of *tikun olam.* Jewish particularists want to believe that our apartness is not a happenstance, is about something more consequential than worshipping God on Saturday rather than on Friday or Sunday. In their search for Jewish meaning, some continue to accept that the Jews are Chosen. But most cannot, except perhaps in some vague metaphoric way; they cannot believe that God's "special relationship" with the Jews is not mirrored by equally special relationships with all His creatures. So they speak to the situation of the Jews, and to the shared interests that arise from it. But most recognize that in the light of Jewish claims, interests are an inadequate definition of purpose.

The assertion that it is our commitment to *tikun olam* that binds us, or might, seems to solve the problem. It has the weight of authentic history behind it, it offers us contemporary meaning, and its appeal is transdenominational. But hard on the heels of that assertion come questions, and then more questions: Since others, too, are engaged in "completing the work of creation," even if they use different words and metaphors to describe what they are doing, how can we speak of *tikun olam* as a distinctive Jewish commitment? In the light of Jewish needs, are not Jews first required to "take care" of other Jews? After all, there are enough "others" to worry about the rest of the world. Who worries about the Jews? Why should we feel we "owe" the world, the world that turned its back on the Jews in our time of need, that is still indifferent to the fate of the Jews?

These are the questions of the particularist; as often, when I try to make the case for "life at the intersection," for a balance between *tikun olam* as end and community as means, it is the universalist who speaks out: If a member of the Jewish family finds a way to help repair the world, if his/her life is lived as an answer to the question "Where are you?," who is to say, and why, that such a life is Judaically inadequate? Is one not a good Jew who takes Micah's three precepts as his own: to do justice, to love mercy, to walk humbly with our God? Is any more required in this, our world, so brutally disordered that there are a dozen points of entry to its repair? If a member of the Jewish family helps, in any serious way, to repair and complete the work of creation, is it not the language of the Jews he speaks, she speaks, is that not the mandate of Judaism?

Listen to the Italian anti-Fascist Nello Rosselli:

> I am a Jew who does not go to temple on Saturday, who does not know Hebrew, who does not observe any religious practice. I call myself a Jew . . . because . . . the monotheistic conscience is indestructible in me . . . because every even disguised form of idolatry repels me . . . because I regard with Jewish severity the duties of our lives on earth, and with Jewish serenity the mystery of beyond the tomb—because I love all men as in Israel it was commanded . . . and I have therefore that social conception which it seems to me descends from our best traditions.

If Judaism's central claims are ethical, is Nello Rosselli not a good Jew? But if Nello Rosselli, who does not go to temple on Saturday, who does not know Hebrew, who does not observe any religious practice—in short, who we may assume in no way identifies with the Jewish community—is a good Jew, what will become of the Jewish community, of the Jewish people? Rosselli tell us that he calls himself a Jew; shall we call him a Jew? The community is puzzled and offended when a Jew makes his way into the larger world, there to do good works, but never thinks to acknowledge his origins, to pay attention to his people, and to see to their welfare, too. Their names are legion; they win Nobel prizes and they die in the American South in the name of freedom; they are brilliant musicians, distinguished jurists. We know their names, we claim them as our own—they have heard the call, have they not?—but we are decidedly unhappy with them. We believe (even if they do not) that who they are and what they are is connected, in some way, to the fact of their Jewishness, and that it is only fair that they give something—say, loyalty—back.

Questions such as these, now from the one side, now from the other, haunt America's Jews, and their answers are elusive, since the dialectics of life at the intersection are necessarily complex. At stake here are both Judaism's mandate and its method. To the particularist who asserts that *halachah,* the corpus of Jewish law, is all we need to know of "method," that it is in the commandments and their interpretation that Judaism is taught and transmitted, we must point to the actual ways in which many Jews over these last several centuries have chosen to live—and I mean here caring Jews, committed Jews, I mean here David Ben Gurion and Louis Brandeis, I mean Albert Einstein and Janusz Korczak and Nello Rosselli and some millions of other decidedly non-*halachic* Jews. If what they have done with their lives is taken, as it should be, as an affirmation of Judaism's deepest convictions, then *halachah* must be seen as only one of an array of Judaic methods.* And if there is a core around

*Gershom Scholem wrote that "the halachah is certainly an overwhelmingly important aspect of Judaism as a historical phenomenon, but it is not at all identical with the phenomenon of Judaism per se. Judaism has taken on many varied forms, and to think of it as only a legislative body of precepts seems to me as a historian and as a historian of ideas utter nonsense."

which they all cluster, it must be an inclusive, not an exclusive, core.

The core method is community, of course, and to the universalist who raises the "Rosselli problem," we say that those who pursue the mandate but ignore its core method weaken the community that nurtures the mandate, that creates the schools and the liturgies and the fraternal societies and the philanthropies and the study groups and the rituals and all the other devices through which the mandate is protected, extended, transmitted to new generations. In the name of universalism, they may leap to the defense of every oppressed and beleaguered group. But they do not count the Jews among the oppressed and beleaguered, nor do they acknowledge that the community that helped inspire their devotion requires (or even deserves) their commitment.

The dialectic continues: We speak of pluralism, we assert that Jewish is what Jews are, and Judaism is the name we give to what Jews do. Even if there be nothing distinctive, let alone exceptional, in the Jewish understanding or experience, nothing, that is, beyond the religious insight Judaism shares with other faiths, the life that has been given us to live is a Jewish life. There are, indeed, many mansions in our Father's house; Judaism is the one into which we were born, and there is no reason to seek more popular or more luxurious or more spacious quarters. And surely there are no houses more interesting. We need only strive not to be hunters; we need not wish to be the only non-hunters.

Then we speak of how education happens: Caring is a cultural value that can be learned deductively or inductively. The deductive method, much favored these days, focuses on formal instruction in the principle, followed by the more or less vigorous pursuit of its application. The Jews have favored the inductive method: first the application, then the principle.* The path to responsibility for the whole of humankind leads from the experience of responsibility for the family and the intimate community. Yes, community is a dangerous undertaking, so easily does it lead to insularity. The turn inward can and often does become a way of making a looking glass out of our window, of throwing ourselves out of balance, of moving

---

*At the base of Sinai, the people responded, *'na'asaeh v'nishma'*—literally, "We will do and we will hear," idiomatically translated as "We will faithfully do." The conventional *midrash* is that in order to "hear"—that is, to understand—we must first do.

not to self-respect but to narcissistic preoccupation with self. But universalism, too, is hazardous. To look out at a larger world, there must be a place to look out from. And it is all too tempting, once you have been blessed with the universalist dispensation, once you have attained that level of ethical sophistication, to look down rather than out and around. The answer is to live at the intersection—call it a dialectic, or call it simply life as a response to both of Hillel's questions. *This* community, *this* people has been for very many decent folk their point of departure toward a life of repair.

Then there is the answer from history: There is something special about the Jews after all. We stand as history's most stunning example of the resistance to despair, of the tenacity of hope. It is not that we are so clever or so talented, but simply that we are so very stubborn. No one has had more ample reason to lapse into cynicism or to collapse into despair; we have chosen otherwise. By the rivers of Babylon, we wept when we remembered Zion; our tears dried, we returned to restore it. And then again. We write songs and walk picket lines and buy new furniture; we teach and we dream and we raise children. Ours is a tradition that insists on hope and hope itself is fixative in a world that knows such vast despair. Who can say with any confidence how much cumulative hope there must be to ensure the safety of the species, which surely cannot live long in hopelessness?

And finally, there is the answer that merges these all: If, as I believe, the commitment to *tikun olam* is a calling, a vocation, then the history of the Jewish people, of its traditions and of its responses, may correctly be read as the history of a distinguished institution of vocational education. Its demanding curriculum offers an array of courses in which it is almost impossible to disentangle pedagogic technique from educational substance: interpretations of history and holidays, *midrash,* courses on memory and hope and decency and ritual and responsibility. To enroll, you must call yourself a Jew; to graduate, you must be called as a Jew. And to graduate with honors, you must act on the call.

And yes, the tuition fees are sometimes very high.

A commentary: How shall we see to the welfare of the institution, preserve its curriculum? The American Jewish community is very young. Until the end of World War II, a majority of America's Jews were foreign-born; we are only now beginning to move into a third and a fourth generation of native-born Jews, generations that do not know their immigrant grandparents (because their grandparents were not immigrants). Moreover, the Jewish world has experienced such profound shocks these last 200 years that we are understandably off balance. Our accession to citizenship, the mass migration to America, the murder of East European Jewry and with it of Yiddish culture, the rebirth of national independence: any one of these would have been sufficient to disorient us. Together, they make confusion inevitable.

It follows that we are a people still very much in flux. It may be that assimilation is inevitable, that we will absorb American values as far as they take us, recall Jewish values to fill in a part of the gap that remains, turn elsewhere—or nowhere—for the balance. Or it may be that after a bit more time to find our feet, we will become craftier at making new ways to safeguard those values we deem appropriate to our time, our place. There is an element of choice here. Human beings are not (unless by default) sociological tokens. We are (if we choose to be) more than the sum of our exposures to multiple social forces, we are more than flesh-and-blood receivers for the signals that are beamed our way. As individuals, we lack full autonomy; that is what being part of a culture means. But the fact that we are not wholly autonomous does not mean that we are impotent; in particular, the communities we join, and even the affiliations we make, can reflect our conscious decisions to hear or not to hear, to respond or fail to respond, to search or to settle.

So we stand, unsteadily, at yet another intersection. Enough of the articulated tradition remains so that we cannot plead total ignorance of it. We may not know the sources and the citations—we do not know them—but we know, at least roughly, what the last several generations have made of them, the uses to which they were put, the directions in which they pointed, the values and commitments to which they helped give rise. In the absence of an intimate Jewish culture, we may either decide self-consciously to study and absorb—and, inevitably, to modify—those values and commitments, or we may let inertia be our guide, and drift ever farther from them.

In short, in a time when being Jewish in any active way has become an option, and in a place where there is scarcely any penalty exacted either for exercising that option or for failing to exercise it, it has become both appropriate and necessary to speak of Jewishness by choice. Today, we use the term "Jew by choice" to describe converts to Judaism; in another generation, or two, or five, all of us will have become Jews by choice, or ceased to be Jews at all. Once, it was enough that others called us Jews; today, it is for us to choose. If we remain Jews, it will be both because enough of us have willed it, and because the agencies and institutions of the Jewish community have become aware that their responsibilities extend beyond the defense of Jewish interests, extend as well into the domain of Jewish values.

As I have said, it is unlikely the Jews can survive, and it would be unseemly if they did, except as a community organized around values and committed to *tikun olam.* I have also said that a culture of organizations is not a culture congenial to the preservation and transmission of values; it lacks the required nutrients. Yet it will not help to rail against modern culture, to urge a return to the simpler and allegedly more intimate days of yore, to press for the re-creation of the small village where we knew everyone by name and left our doors unlocked. Those places, insofar as they ever existed, exacted a dreadfully high price in human freedom in return for the community they offered. In any event, whatever their virtues after their considerable liabilities are discounted, they are not available to more than a handful of us, and we cannot yearn our way back to them.

Moreover, there is still enough that is distinctive in the behavior of America's Jews to suggest that we may speak, hesitantly, of an American Jewish value system. The divorce rate among Jews remains about half the rate for the nation as a whole, suggesting that the much-noted Jewish emphasis on family survives. Jewish philanthropy in America is an extraordinary—perhaps the most characteristic—expression of our traditional value of mutual responsibility.

We have considerable data on political behavior to show that Jewish political behavior is driven as much or more by values as by interests. We have a continuing disproportionate involvement of Jews in the public service sector of society. (Others would add other examples; my purpose here is illustrative, not exhaustive.)

We may think of these as merely a residue, left over from earlier and more intimate days. That is how they are often viewed. But I prefer to think of them as a foundation, a place to start from and then to introduce such changes and modifications and expansions as will, in time, suit our informed intentions.

Here and there, that is happening. Some number of Jews have in recent years rediscovered intimate community through the creation of what are known as *havurot*—small groups of people who gather, principally for study and/or worship, either independently or within the context of an institution such as a synagogue. Frequently, the original impetus is innocent, a straightforward pursuit of adult education. But the dynamic of community is rarely denied; what begins with study grows into an extensive and ambitious support system. And sometimes, such a system is the stated purpose of the effort.

In 1969, for example, in an affluent suburban Boston neighborhood, a few friends stumbled onto the fact that none of them had read the Bible since childhood. They decided to convene a somewhat expanded group, and soon ten couples, in the thirty-five to forty-five age range, began to meet and to study the Bible together. They have continued meeting, every second Saturday afternoon, all these years. One couple moved away, another was divorced; new members were added to replace them. The group includes atheists and believers and represents a range of professions and occupations. It has no teacher; responsibility for "presenting" a session rotates among the members, all of whom are college graduates, comfortable doing their own research. Nor is there any standard approach to the material; each presenter is free to draw on his or her own preferred sources. Soon after they began, the bimonthly meetings were expanded to embrace holiday celebrations as well; by now, the group has also had occasion to celebrate birth and marriage and to mourn death. It has become, for all its members, the principal expression of their Jewishness, a place both to study and to be, and groups like it have proliferated all over the country; there is even now an annual conference for their representatives, as eclectic a collection of American Jews as one may encounter anywhere, united only in their ongoing search.

Such *havurot* are a beginning. They move beyond pediatric Judaism ("It's good for the children") and cardiac Judaism ("It's enough that I feel Jewish") and nostalgic and gastronomic and all the other empty expressions of residual Judaism that remain so very popular as substitutes for a Judaism of purpose, of commitment. But the *havurot* have yet to show that they can move beyond their own confined boundaries, beyond the pleasures of learning and the benefits of intimacy and on into the work of repair. Their members are plainly Jews by choice; on the whole, they are not yet Jews by calling. Theirs is so far more an experience in propinquity than in passion. Too often, they mistake the meaning of the Sabbath; it was intended not as a stopping place but as a resting place.

Still, the *havurot* offer a partial solution to the dilemmas I have been discussing. The identification and articulation of Jewish values in the American context depends on the existence of such nurturing Jewish communities, of people who may come together initially to seek human solidarity, personal support, and Jewish learning, and who then figure out how to search for godliness, too. The *havura* has the capacity to become the place where American Jewish values are organically developed and nourished.

We cannot permit the possibilities of *havura* to deflect us from concern with the far larger associational network of American Jews. The *havura* movement involves a tiny, though still growing, fraction of America's Jews. It is quite unlikely that they or their equivalents will ever capture the imagination of very large numbers of Jews.

In the larger community, with all its limitations, there are still snatches of melody to start from. It is encouraging to witness the response of America's Jews to a Jewish crisis in a far-off land. When, in 1984 and 1985, the plight of Ethiopian Jewry became apparent and dollars were needed in order to help rescue and resettle thousands of our distant kinsfolk, the Jewish community in six months raised $40 million to meet the need. For many years now, thousands of Jews have given tens of thousands of hours to the cause of Soviet Jewry. We may call attention to the vast sums that American Jews contribute to diverse philanthropic purposes, still more to the extravagant energies the raising of those dollars involves; by and large, our philanthropies are based on peer rather than professional solicitation, and no one who has sat through the endless meetings that are required to raise money and to spend it wisely can fail to be moved by the devotion that is apparent there.

Yet praiseworthy though such efforts are, raising dollars and signing petitions and even chaining yourself to the gates of the Soviet or South African Embassy do not exhaust the agenda of a people that declares, as assertively as we do, that the tradition we honor and seek to preserve is a tradition of profound and enduring concern with ethics, that what we are here to do is to mend the world.

The more so if we take seriously yet another paragraph from the Ahad Ha'Am essay I cited earlier:

> It was for moral development that Israel was chosen by God, "to be a peculiar people unto Himself . . . and to keep all His commandments"; that is, to give concrete expression in every generation to the highest type of morality, to submit always to the yoke of the most exacting moral obligations, and this without any regard to the gain or loss of the rest of mankind, but solely for the sake of the existence of this supreme type. This consciousness of its moral election has been preserved by the Jewish people throughout its history, and has been its solace in all its sufferings. . . . [Judaism] distinguishes the Jews from the rest of mankind only in that it imposes on them exacting and arduous obligations. . . . The Prophets no doubt gave utterance to the hope that Judaism would exert an influence on the moral condition of other nations; but their idea was that this result would follow naturally from the existence among the Jews of the highest type of morality, not that the Jews existed solely for the purpose of striving to exert this influence. "Come ye and let us go up to the mountain of the Lord . . . and He will teach us of His ways and we will walk in His paths." We do not find that Israel is to say, "Come, let us go out to the nations and teach them the ways of the Lord, that they may walk in His paths."

I have problems with Ahad Ha'Am's notion that the Jews are distinguished from the rest of mankind by the rigor of their moral obligations. In fact, I suspect that those Jews who choose to live according to the highest moral standards will find themselves linked to, rather than separated from, people of other communities who take their own moral codes and commitments every bit as seriously as we do ours. I cite the Ahad Ha'Am statement because it calls on the Jews to be true to themselves, independent of whether they serve others as an inspiration. And I would go beyond his statement in one respect: Borrowing the form of his own aphorism that "more than the Jews have kept the Sabbath, the Sabbath has kept the Jews," I would propose that more than "this consciousness of its moral election has been preserved by the Jewish people," the Jewish people has been preserved by this consciousness of its moral election. It has been more than a solace; it has been a raison d'etre.

But, as I have said, the sense of moral election is not yet the substance of it. A would-be community of ethical excellence, a network of organizations that seeks to revive the intensity of community, has as its first priority an internal task. That task is to comfort the bereaved, and to visit the sick, and to refrain from gossip. It is to teach these things, inductively and deductively, to our children, to raise up a generation that knows no higher joy than to help, in these ways among others, complete the work of creation.

Such things are always and everywhere best taught by doing them; talking about their importance is a very distant second-best. Yet looking about the Jewish community and its institutions—schools, synagogues, even its philanthropic organizations—there is little evidence that ethical concern is writ large on their agendas. The "be a good person" rhetoric is there, to be sure, and the sense of ethical election. But the sense of it is not the substance of it; there is not sufficient attention to institutional mores to move us beyond coasting on memory, to move us toward sustaining community.

What Ahad Ha'Am did not know, could not have known, was that there would soon emerge a second and equally compelling priority, that there would come a time and a place for us to take our values from the community to the metropolis, from the pulpit to the public square. That is what is expected of an empowered community in a pluralistic democracy, and that means that our new priority is to extend the scope of our ethical concern beyond the traditional ethics of communal compassion to the needed ethics of worldly wisdom, wrestling with the vexing questions of our tangled new age, drawing on precedent and analogy where we can, knowing that often we will find no map to help chart our path, merely a compass to fix its direction. A compass, and, if we so will it, perhaps even a community. For the way to build community is to engage together in shared endeavor; the way to build a Jewish community of meaning is to get on with the work of repair, and in that work to discover one another. *Na'aseh v'nishma.*

I have been arguing throughout these pages that for the sake of Jewish continuity we must be concerned with Jewish ethical values, more specifically that Jewish continuity requires a corollary commitment to *tikun olam.* There is a different and substantially more straightforward argument I might have made on behalf of those values and that commitment: The moral life is the good life, the proper life; it is the right way to live whether or not it promotes Jewish continuity or anything else outside itself. That argument, I trust, requires no elaboration; the relationship of Jewish ethics to Jewish interests is less obvious. In fact, there has lately emerged a vigorous debate regarding the connection between the two. Specifically, Jewish neo-conservatives have charged that the Jewish liberal's emphasis on *tikun olam* implies an indifference to Jewish interests. Writing of Jewish liberals, Murray Friedman holds that "Few groups in America have been as willing to set aside their group interests on behalf of what they deem to be the public good." He intends his statement as an indictment of Jewish naivete, and many of the Jewish neo-conservatives have expressed similar views. Jewish liberals are "moralistic" rather than "realistic," "idealistic" rather than "pragmatic." One might, of course, think it a compliment that Jews are selfless in their political behavior, so it says something about the nature of neo-conservative thought that it regards such selflessness—if that is what it is—as a mistake. But that is beside my present point, which is about the implicit assumption of such criticism—to wit, that there is an inherent dichotomy between Jewish "group interests" and "the public good" as liberals have traditionally conceived it, between "idealism" and "realism" as the neo-conservatives defined it. That assumption is at the heart of the current debate between Jewish liberals and Jewish neo-conservatives. If the neo-conservatives are right, then all the talk of *tikun olam* is idle, bloated. We are a group, not a religious civilization; as a group, we are required to analyze our interests and to defend them. "Is it good for the Jews?" is restored, not as grandmother's question but as the savvy realist's criterion for making political judgments.

I, too, care whether "it is good for the Jews." But I understand that question quite differently from the way it is understood by the neo-conservatives. When I say that without a purpose beyond its own defense, without moral and ethical ambition, the American Jewish community will not survive, I am not preaching a sermon; I am making an analytic statement. The analysis can be debated, but it misses the point to dismiss it as idle moralizing. In my view, Jewish interests and Jewish ethics cannot be disentangled, and should not be. In my view, what is good for the Jews is to practice what they have preached, and not, as the neo-conservatives in effect insist, to adjust their preachings to fit their practice. I have cast my argument in instrumental terms because I do not accept that defending Jewish turf while ignoring Jewish truth will preserve the Jews. I believe that what is good for the Jews, even best for the Jews, is to devote their energies, in their own community and in the larger public square, to making the world whole again. For in order to survive, a people needs more than a strategy; it needs a reason.

Jewish history has been a cruel teacher, but it has not been our only teacher. We have not only history but also memory; of the two, our memory is the larger, for it contains our history *and* our dreams. *We remember tomorrow.* And because the tomorrow we remember is a different and better tomorrow, it calls us back to a promise we made long before there were such words as "liberal" or "conservative," long before there was a political right or a political left. It is not possible to contemplate the mystery of the Jewish experience, to fathom how the Jews have lasted this long, without acknowledging the force of our dreams. For centuries, they were what sustained us. And while some Jews in our time have been relieved to exchange the dreams for muscles and guns, it would be a mistake to underestimate the holding power of the dreams. They have been our reason.

The reality of Jewish life—its political and social reality as well as its religious reality—cannot be measured in terms of Jewish firepower. That is what Y. L. Peretz understood and why he stopped counting calories and started listening to stories and writing them, and Jacob understood it when he wrestled with the angel and gave to all of us the name he took in his dream. It was a dream that enabled the anemic youngsters from East Europe to reclaim the barren wastes of the Promised Land. Jewish life has always been about tomorrow. It has been about the world that might yet be, the world beyond the River Jordan. It has been about God, and about godliness. And it will not do to say that if you're talking about Jewish interests, you can't drag such terms into the conversation. Quite the reverse, in fact: If you want to have a serious conversation about Jewish interests, you cannot exclude Judaism from that conversation. The Jewish imagination is as much a part of the Jewish reality as the Jewish belly is. And Judaism is the name we give our organized imagination.

Here is the heart of the dispute between Jewish liberals and Jewish neo-conservatives. The dispute is not about the extent of black anti-Semitism or the sincerity of the Christian right; it is not about the wisdom of affirmative action or about the threat of the Soviet Union. These are all important issues, but the prior issue is the character and the meaning, hence also the interests, of Judaism. Is history inevitably our enemy or can we, by bringing our God to that history, make it our friend?

The argument goes back a very long way, and it will never be finally settled. "We are talking," Irving Kristol says, "about the nature of reality, about the nature of human authenticity," and he is quite right. Kristol believes that "evils exist, that we don't know why they exist, and that we have to have faith that, in some larger sense, they contribute to the glory of the world." Most simply, "Human nature and human reality are never transformed." Adhering to so stoic a doctrine, he has scorn for those who believe, instead, that "the proper and truly authentic human response to a world of multiplicity, division, conflict, suffering and death is some kind of indignant metaphysical rebellion." It is not merely wrong to hold that view, Kristol argues; it is unrealistic, and dangerous.

The question of realism is not easily settled. Kristol's well-known line, "A neoconservative is a liberal who's been mugged by reality," suggests the general stereotype: liberals are soft and vague, conservatives are tough and precise. Above all, liberals are dreamy, while conservatives are practical. The conflict is classic: It is, as Kristol observes, the contemporary expression of the ancient conflict between the prophetic tradition and the rabbinic tradition, and it is "absolutely crucial to an understanding of the relationship between any religion and the real world—the real world of politics, the real world of social life."*

Amen. But it is also absolutely crucial to understand that the central reason we remember the prophets as keenly as we do is precisely that they stood at the intersection of the world of religion and "the real world"—yes, the real world of politics, the real world of society—and did not flinch. Their power derives from the fact that they brought the two worlds into intimate conversation. It is simply not the case that the prophets were victims of unanchored fervor, that they were escapists who responded to human misery by preaching of good (and just, and peaceful, and make-believe) times to come, realism be damned. That is not how they saw themselves, and that is not how they were heard.

It is easy to be misled into a mistaken view of the prophets. Their poetry was so powerful, their depiction of the future so compelling, that we are caught up in the imagery; what they say speaks so movingly to us that it seems timeless. But the prophets were not speaking for the ages; they spoke for their times, their places. In the context of those times and places, their words were chosen for

*The rabbinic mode "engenders a somewhat stoical temper toward the evils of the world"; the prophetic mode rebels against them. Kristol makes much of the distinction; in his "Christianity, Judaism, and Socialism," he argues that the tension between the two is "eternal" and is mirrored in all religions.

immediate political effect. In his *Power and Powerlessness in Jewish History,* David Biale makes the point clearly:

> Prophets such as Isaiah and Jeremiah were neither pacifists nor apolitical moralists. They were part of the Judaean political establishment, and their preaching was the theological expression of their shrewd policy of neutralism and accommodation to the imperial world. . . . In one of the most famous passages in Jeremiah, the prophet writes to those in exile: "Build houses, settle down . . . work for the good of the country to which I have exiled you; pray to the Lord on its behalf, since on its welfare yours depends." Far from advocating a withdrawal from politics, Jeremiah was suggesting the very kind of political activism that several generations later led to the successful return from Babylonia, a return predicated on the political successes of the Jews in the Persian court.

Whether the substantive teachings of the prophets are deemed wise or foolish, they were political teachings, not sentimental moralizings. Their commanding claim on our attention and respect derives from their central insight: the welfare of a society, in the most pragmatic terms, cannot be separated from the moral quality of that society. The prophets took account of both muscles and morals.

They took account, as well, of their audience. "Prophecy," writes Michael Walzer,

> is a special kind of talking, not so much an educated as an inspired and a poetic version of what must have been at least sometimes, among some significant part of the prophet's audience, ordinary discourse. . . . Prophecy aims to arouse remembrance, recognition, indignation, repentance. . . . The power of a prophet like Amos derives from his ability to say what oppression means, how it is experienced, in this time and place, and to explain how it is connected with other features of a shared social life.

If you seek to move people through language, you must speak a language they understand. God-talk is the language Jews have traditionally understood.

But what of the prophetic focus on millennial times, on the end of days? Is that not a prescription for escape? How can it be thought realistic, for example, to hold out to the people—to any people—so utopian a vision as Isaiah offers us in Chapter 65:

For behold! I am creating
A new heaven and a new earth;
The former things shall not be remembered,
They shall never come to mind.
Be glad, then, and rejoice forever
In what I am creating.
For I shall create Jerusalem as a joy,
And her people as a delight;
And I will rejoice in Jerusalem
And delight in her people.
Never again shall be heard there
The sounds of weeping and wailing,
No more shall there be an infant or graybeard
Who does not live out his days.
He who dies at a hundred years
Shall be reckoned a youth,
And he who fails to reach a hundred
Shall be reckoned accursed.
They shall plant vineyards and enjoy their fruit.
They shall not build for others to dwell in,
Or plant for others to enjoy.
For the days of my people shall be
As long as the days of a tree,
My chosen ones shall outlive
The work of their hands.
They shall not toil to no purpose;
They shall not bear children for terror,
But they shall be a people blessed by the Lord,
And their offspring shall remain with them.
Before they pray, I will answer;
While they are still speaking, I will respond.
The wolf and the lamb shall graze together,
And the lion shall eat straw like the ox,
And the serpent's food shall be earth.
In all My sacred mount
Nothing evil or vile shall be done
                                        —said the Lord.

Is not this promise of universal regeneration an example of naive (or manipulative) utopianism? Can such language properly be called, by any standard, realistic?

But read once more the last two lines—"In all My sacred mount/ Nothing evil or vile shall be done"—and insert before them the conditional "If." Over and over and over again, that is the prophetic message: *If* you do the thing you have been told to do, and refrain from doing the things you have been told not to do, *then* a new day will dawn. The weight of the prophetic argument is that the time of the wolf and the lamb, the end of days, is not an arbitrary or whimsical gift of God's grace; it is God's part of a covenantal bargain.

The character of that bargain is nowhere better captured than in Isaiah 58, from which I quoted in the Introduction:

> Cry with full throat, without restraint;
> Raise your voice like a ram's horn!
> Declare to My people their transgression,
> To the House of Jacob their sin.
> To be sure, they seek Me daily,
> Eager to learn My ways.
> Like a nation that does what is right,
> That has not abandoned the laws of its God,
> They ask Me for the right way,
> They are eager for the nearness of God:
> "Why, when we fasted, did You not see?
> When we starved our bodies, did You pay no heed?"
> Because on your fast day
> You see to your business
> And oppress all your laborers!
> Because you fast in strife and contention,
> And you strike with a wicked fist!
> Your fasting today is not such
> As to make your voice heard on high.
> Is such the fast I desire,
> A day for men to starve their bodies?
> Is it bowing the head like a bulrush
> And lying in sackcloth and ashes?
> Do you call that a fast,
> A day when the Lord is favorable?
> No, this is the fast I desire:
> To unlock the fetters of wickedness,
> And untie the cords of the yoke
> To let the oppressed go free;
> To break off every yoke.
> It is to share your bread with the hungry,

And to take the wretched poor into your home;
When you see the naked, to clothe him,
And not to ignore your own kin.

Then shall your light burst through like the dawn
And your healing spring up quickly;
Your Vindicator shall march before you,
The Presence of the Lord shall be your rear guard.
Then, when you call, the Lord will answer;
When you cry, He will say: Here I am.

Here the "if-then" relationship is virtually explicit: God's "Here I am" comes only as a response to man's. That is the heart of the Jewish religious understanding, rabbinic and prophetic alike, and the Jewish religious understanding is (or is supposed to be) at the heart of the Jewish political understanding. (Kafka put it more emphatically: "The Messiah will come only when he is no longer necessary; he will come only on the day after his arrival; he will come, not on the last day, but on the very last.")

There is, nonetheless, a tension between prophetic and rabbinic Judaism, at least as they have been received. The prophets spoke during a time when Jews governed themselves; they were concerned with stability, but they are remembered chiefly for their activism, their passion, their obsession with justice. The rabbis wrote after the Jews were exiled from their land; they cared about justice, but their teachings are more quietistic, stoic, concerned with stability. Irving Kristol prefers the rabbinic tradition, a choice he is, of course, entitled to make; it is the choice Jews made for some 1,500 years. But for the last 200 years, Jews have been struggling to come to terms with the Emancipation, which marked the end to their exclusion from civic affairs. And for the last fifty years, America's Jews have been wrestling with what it means not merely that their exclusion is over, but that they have actually come to a measure of power. That is a condition that rabbinic Judaism did not foresee and for which it did not prescribe, except coincidentally. And one of the principal ways in which most Jews these last two centuries have tried to come to terms with the radical change in their circumstance is reflected in their rediscovery of prophetic Judaism.

The critics of that rediscovery, arguing principally from a conservative perspective, quite correctly observe that it has often served as an excuse to deny Jewish particularity. That is plainly a distortion of the prophetic message. But one need not rebury the prophets in order to repair the distortion; one need only take seriously their teaching of the reciprocal significance of the particular and the universal.

So, too, Jewish neo-conservatives may choose to disagree with Isaiah, to deny the linkage between social and political morality, on the one hand, and peace and plenty, on the other. But they cannot simply dismiss Isaiah's argument on the grounds that since it is religious (and compassionate, to boot), it must therefore be unrealistic, apolitical, or even anti-political. The choice between indignation and stoicism is a profoundly pragmatic choice, rich with political implication.

I believe that Judaism in our time, as it was in the time of Amos and Isaiah, is on the side of indignation, hence also of political activism. The moment I take seriously the religious injunction to heed the needs of the stranger, I enter the political realm. As Michael Igantieff wisely observes, "The moral relations that exist between my income and the needs of strangers at my door pass through the arteries of the state."

One can play an endless game of citation here, bringing this text or that to bear, and then its equally cogent contradiction. There was Hillel and there was Shamai, there were the Pharisees and the Sadducees, there is rabbinic Judaism and there is prophetic Judaism, the sources are confoundingly rich. Sometimes it seems as if Jewish life is an ongoing search for the finally unanswerable citation.

But, of course, there is none. There is only how a community of Jews, bounded by space and by time but not fettered by either, try to understand who and why and where they are. And from that understanding, what their interests are.

The citations that most of America's Jews have chosen as their controlling ones have been profoundly influenced by their experience of modernity in America. It does not much matter, except to the curious, that when Rabbi Akiba, quoting Leviticus, said, "Thou shalt love thy neighbor as thyself," he was almost surely referring exclusively to "thy Jewish neighbor." What matters is how we have chosen to understand the words, not how Akiba meant them. For our effort has been and must be to reach into our own souls, not into the minds of those who came before. And the way we have chosen to understand the words of Rabbi Akiba is that they apply to all the children of God.

Of course there are sources that point us in the direction of political quietism as powerfully as Isaiah points us toward activism. (From the *Ethics of the Fathers:* "Pray for the welfare of the government, since but for the fear of it men would swallow each other alive." Or: "The laws of the state are the laws.") But if we spend our time trading sources, the argument will never be resolved. Accurately cited, all are authentic, even in the face of their contradictions and sometime ambiguities; the search for *the* right source is a futile and mistaken search. The question is not which source is the weightier, which the more authentic; the search is for a way to choose among them.

We are that way. Our search is not for sources to cite but for *midrash* to write. We pick up those threads of the tradition that seem to us most suited for this time, this place, this people. Inevitably, the way we choose to understand Akiba's words derives from the way in which we understand ourselves. Again, we are the text. And America, in the closing decades of the twentieth century, is the context.

11

Politics as Vocation

Harold Lasswell defined politics as "the displacement of private motives onto public objects," and out of that definition, a whole new school of political analysis was born. Lasswell had in mind, mostly, that individuals who enter the world of politics use that world to deal with deeply personal matters. I want to make a parallel argument here: The hyperinvolvement of Jews in American politics reflects the displacement of the collective motives of an entire community rather than the private motives of its individual members. Jews enter the world of politics, and there act as they do, because there they can address, both symbolically and practically, fundamental questions of Jewish identity—the tension between interests and values and the commitment to *tikun olam.* It is in the public square, in the realm of the political, that we find the most precise articulation of the American Jewish synthesis. There the Jews defend their particular interests, and there the Jews pursue their universal concerns. There they offer their answer to Hillel's third question, the question that forbids us to be disabled by the enduring dialectical tension of his first two questions: *If not now, when?* There is where we most directly discover the American Jew. Politics, for Jews, is the displacement of Jewish motives onto public objects.

What are those motives? To be a Jew means to belong to a people, not merely to adhere to a doctrine. It means, more specifically, to belong to a people that has perforce developed special sensitivities, through the course of its wanderings, to the acts of rulers and governments. It means, therefore, that the Jew *as Jew* has learned to pay attention to the political, to engage with it in order to ensure that princes and parliaments do not, wittingly or casually, do harm to one's people.

But there is much more to it than that. For the Jew is also part of a people that has for 3,200 years (ever since Sinai) been committed to building the kingdom of heaven here on earth. Before we were invited to political participation, before we gained access to the realm of state power, that commitment could not find political expression. Now, in the era of the modern state, there is no path to the kingdom that does not pass through the halls of government. I say "pass through"; the state is not the kingdom, actual or potential, the chief of state is not the king. But the modern state is so pervasive, its public policies so comprehensive, that there is no detour around it that will lead to the kingdom.

There's great temptation to walk away from politics; with each new revelation of political malfeasance, misfeasance, nonfeasance, it becomes harder to stay with it. The halls of Congress, of all the parliaments, for all their domes and pillars, can scarcely be mistaken for the anterooms of God, particularly these days. One can—some do—choose to search instead for personal redemption, avoiding the lofty utopian ambitions that seem doomed to disappointment. But though Judaism has known and admired its saintly isolates, the center of its gravity has been with the people, inside the community and in the public place. Justice is no private virtue; it is meted out at the gates of the city, there where the traffic is thickest.

And here in America, where the nation's leaders have since our beginnings and on unto the present day cast their arguments in religious terms, the political purposes of the Jewish tradition have been reinforced. American political rhetoric has not merely been congenial to the Jewish temper; it has used the very same metaphors and images, drawn explicitly from the Jewish tradition. This, Americans (we among them) have sung, is God's country—and God's nation, too. The nation's work is, then, God's own work; it is the work of the heavenly kingdom, no less.

How appealing this is to the Jew, the more so to the Jew who can no longer quite figure out what else Judaism means. If, for whatever reason, the classical God is inaccessible to you (or you to God), politics can become your religion, your vocation. Is not political activity ever so much more modern a way to engage in the work of redemption than, say, praying for the coming of the Messiah? As Milton Himmelfarb has suggested, "The zeal of untraditional Jews for politics is their de facto religion. With all they've gone through, those Jews are still messianic, and their religion is politics." Better, though, to say "unobservant" than "untraditional," for Judaism, so rich with reference to justice in the here and now, appears to permit, even to encourage, a passion for politics. That passion is not new, not outside the scope of the tradition; what is new is the opportunity for its sanctioned expression. Little wonder that Jews have seized the opportunity, invested politics with quasi-religious significance, and engaged in politics with holy zeal.

Politics is our religion; our preferred political denomination is liberalism. In Lakeville, the pseudonymous Middle Western suburb where in the 1950s Sklare and Greenblum turned up such a rich lode of Jewish universalism, nearly a third of the respondents felt that "being a liberal on political and economic issues" is essential to being a "good Jew," and another third felt it was at least desirable. As Steven M. Cohen puts it, "Many American Jews were raised with the understanding that liberalism or political radicalism constituted the very essence of Judaism, that all the rest—the rituals, liturgy, communal organizations—were outdated, vestigial trappings for a religion with a great moral and political message embodied in liberalism."

Why should that be so? What is there about liberalism that has made it so congenial to the Jews? What connection, if any, does liberalism have to the themes we have been discussing? Is the connection a temporary coincidence, or is it intrinsic? What accounts for the widespread perception that Jewish liberalism is finally waning? Is the perception accurate, or is it wishful thinking? These days, Jews from the left rail against the supposed rightward lurch of the mass of Jews, against their resurgent particularism, their hypocritical mix of high-minded rhetoric and beer-bellied behavior. At the same time, neo-conservative Jews scratch their heads in puzzlement at the obduracy of Jewish liberalism, at its mulish naivete and its obsessive nostalgia. Only yesterday, it seems, the neo-conservatives were certain they were the wave of the Jewish political future. Now, recognizing that they did not prevail, that they are a mere wavelet, they denounce the "leftist mindset" of American Jews and lament its "ineradicability." What shall we make of all this, and how does it fit into the story of the Jewish search for meaning?

Two circumstances account for the perception—and it is an accurate perception—that, at least until quite recently, Jews have been wedded to the left. The first of these is the astonishingly high level of Jewish participation in left-radical movements from mid-nineteenth-century Europe to at least mid-twentieth-century America; the second is Jewish voting behavior in this country, the fact, as Milton Himmelfarb has felicitously put it, that though the Jews earn like Episcopalians, they vote like Puerto Ricans.

There is scarcely need, yet again, to recite the names of all those Jews who helped shape the left in Russia, in Poland, in Germany, in France, in other European countries. The names—from Trotsky, Léon Blum, Rosa Luxemburg, Ferdinand Lassalle, Eduard Bernstein, and so very many more, all the way to Daniel Cohn-Bendit ("Danny the Red"), leader of the French student uprising of 1968—remain familiar even as their beliefs and behaviors have largely been forgotten. (Among the less-remembered but interesting names are those of Shmuel Weizmann, brother of the long-time Zionist leader who was to become Israel's first president, and Werner Scholem, brother of the great scholar Gershom Scholem. Weizmann was—unlike his more famous and considerably more moderate sibling—a revolutionary Socialist, and Scholem sat in the Weimar parliament as a delegate of the Communists.)

In this country the European radical tradition persisted. In 1934, the Communist Party controlled newspapers that published daily or weekly in twenty-one languages. Its flagship paper, *The Daily Worker,* had sales of 50,000; its Yiddish paper, *Freiheit,* was next with 22,000. Some 15 percent of the members of the Communist Party were Jews, and a vastly higher proportion of its leadership. (Harvey

Klehr, in *The Heyday of American Communism,* tells how the New York Young Communist League, in late 1929, reported its recruitment of 117 new members: "The results are also good in national composition, the majority of the new recruits being young Americans and not Jewish.") The only two members of the Socialist Party elected to the U.S. House of Representatives were Jews; Emma Goldman, the anarchist, was a Jew; in the 1920 presidential election, Eugene Victor Debs, the Socialist candidate, won 38 percent of the Jewish vote.

And so forth. Again, the facts of Jewish activity on the left in the days of the (largely) immigrant generations are too well known to require detailed recital. Nor are the reasons for that activity much of a mystery. There was the pull of the left, with its promise of a politics of reason and of inclusion. And there was the push of the right; as Nathan Glazer has observed, "The Jews are a people of the Left. And why not? The right means only indifference to the demands of the workers and the poor—Jews are no longer workers or poor—but it has also meant, since the French revolution, a susceptibility to medievalism, romanticism, blood and soil, racism—and anti-Semitism." Jews, then, preferred the left not only because of what it promised to do *for* them but also because of what the right had done *to* them.

All this might well have been assigned to an earlier history of the Jews, interesting as the story of one of the places we have been in our crazy-quilt past but not any longer relevant, had the 1960s not unfolded in the way they did. By decade's end, there was no denying that the old-time religion of radicalism was still surprisingly alive. A majority of the freedom riders to the South at the height of the civil rights struggle were Jews, and Andrew Goodman and Michael Schwerner, who were murdered along with James Chaney in Mississippi in 1964 while conducting a voter registration campaign among blacks, were Jews, and more than half the delegates to the 1965 national convention of SDS, the Students for a Democratic Society, were Jews, and six of the eleven members of the steering committee of Berkeley's Free Speech Movement—with which the student unrest in America began—were Jews, and Mark Rudd, who led the Columbia University student uprising in 1968, was a Jew, and so were Abbie Hoffman and Jerry Rubin, and so were I. F. Stone and Noam Chomsky and Herbert Marcuse, who provided much of the intellectual grist for the student mill, and so were William Kunstler and Leonard Boudin, the attorneys most active in defending accused radicals, and so was Daniel Ellsberg, he of the Pentagon Papers, and so were the principals of the Institute for Policy Studies, the "think tank" of the left, and so also, but hardly finally, were most of the leading intellectuals who helped launch the feminist movement, such as Susan Brownmiller and Shulamith Firestone, and, of course, Betty Friedan.

One interesting question is whether the 1960s were the last gasp of an activist radical subculture among the Jews, or simply another installment in an ongoing saga. That is not a question I know how to answer; in any event, though interesting, it is not an especially relevant question here. While yesterday's radical Jews were a large fraction of American radicals, they were a tiny fraction of America's Jews; most likely, tomorrow's Jewish radicals will be no larger. Their high profile cast a redder hue over America's Jews than the facts of Jewish political orientation warranted, then or today. It is those facts that are here our concern.

The first and foremost of those facts is the continuing liberalism of the Jews, all the rumors of their incipient conservatism notwithstanding. But the rumors have gained such currency that one can no longer simply assert the fact of Jewish liberalism and let it go at that. What is the evidence that supports the fact?

In the late nineteenth century, most Jews perceived the Republican Party as the progressive option at the national level. The Republicans were anti-slavery, while a number of very voluble populist anti-Semites were associated with the Democrats. The Jewish shift to the Democratic Party began with the election of 1912. Woodrow Wilson, the intellectual internationalist, won 55 percent of the Jewish vote, his Republican, Progressive, and Socialist opponents dividing the balance. In 1928, with the candidacy of Al Smith, the Jewish relationship with the Democratic Party was cemented: Smith won 72 percent of the Jewish vote. Franklin Delano Roosevelt, in the four elections he stood, won 82 percent, 85 percent, 90 percent, and

90 percent. In 1948, Truman won 75 percent, and Henry Wallace another 15 percent; once again, the Republican candidate—Thomas Dewey—took only 10 percent of the Jewish vote.

And then there was a correction. Most analyses of the shifts in Jewish voting patterns use as their baseline measures the 1960 election of John F. Kennedy, in which Kennedy took 82 percent of the Jewish vote (a higher level of support than he won from Catholic voters), the election of 1964, when Lyndon Johnson bested Barry Goldwater among the Jews by a 90–10 margin, and then the 1968 election, in which Hubert Humphrey won 81 percent of the Jewish vote. They then look at the results of the elections from 1972 to 1984, in which the Republican candidates won 35 percent (Nixon in 1972), 28 percent (Ford in 1976), 39 percent (Reagan in 1980), and 34 percent (Reagan in 1984), and they conclude that there has been a significant shift in Jewish political orientation; that is where the rumors start. As Nathan Perlmutter put it, "The 1970s . . . ushered in a significant change in Jewish voting patterns. . . . The plain arithmetic is that in a score of years the percentage of Jews voting for a Republican candidate for the Presidency has doubled."

But this view, which is quite widely accepted, conveniently ignores the longer-term pattern and, specifically, the years between Truman and Kennedy, the Eisenhower years. Running against the uncommonly urbane Adlai Stevenson, who might well have been thought the nearly ideal "Jewish" candidate, Dwight Eisenhower took 36 percent of the Jewish vote in 1952 and 40 percent in 1956. There is no reason not to take those two elections as our baseline, to assume that roughly 30 to 35 percent of Jewish voters are, under "normal" circumstances, prepared to vote for a Republican candidate for president.

By "normal circumstances" I mean peacetime elections in which the Republican candidate is not perceived as a radical extremist. The Richard Nixon of 1960 and of 1968 (18 percent, then 17 percent of the Jewish vote) was so perceived; the Richard Nixon of 1972 was not, especially when compared to George McGovern, the Democratic candidate.

More important still, it is folly to plot the Jewish vote over the years as if it were happening in a political vacuum. The Jews, after all, experience the same political environment that all citizens do; if the country as a whole moves in one direction or another, we can generally expect that the Jews will move in the same direction. So the question is not how the Jewish vote divides, but how the Jewish vote compares to the general vote. When we make that comparison, we find that the Jewish "surplus" for the Democratic candidate— that is, the amount by which the Jewish vote for the Democratic candidate has exceeded the general vote for that candidate—has ranged from a low of 18 percent to a high of 36 percent. The low was 1956, when 42 percent of the voters—and 60 percent of the Jewish voters—preferred Stevenson to Eisenhower; the high was 1944, when 54 percent of the voters—and 90 percent of the Jewish voters—chose Roosevelt over Dewey.

In fact, if we track that differential support over the years, we find that there has been no Jewish shift at all from the Democratic Party. If the nation as a whole had given him the same support he won from the Jews, George McGovern would have been elected by one of the largest popular landslides in American history. The Jewish vote for Ronald Reagan in both his elections was more than 20 percent below the general vote—about the same level of difference as in the first two Roosevelt elections. In political terms, these are landslide differences. Which is to say, insofar as the presidential vote is a measure of liberalism, America's Jews in the 1980s remain as much more liberal than the population as a whole as they were in the 1930s.

Nor can we be satisfied, in any case, with the vote for president. It is a serious error to imply that when we have reviewed the behavior of a group in presidential elections, we have captured an adequate political profile of that group. The high drama that surrounds presidential elections may well distort rather than clarify ongoing political dispositions. Look instead to the aggregate behavior of the group with regard to congressional elections, or—better yet—look to the sentiments it expresses with regard to policy issues that are addressed either in surveys of public opinion or in referenda in the several states.

In the congressional elections of 1986, the general electorate gave 52 percent of its votes for the House of Representatives to Democratic candidates; the Jews gave Democrats 70 percent of their vote, a 28 point difference. (From 1960 to 1980, Jews voted Democratic in elections to the House about 24 percentage points higher than the rest of the country did.) In California, Alan Cranston was re-elected to the Senate with 51 percent of the popular vote; he won roughly 80 percent of the Jewish vote. In Florida, Bob Graham defeated Paula Hawkins by a 55–45 margin; the Jews went 76 percent for Graham. In New York, Alfonse D'Amato won re-election with 58 percent of the vote; the Jews gave him 34 percent of their vote, 64 percent preferring his liberal opponent, Mark Green. In 1982, Tom Bradley was defeated as the Democratic gubernatorial candidate in California, although he took 81 percent of the Jewish vote; by 1986, he was running against an incumbent, and some Jewish voters had become disenchanted with him because of his response to Louis Farrakhan. His support among Jewish voters dropped to 63 per-cent—but the population at large gave Bradley only 38 percent in 1986. In 1983, the candidates for mayor of Chicago were a tainted black Democrat and a tainted Jewish Republican. Slightly less than half the Jews voted for the Democrat—but that was two and a half times more support than other whites gave him. And in 1987 again, while 10 percent of the white Catholics and 25 percent of the white Protestants were voting for the now incumbent black mayor—Har-old Washington—47 percent of the Jews voted for him.

Some part of this extraordinary level of support for Democratic candidates may be explained by inertia: most people inherit their political preference from their parents. But if we look more closely, we learn that while Jews think Democrats are good, they think liberal Democrats are even better; in party primaries pitting a liberal Democrat against a centrist or conservative Democrat, it is almost invariably the liberal who wins the lion's share of the Jewish vote. And when, as sometimes happens, an election pits a liberal Republi-can against a conservative Democrat, the Democratic share of the Jewish vote drops dramatically.

In short, over and over again, and without any apparent diminu-tion, we find that America's Jews are decisively more liberal in their political preferences than are their neighbors.

So, too, when we look to questions of public policy. Alan Fisher has examined the vote on the several initiatives put before California voters in 1982. On the nuclear freeze, 52 percent of the electorate—and 73 percent of the Jews—were in favor; on handgun control, 37 percent of the voters were in favor—and 71 percent of the Jews. In a 1984 study of Jewish "young leaders," philanthropic activists of generally very high income, Deborah Lipstadt, Charles Pruitt, and Jonathan Woocher found that 56 percent were in favor of more government spending on social welfare programs (18 percent favored less spending); 63 percent wanted less spending on national defense, as compared to 8 percent who wanted more; the break in favor of more health care for the poor was 54–10; in favor of more health care for the elderly, 64–5; in favor of more spending for education, 83–2. Seventy-two percent were for government aid for abortion; 94 percent opposed prayer in the public schools; 85 percent were for a verifiable nuclear freeze. (Yet these people, 63 percent of whom hold post-graduate degrees, 35 percent of whom have family incomes in excess of $75,000 a year, do not invariably take the liberal position. They split evenly on the question of whether government has gone too far in regulating business, and they split 43 percent to 32 percent in favor of aid to the anti-Communist forces in Central America and 57 percent to 26 percent in favor of the death penalty.)

In his 1984 survey, Steven M. Cohen found that 35 percent of the Jews identified themselves as liberals, 24 percent as conservatives. Plainly, however, the self-described "middle-of-the-roaders" in his survey are, by any conventional standard, liberal. For how else can we explain that 70 percent of his respondents favor affirmative action? Or that 87 percent are for equal rights for homosexuals, 81 percent endorse government aid for abortions, 84 percent favor a nuclear freeze, and 70 percent oppose a moment of silent meditation in the public schools?

After 1980, before the 1984 election, the expectation was widespread that the Jews would, in fact, move rightward. There was an air of anticipatory triumph among Jewish conservatives. Jimmy Carter was the first Democratic candidate in modern times to win less than a majority of the Jewish vote (the balance having been divided between Reagan and John Anderson), and it was supposed that now that so many Jews had lost their political virginity, had managed to force their hand to pull a non-Democratic lever, they'd find it easier the next time out. As Milton Himmelfarb had put it back in 1981, "No matter what happens in 1982 and 1984, for the first time most [Jews] will have experienced in their own flesh that the right hand need not wither if it strays from the Democratic lever." Or Nathan Glazer: "For decades Jews have voted against their economic interests. . . . It seemed to be only a matter of time before their economic interests would wear down the nostalgic heritage of the past, when Jews voted Socialist, and then for liberal Democrats, and their voting would come in line with their economic interests. The 1984 election was to be the conclusion of that process."

But that was not what happened. In 1984, Ronald Reagan, widely perceived by Jews as a truly splendid friend of Israel, won less of the Jewish vote than he had in 1980. A puzzlement, and an irritating disappointment to conservative Jewish intellectuals such as David Sidorsky, who in the aftermath of the election complained that American Jews, despite their devotion to Israel's security and to Soviet Jewry, had preferred a party "antagonistic to the security needs of Israel" and given to "the most accommodationist approaches to the Soviet Union."

The historian Lucy Dawidowicz summarized the neo-conservative view:

> The Jewish agenda requires a strong government in the United States to insure Israel's security. Jews who care about Israel are obliged to use their vote to that end. They did so four years ago, when for the first time in over fifty years the Democratic candidate for the Presidency, Jimmy Carter, failed to win a majority of the Jewish vote. In 1984, by contrast, a great many Jews seemed willing to ignore the drift of the Democratic party into isolationism and defeatism, not to mention the party's embrace of Jesse Jackson, a man overtly hostile to a strong America and a strong Israel.

The year 1980 was not, then, the beginning of a trend; it was an ephemeral anomaly. Milton Himmelfarb concluded that "what misled the forecasters was the exceptionalness of 1980. It now seems clear that a big part of the 1980 Jewish vote for Reagan was the

desire of many Jews to punish Carter." In 1984, Jews defied logic—
as conservatives had defined it—and reverted to their perverse behavior. The Jews had become comfortable but not conservative, rich
but not Republican.

So much for the fact of American Jewish liberalism. But we have
yet to look to its history and logic. Only if we understand why
liberalism has been the political religion of America's Jews will we
be able to assess the neo-conservative claim that it is (yet another)
god that has failed.

When Rabbi Dov Meisels was elected to the provisional Austrian
Reichsrat of 1848 and seated himself to the left of the aisle, with the
liberals, he explained his behavior with a play on words: *"Juden haben
keine Rechte*—Jews have no Right(s)." But Jews did, as it were, have
many lefts. By the turn of the century, there were Social Democrats
and anarchists, Communists and Bundists and Labor Zionists and
more, each with its own divisions and subdivisions, a chaos of
parties, groups, cells, mimeograph machines. The non-rightness of
the left was a major attraction; so were the reformist dreams that
were so vivid a part of the European political drama of the time.
Each new doctrine and all its variants promised a just society.

But there was (and is) a fundamental difference between the
revolutionary left and the liberal left. Liberalism, which is essentially ameliorative in its intentions, requires the very stability that
revolutionism seeks to undermine. In the American context, it was
liberalism that became the doctrine of Jewish choice. The Jews have
learned many lessons in this noisy century. They have learned that
the right has no monopoly on anti-Semitism, and that "left" does
not necessarily mean liberal. They have learned to be less sanguine
about the consequences of revolution. (As Yeats put it, "Hurrah for
revolution and cannon come again! The beggars have changed
places, but the lash goes on.") But over and above all such lessons
from history, whether well or poorly learned, America's Jews have
learned a lesson from their lives as Americans. In this country, both
the welfare of the Jews and the condition of justice depend on the
health of liberal, democratic pluralism.

We are, at last, at home in America, as at home as Jews can feel,
more at home than in any of the lands of our wandering. The

surprise of our at-homeness has worn off, and we now have time to look about, to examine the foundation and the furniture of this blessed house. And when we do, what we find, over and over and over again, is that the foundation on which the house is built is pluralism. Here, the state leaves space for the group to flourish; it does not claim its citizens' exclusive loyalty. And that, it turns out, makes nearly all the difference that matters.

So here, its sometime radicalism is not the remarkable aspect of the Jewish political disposition. If we perceive danger here, it is not so much from the traditional enemy—the radical right—or from the new enemy—the radical left—as it is from the kind of prolonged instability, whatever its source, that might threaten the pluralist tradition.

How to protect against that instability? By and large, Jews have supposed that the best defense against it is a politics that speaks to the needs of those who have been left out or left behind, a politics of inclusion. And while it can be and is argued, these days, that many Americans feel themselves left out precisely on account of the establishment of liberal policies that are at odds with their own values, it remains chiefly the weak, the poor, the otherwise un-protected who engage Jewish sympathy and attention.

Nor does it derogate one whit from the Jewish concern for justice to observe that there is a considerable perceived self-interest here: Better to attend the unwashed hordes, for it is we who will be their first targets if their only escape from their enclaves is to break out of them. It is we they will attack not because we are the pawn-brokers but because we are the pawns, the sop the powerbrokers will throw to distract the vandals, to pacify the mob. And the mob will swallow us alive, for it knows that we are impostors, we who claim from high up on the hill that we are their kinsfolk, that we, too, have suffered; they will scoff at our claim, the claim of those who shed their tears for the down-and-out as they climb aboard the 5:09 for Scarsdale. We do not belong with them, and we do not belong where we are. We have been waiting for them, for the Cossacks, we knew this could not last. So the Jewish hero of Morde-chai Richler's *St. Urbain's Horseman:* "From the earliest, halcyon days . . . he had expected the coming of the vandals. Above all, the

injustice-collectors. The concentration camp survivors. The ema-
ciated millions of India. The starvelings of Africa. . . . The demented
Red Guards of China are going to come, demanding theirs, followed
by the black fanatics, who live only for vengeance. The thalidomide
babies, the paraplegics. The insulted, the injured."

We remember. We fear the princes of the boardroom and the
paupers of the barroom. And we remember the role we have played
for both in history's most enduring ritual of hate. So we seek peace
and quiet. The most comprehensive statement of the organized
Jewish community's views on American public policy is called the
"Joint Program Plan." Published annually, it is a product of the
National Jewish Community Relations Advisory Council, an umbrella organization of 11 national and 113 local Jewish community
relations agencies and organizations. In its 1987 edition, the Plan
observed that "The fundamental premise of the field of Jewish
community relations is to foster conditions conducive to Jewish
security and creative Jewish living in a free society. Such conditions
require a society committed to equal rights, justice, and opportunity. Their denial breeds social tensions, conflicts, and dislocations,
and has led to threats to the democratic process in general, and to
the Jewish community in particular."

But we remember, too, that we were strangers in Egypt, and
slaves. We know what it is to be a stranger, and we know as well
that no modern society can long survive half-slave and half-free.
The NJCRAC Plan goes on to assert that "The stake of the American
Jewish community in a strong democratic society is reinforced by
the moral imperative on the Jewish community to pursue social
justice. This commitment flows from Jewish religious mandates,
tradition, and the millennial experience of the Jewish people."

Our interests and our ethics both point in the same direction, help
lead us to the same conclusion—a politics that defends pluralism
and supports social justice. We have taken the prophets' teaching
to heart: Justice and stability are two sides of the same precious coin.

So stated, the dominant Jewish political disposition may seem a
bore, too obvious to merit notice, too anemic to warrant respect.
Who is hostile to stability, who opposes pluralism, who stands
against social justice? Yet the commitment is not at all so obvious.

Classically and characteristically, the right has held that stability is the precondition for justice, and it brings as evidence the injustice that is so often a consequence of instability. Classically and characteristically, the left has held that there can be no stability without justice, and its evidence, too, is considerable: Does justice denied not one day explode? Is not "stability first" merely a rationalization on behalf of those who benefit from injustice?

Although a politics of amelioration may seem gutless to the radical and sentimental to the reactionary, it is an effort to draw on both bodies of evidence, to tie stability and justice together in a dynamic way, in a way that will prevent them from becoming each other's enemies. True, it replaces utopian fervor with such things as entitlement programs, which can readily be dismissed as a trivial politics of tea and sympathy rather than promoted as a powerful politics of sober compassion. But its very sobriety is what gives it bite. In that sense—and I take it to be a powerfully important sense—Jewish politics in America is informed by both the Jewish rabbinic and the Jewish prophetic traditions.

Little wonder. For "stability," so emphasized by the rabbinic tradition, read "community"; for "justice," central to the prophetic tradition, read "liberty." The terms are not identical, but they are close enough, and Jews, as I showed in the last chapter, have long sought the political environment that would permit them to pursue both. In pluralist America, they have found it.

In 1974, Lucy Dawidowicz and Leon S. Goldstein concluded their review of the American Jewish liberal tradition by suggesting that its formative elements were fading:

> Memories of unemployment and poverty may still linger among the many American Jews who experienced the Depression of the 1930's or witnessed the economic hardships of immigrant parents, but such recollections . . . are increasingly becoming part of a distant and even irrelevant past. The decline of overt anti-Semitism, the growing acceptance of Jews in nearly all occupations and at nearly all levels, will also probably affect the political behavior of Jews. If Jews find themselves wholeheartedly accepted, socially as well as professionally, by Gentiles whose class and status have made them

Republican, the Jewish political style may change. The identification of the political right with anti-Semitism—an identification
based almost exclusively on European politics—may then lose its
meaning. Acculturation and full acceptance by Christians may in
time deaden or at least dull Jewish sensitivity and feelings of insecurity. When this happens, class interests will probably affect
voting more than Jewish group identity.

As we have seen, the prognosis was wrong. So far, at least, it is
"Jewish group identity" rather than "class interests" that most af-
fects Jewish voting and, more generally, Jewish political attitudes.
That is, in fact, the most remarked-upon aspect of Jewish political
life in America: though most Jews have "made it" and their memories of the sweatshops have by now been reduced to no more than
a nostalgic blip in the far distance from their suburban picture
windows, they do not vote their class interests.

Class interests, however, are not the only interests people have.
In the case of the Jews, one might have thought that even if they
were not moved rightward by their class interests, the interests
arising from their Jewish group identity would by now have led
them to abandon their attachment to liberalism. Israel's precarious
circumstance and, specifically, Israel's dependence on America for
state-of-the-art weapons, should have forced them to reassess their
view of the Pentagon budget, and Soviet anti-Semitism should have
turned them from detente toward confrontation. Their abhorrence
of quota systems should have led them to oppose affirmative action,
so thin is the line that separates it from quotas. Jesse Jackson's
blurted "Hymie" and Louis Farrakhan's blatant hatred cannot
safely be dismissed as exceptions to the attitude of many blacks;
these should have ended Jewish involvement in the civil rights
movement. The UN's declaration that "Zionism is racism" should
have cured them of their internationalism. Jimmy Carter's and
George McGovern's concern for the Palestinians, in contrast to
Richard Nixon's and Ronald Reagan's consistent and generous support of Israel, should at the least have caused them to reconsider
their loyalty to the Democratic Party. The virtual collapse of the old
coalition that was the heart of the liberal wing of the Democratic
Party—labor, the blacks, the Jews—should have moved them to

seek a new and more cordial political home. Even the evangelicals on the right are fervent friends of Israel, and that should have reduced the classic Jewish fear of the far right.

There is no doubt that such issues have, indeed, disturbed and disconcerted many Jews and caused some of them to reassess their political attachments. As we have seen, however, most have stood fast, apparently convinced that Jewish group interests are best represented in a context that also permits the pursuit of Jewish group values. And the behavior of individual Jews has been mirrored in the actions of Jewish organizations, which have, by and large, remained as steadfastly liberal. True, the Anti-Defamation League, likely the best known of the Jewish organizations that is active on matters of public policy, has become visibly more conservative over the years and has also experienced considerable organizational success. But there is, as I have noted, NJCRAC and its annual "Joint Program Plan," which reads like a classic liberal handbook. The Union of American Hebrew Congregations and the Religious Action Center, arms of the Reform movement, are energetic participants in diverse liberal coalitions. The American Jewish Congress and the National Council of Jewish Women file amicus briefs with the Supreme Court and testify before congressional committees in favor of traditional liberal positions. When the Washington representatives of those Jewish organizations that have offices in the nation's capital meet, as they do monthly, to coordinate their work, there is no debate about, say, whether Jews ought to be for or against an expansion of government's role in social welfare. The debate is about how best to press for such expansion. It is unnecessary to articulate the assumptions that inform their work; they are the traditional liberal assumptions.

Why, then, has the impression of a Jewish rightward lurch gained such currency? And beyond impressions, must not the disarray and the demoralization of American liberalism eventually lead to a decline in Jewish liberal enthusiasm? What does it mean to say the Jews are still liberal at a time when there is such uncertainty regarding what liberalism means? More: What of the issues themselves, those issues that bring neo-conservatives to accuse liberals of be-

traying the Jewish interest and bring liberals to accuse the neo-
conservatives of betraying Jewish values?

Not so long ago, we knew what it meant—or thought we did. The
liberal program meant more concern for the poor and a greater
emphasis on both civil liberties and civil rights. It meant, by and
large, a distinct preference for political rather than military solutions to international problems. It meant a New Deal and a Fair Deal
and a New Frontier and a Great Society. But what does it mean
today, when the federal budget deficit cautions even the most open-
handed liberals to budgetary parsimony, when Democratic leaders
scramble to prove their fiscal conservatism? What does it mean at
a time when, even if it had the fiscal resources, liberalism appears
to lack the needed ideas and energies?

The day before yesterday, we truly believed that the Food for
Peace program, Model Cities and community control, Headstart and
Upward Bound, the War Against Poverty and Medicare were going
to do the job, to fulfill the great promise of this great nation. Now
comes Charles Murray in his *Losing Ground: American Social Policy,
1950–1980* to argue that when "we tried to remove the barriers to
escape from poverty," what in fact happened is that we "inadvert-
ently built a trap." Nor does the average citizen need to depend on
Murray to see that the promised wonders never happened. Here and
there a battle won—but the war? Look at the street people; look at
the path of hunger, as it moves from Appalachia to Iowa, as it
devastates families and communities that have never known it before; look at Boston's 47 percent dropout rate from high school;
count the new poor, witness the hopelessness of the ghetto, weep
for the underclass. Yes, a major part of all that is the consequence
of the large holes in President Reagan's "safety net." But who still
believes that with a stroke of the pen here and a generous allocation
there, all will at last be well?

Perhaps the current liberal disillusion stems from yesteryear's
inflated promises. It is hard to fault those who did the promising;
had they been more circumspect in their assurances, they might well
have been unable to mobilize the nation behind their programs. Yet
the disappointment was inevitable. Some good here, some good

there, but nowhere the promised transformation that had enchanted and inspired us. It is hard now to work up much enthusiasm for programs that seem to offer little more than tinkering; the evident withdrawal from the ambitious reformism of the 1960s reflects a general doubt that what we have to offer, beyond charity, will matter very much. And, more important still, our confidence that what government has to offer, beyond more bureaucracy, more boondoggle, more patchwork, has collapsed.

We have been chastened by the 1960s, that time when tomorrow was now and today was a trap. They have left a bitter aftertaste. Then, heady with ambition and resolve, we marched off behind every new drummer: no censorship, no prayer in public schools, no restrictions on abortion, no Vietnam, no racism, no pollution. A new politics, linked to a new culture (no plastics, either). But no sense whatever of priorities, of balance, of trade-offs, and only contempt for those—the vast majority of all Americans—whose familiar world was shaken by the storm of proposed reforms and innovations.

In the aftermath of the anger and confusion and fatigue, people withdrew from the battle. A handful cling to the old banners, seeking in nuclear weapons or power plants or in acid rain or in Nicaragua or in gay rights or in apartheid a cause to justify their passion. Others wait and wonder, lean to hear the echo of a distant trumpet. Some have brought their zeal to mainstream politics. Some re-entered society with a vengeance, becoming cynics or—not even sufficiently alert to become cynical—becoming yuppies. Others play out their anger as neo-conservatives.

Yes, liberalism is in crisis. But the argument is incomplete, for liberalism's crisis is almost surely a cyclical rather than a linear phenomenon. An aftermath is not a wake; the bell tolls intermission, not death. Some of the liberal programs of the 1960s and 1970s failed, but others succeeded, and partial success is par for the political course. Of those that failed, some failed because they were underfunded, some because they needed more time, some because they were based on bad ideas. The accurate memory is less of failed programs than of disappointed expectations. But there are gathering signs that the wounded hopes are healing now, that liberal instincts are still intact, awaiting only the revival of liberal energies to bring the crisis to its end. In the meanwhile, it is easy to mistake the uncharacteristic silence of liberal Jews for evidence that they have abandoned their old-time religion, and that is one explanation for the fuss that's been made of a Jewish rightward turn.

There's been no such turn, yet the reports persist, encouraged by the emergence of a new voice in Jewish life, a voice that calls on Jews to reassess the wisdom of their longstanding commitment to liberalism, that encourages them to enter a new and ostensibly more congenial political home. I am speaking, of course, of the neo-conservatives, and there is no gainsaying that they have dramatically altered the nature of Jewish political debate. They press upon the Jews a new form of Jewish particularism that is not easily denied; they represent themselves as uniquely willing to ask of public policy whether it's good for the Jews and as uniquely able to answer that question properly.

There is considerable irony in that. The case for Jewish neo-conservatism has been most thoroughly and insistently argued in the pages of *Commentary* magazine, whose editor since 1960, Norman Podhoretz, is among the most influential of the neo-conservatives. Writing in the early 1960s, Podhoretz seemed to endorse the universalism that then dominated Jewish intellectual circles. In commenting on the 1961 symposium of younger Jewish intellectuals from which I quoted earlier, he was "reassured" by the "idealism" of the participants, who believe "that the essence of Judaism is the struggle for human justice and brotherhood," and who "assert over and over again that anyone who fights for the Ideal is to that degree more Jewish than a man who merely observes the rituals or merely identifies himself with the organized Jewish community." In 1963 he wrote, "I think I know why the Jews once wished to survive (although I am less certain as to why we still do)." But by 1971, a dramatic transformation was visible. Reflecting on "The Movement," a term he—and others—used to describe the twin phenomena of the New Left and the counterculture, and specifically on its dismissal of Jewish concerns, Podhoretz wrote:

By anti-Semitism I mean . . . very simply, *against the Jews:* against
their duty and their right to exist, to live and not to die, to look after
themselves and their families, to make the best of their circumstances, to pursue their own interests, to defend themselves and
their own against all who wish for whatever reason to diminish or
destroy them. A person of Jewish birth who consistently violates his
human duty by denying those rights to himself may be said to be
suffering from the sickness of self-hatred; if he extends that denial
to the Jewish people in general, and especially if he does so in the
name of justice, he may also be said to be guilty of the sin of
anti-Semitism.

The shift from fighting for "the Ideal" in 1961 to "looking after
themselves and their families" in 1971 was not Podhoretz's alone;
numbers of Jewish intellectuals traveled the same winding road
through a decade dense with especially unsettling challenge, and
their journey has been chronicled both by the participants and by
their critics. The journey ended, the new *Commentary* has since been
energetically, aggressively, and virtually without demurrer making
the case both for neo-conservatism and for Jewish particularism. In
the name of Jewish self-interest, it urges the abandonment of liberal
universalism, thereby rejecting the delicate balance between universalism and particularism that remains, in my view, so critical to
Jewish survival. As Bernard Avishai has said, it has "sought to
redefine the vocabulary by which American Jews are to consider
their interests. . . . The old *Commentary* had seen us as an eclectic
collection of individuals with incipient purposes—self-criticism, the
study of Jewish history and philosophy, the pursuit of democratic
ethics; the new *Commentary* depicted us as a corporate entity, an
interest group, with an agenda oriented around self-promotion and
gain. Our goals were clear: to make it in America, to learn to use our
elbows."

Commentary was among America's most important intellectual
journals long before the Reagan presidency; during the Reagan
years, its influence expanded beyond its traditional constituency,
into the world of affairs. (Yet it is interesting to note that between
1971 and 1986, *Commentary* lost more than 20,000 subscribers, a drop
in its circulation of nearly 40 percent.) Together with the high
visibility of a number of Jewish neo-conservatives (such as Richard
Perle and Elliot Abrams) in the Reagan administration, it has been

taken as evidence of a significant rightward movement among the Jews. But the most that can be said about its impact is that it has provided legitimacy to Jewish conservatism; its single-minded focus on Jewish interests has caused no audible reverberation in the larger Jewish community. Where a generation and two ago it was the drama of Jewish radicalism that intrigued observers, today it is the neo-conservatives who have taken center stage. But so far, only a scattering of Jews attend their performance. Most are at home, resting, or at the malls, spending; many are waiting for a new and persuasive liberal platform, and more than a few are busy drafting it and doing it.

I do not mean to suggest that America's Jews are an elite liberal vanguard, immune to the tides and trials of our time. Being Jewish is not an inoculation against the politics of selfishness or any of the other diseases that plague the polity. We have yuppies galore, we have know-nothings and care-littles, bigots and philistines. Our liberalism is very often not much more than "bourgeois humanism," as Stephen Whitfield has aptly put it. But I take as my clue the way in which Lucy Dawidowicz, herself a neo-conservative, chose to conclude her mistaken prognosis that we would soon move right-ward: "Class interests," she wrote (with Leon Goldstein) "will probably affect [Jewish] voting more than Jewish group identity." On the evidence, most Jews evidently continue to understand their group identity as I have here sought to define it: a commitment both to Jewish interests and to Jewish values, perhaps even an under-standing that our principal interest as a group is the promotion of the values we hold dear. There are ebbs and flows to the energies with which we pursue the commitment, and one may lament its relative recession in recent years. But the common prediction that sooner or later their "class interests" will catch up with the Jews misses the mark; their class interests are offset by their resurgent sense of group identity, and that identity teaches that while one is permitted to be rich, one is not permitted to be comfortable. The commitment to the tradition of liberalism, and perhaps even to *tikun olam,* as evidenced in voting behavior, in attitudes, in organizational activity, persists.

The neo-conservatives themselves know that. They complain

often of the "innocence" or "naivete" of the Jews, who resist neo-conservative blandishments and persist in their liberal error. Typically, they attribute the error to cultural lag. In a major statement of this position, in the July 1984 issue of *Commentary*, Irving Kristol argued that, "while American Jews have for the most part persisted in their loyalty to the politics of American liberalism, that politics has blandly and remorselessly distanced itself from them." The Jews "stubbornly stick their heads in the sand and hope that yesteryear's realities will return," despite the fact that "over the past two decades, the political landscape with which American Jews are familiar, and in which they are accustomed to take their bearings, has been shifting in all sorts of unexpected ways."

Kristol is right about that; the landscape has been shifting. I said at the outset that issues have arisen that have caused many of us to be disturbed and disconcerted. By reviewing several of these issues, we may reach a more precise understanding of the relationship between Jewish values and Jewish interests, as well as of the likely political trajectory of America's Jews.

12

Is It Good for the Jews?

LATELY, AMERICAN JEWS have been urged to set aside their traditional apprehension of the Christian right. Some of its most important leaders are militant supporters of Israel, and, at a time when Israel's standing in liberal circles has suffered erosion, we cannot afford to reject the hand of friendship they extend; in Irving Kristol's view, that support could prove "decisive for the very existence of Israel." Hence on grounds of expediency alone, we should move from hostility to embrace. Moreover, Kristol argues, those of us who are determined to oppose the domestic social program of the Christian right may relax; the campaign for that program has failed. In any case, he continues, "expediency or no expediency," it is time for us to rethink our own position on some parts of that program: "Ever since the Holocaust and the emergence of the state of Israel, American Jews have been reaching toward a more explicit and meaningful Jewish identity and have been moving away from the universalist secular humanism that was so prominent a feature in their prewar thinking. But while American Jews want to become more Jewish, they do not want American Christians to become more Christian."

The argument that in politics one should take one's friends where one can is particularly appealing to Jews, whose friends are rather less than legion. Yet there is probably no domestic issue on which the Jewish consensus is broader and deeper: Jews are suspicious of the Christian right, of its intentions and of its programs. They do not perceive it as an acceptable partner, despite its stated friendship toward Israel. Cohen (1983) found that 69 percent of America's Jews had an unfavorable opinion of the Moral Majority; only 7 percent held a favorable opinion. (The rest were either mixed or had no impression.) The only other group that elicited anywhere near the same unfavorable consensus was the Jewish Defense League, regarded unfavorably by 41 percent of the survey respondents. (By contrast, only 11 percent held an unfavorable view of the National Organization of Women and 12 percent of the NAACP.)

Is this an example of "cultural lag" or is there something else at stake?

The first thing to be said is that American Jews don't much care, one way or the other, how Christian American Christians become. The Jewish concern is not with Christians, but with America; our objection is to *America* becoming more Christian—and not merely "more Christian," but more formally Christian, and more formally Christian as some Christians define Christianity. And the reasons for our objection are obvious, even if the policies that flow from it are not always clear. The Jewish concern is with the preservation of a pluralistic America, one in which Jews are free to pursue their particularity. And most Jews share an abiding conviction that an America in which Christian symbols are confused with state symbols would be an America less hospitable to that particularity.

Irving Kristol asks, "Why should there be a Hanukkah candelabrum at Central Park, as there is, but no Christmas creche?" And the answer most Jews would surely give is that there shouldn't be a Hanukkah candelabrum at Central Park. (In recent months, some Jewish organizations have finally overcome their inhibitions and have filed suit against those municipalities that, at the insistence of Orthodox Jewish organizations—notably the Lubavitch Hasidim— have permitted Hanukkah menorahs on public property.)

Nor do Jews perceive that it is the Christianity of the Christian right that threatens America; it is their rightness. There are, after all, other Christians, as devout, who are not viewed as a danger. Jews fear that the right in general, the Christian right in particular, is weak in its commitment to precisely that pluralism which they understand as their first line of defense. The interest of the Jews is in protecting that line, in ensuring that it is the Constitution and not the New Testament that serves as this nation's organizing document. That is pluralism's promise.

Where, precisely, the line of defense falls is a prudential matter on which there is considerable disagreement. But there is virtually no disagreement that, despite the Christian right's embrace of Israel, the line falls far short of its stated positions on public policy.

Moreover, most Jews are at best of mixed mind on the reliability of the love the Christian right expresses for Israel. We see ourselves as unwilling actors in other people's eschatological fantasies, assigned a sacrificial role that will bring redemption to others who need us but who do not and cannot accept or respect us. As Leon Wieseltier has observed, "I do not see tolerance and unconditional respect in the churches of the fundamentalists. (Their respect for the Jews is conditional upon the tarrying of the end of days, at which point Gog and Magog will get Irving Kristol, too.)"

As Jews see it, then, the Christian right is no friend of pluralism and no friend of Israel, and they surely do not believe it is a friend of the Jews. A recent survey of evangelical and fundamentalist attitudes toward the Jews, sponsored by the Anti-Defamation League (ADL), bears notice here. The report reveals a remarkable absence of anti-Semitism—alongside a pronounced Christian dogmatism. Eighty-nine percent of the respondents agree that "a person needs to personally accept Jesus Christ as his or her personal savior in order to have eternal salvation and to be saved from eternal hell"; 78 percent reject the notion that "many different religions may have some truth or correctness in the eyes of God," agreeing instead that "there is no doubt that the only true or correct religion is belief in Jesus Christ as personal savior."

Even so, the sample is only mildly tainted by traditional anti-Semitic attitudes, and that was the finding that the ADL—an enthusiastic proponent of increased Jewish contacts with the evangelical right—emphasized in its press release on the matter. Given the propensity of Jews to assume anti-Semitism as a correlate of fundamentalism, one can understand why the ADL chose the emphasis it did.

Still, half the sample believe that "Christians should actively witness to Jews and actively help lead Jews to accept Jesus Christ as savior." One may draw some comfort from the fact that a fundamentalist religious orientation does not, as might have been supposed, imply anti-Semitism, and one may applaud the readiness of the ADL to build on that fact. But one will also understand if Jews are less than enthusiastic about seeking an intimate political alliance with people who, whether or not anti-Semitic, take it as their mission to convert the Jews and of whom 59 percent agree that "Jews can never be forgiven for what they did to Jesus until they accept him as the true savior." Perhaps, as the authors of the report claim, that doesn't mean anti-Semitism; most Jews will think it comes close enough, that it suggests at the very least a considerable potential for anti-Semitism.

Finally, aside from any linkage between fundamentalist theology and anti-Semitism, there's the question of the fundamentalism of the fundamentalists—that is, of their way of looking at the world, including its Jews. In an earlier chapter, I wrote of the problems most Jews have with Jewish fundamentalism—and I note once again that I use that term to describe how ultra-Orthodox Jews are quite widely perceived, whether or not it is accurate or fair to lump them together with Christian fundamentalists. Those problems, however, are mitigated by a sense of shared history and destiny, even if not of shared world view. With regard to Christian fundamentalists, there is nothing to bridge the gap.

That, I suspect, is why the efforts of some Jewish leaders to enter into dialogue with fundamentalist Christians evoke so little enthusiasm from American Jews. If Menachem Begin feels, for whatever reason, that it is appropriate to reward the Reverend Jerry Falwell for his "distinguished services to the Jewish people"—whatever it was that Begin had in mind when he did that in 1980—Jews will, by and large, indulge him his extravagance. Their own sentiments are more accurately reflected in the near-universal and quite visceral

negative reaction to the fundamentalist rhetoric at the Republican
National Convention in 1984. There are students of that election
who believe that until the time that its prayer breakfast was nation-
ally televised, the Republicans were winning among the Jews; it was
only when Jewish antipathy to Jesse Jackson was offset by Jewish
fear of Jerry Falwell et al. that the Democrats won out.

Why prefer Jackson to Falwell? It is not that the fear of Christian
anti-Semitism is older, hence better established, than the fear of
black anti-Semitism, though obviously it is. The difference is really
much simpler than that. It is that Jerry Falwell is perceived as a more
accurate reflection of Republican sentiment than Jesse Jackson is of
Democratic sentiment. When Walter Mondale embraced Jesse Jackson, Jews were unhappy, but they supposed that Mr. Mondale was
also unhappy; when Ronald Reagan embraced Jerry Falwell, Jews
were unhappy, but they had no reason to suppose that Mr. Reagan
was. The Democratic Party is still perceived by very many Jews as
the party of Ellis Island, the swarthy party; the Republicans are the
party of the Los Angeles Olympics, all blond and bland, alien. We
look at the Jewish neo-conservatives, and wonder how they have
come to feel at home there; truth to tell, we suspect they have not.
(Indeed, we suspect that they want us to join them because they
yearn for both vindication and company. In the nineteenth century,
two Jews who had not seen each other in many years met on a street
in Berlin. "What's new?" asked the first. "What's new," his old
classmate said, "is that I've converted. I've become a Christian."
"Oh, how interesting." "Yes, and now I have one favor to ask of
you. I want you to convert also." "Me? Why in the world should
I convert?" "Because I'd like at least one Christian friend.") Even
though we've by now met Republicans who don't make us feel like
foreigners in America, the sight and sound of the fundamentalist
preachers at the Republican Convention evoked every old and
negative stereotype. If this is where the fundamentalists belong,
how can we, too, belong there? Call it cultural lag if you will, or
call it a recognition of abiding cultural and political differences in
America.

Still, for all that our values and our interests (along with our
viscera) point us toward a rejection of the Christian right, there

remains the issue of Israel. Given the urgency of Israel's need for support, should not that interest outweigh the rest? Liberal Jewish organizations have generally taken the position that if the Christian right, for its own theological or political reasons, wants to lend Israel a hand, that is all to the good. But if it expects reciprocity, it will be disappointed; we may, as a matter of courtesy, try to avoid biting the hand that reaches out to Israel, but neither will we clasp that hand in ours. The Christian right acts for its reasons, we for ours. And of all our reasons, as American Jews, none is more central than the defense of pluralism. So Shylock's distinction is drawn still tighter: We will talk with them, but that is all. We will not walk with them, nor drink with them, nor pray with them.

With regard to the Christian right, we are asked to make of an old enemy a new friend. With regard to black Americans, the question is whether an old friend has become a new enemy. The historic alliance between blacks and Jews in this country has been much remarked, and with good reason: despite the tensions and the fallings out, despite the misunderstandings and the lingering stereotypes, it was a proud chapter in American group history. From the time of the founding of the NAACP in 1909 through the Mississippi summer of 1964, the Jews were the blacks' most dependable companions in the struggle for civil rights.

Now, we are told, the alliance is done, battered by the continuing disputes over affirmative action and Israel's relationship with South Africa, beaten by the wounds it suffered during the urban riots of the 1960s, during the New York City schoolteachers' strike of 1968, during the Andrew Young affair in 1979, gravely wounded by Jesse Jackson's "Hymie" in 1984 and by the failure of black leaders to condemn Louis Farrakhan in 1980, when he first attracted national attention.

While the old alliance is plainly hurting, it seems to me a mistake to think it dead. It has suffered, no doubt, from all the issues and events I have recited, and more, and it surely has not been helped by the fact that the liberal coalition, so rudely knocked down during the Reagan years, is only now and somewhat woozily preparing to enter the ring again. But around the country, Jews and blacks in local communities continue to try to work together. When the Congress voted, in 1981, on whether to sell the AWACS system to Saudi Arabia, the black congressional delegation stood unanimously with the Jews in opposition to the sale (while of the twenty-eight senators usually associated with the "New Right," twenty-six voted for it). In the summer of 1987, black and Jewish organizations (including among others the Jewish War Veterans of America) worked in tandem to block Senate approval of Judge Robert Bork to the Supreme Court, perhaps learning again that an alliance, like a community, is better nourished by working together on its shared agenda than by convening yet more introspective conferences on its own health.

I want to step back from the ups and the downs of the relationship to raise a question that is often neglected in the rush of condemnation or in the work of repair and that seems to me critical to an understanding of its condition. On the surface, a black-Jewish alliance in America seems an unlikely thing. How and why should two communities so different in circumstance as these be expected to work together? Why is so much emotion attached to the condition of an alliance that objectively appears so unlikely? The Jews came from Europe's oppression to America's freedom; the blacks came from Africa's freedom to America's slavery. Today, though there are more poor Jews than is often recognized, Jews are decisively among the haves, while blacks remain decisively among the have-nots. Jewish children worry which college to attend, black children about joblessness. A day or two a year, Jews and blacks meet to talk their problems through; the rest of the days of our years we live in different worlds, in ignorance of and indifference to one another. What is it, then, that makes the condition of the black-Jewish alliance an object of such passionate ongoing concern?

I leave aside the answers historical and geographical, much discussed in the extensive literature on the relationship. The more interesting and, I think, important answers have to do with the ways in which blacks and Jews each see themselves mirrored in the experience of the other.

The traditional liberal conviction was that the battle for civil rights was a battle for desegregation. The problem, then, was a legal one, to be fought in the courts and in the legislative bodies of the land. Progress toward desegregation could be and was measured by evidence of movement toward integration—that is, toward a condition in which blackness had become irrelevant in determining where one lived, went to school, or worked. The goal was a truly color-blind society. When, in 1963, Norman Podhoretz proposed miscegenation as the only solution to "the Negro problem," he was drawing an unconventional but logical conclusion from the conventional liberal understanding. Color was to become irrelevant.

If white American society had mustered the intellectual and moral resources necessary to deliver on its promise of integration, blacks might have been swallowed up in the embrace of thorough assimilation and the ideological turn they have taken these last two decades or so might have been preempted. Obviously, however, white America did not deliver on the integrationist promise. The fundamental reason was and remains simple: Blacks are black. The society that promised to see the person and not the color reneged on its promise; it could not bring itself to see beyond the color.

And so the black effort was redirected. If white color blindness was not possible, then let blackness be transformed from a stigma into a badge of pride. Let black be beautiful. And since the day that Stokley Carmichael first insisted that black *is* beautiful, Americans in general, and American Jews in particular, have had to re-examine their assumptions not only about the meaning of blackness but also about the intended texture of American society.

I say "Jews in particular" because Jews have had special reason to attend the stirrings of black separatism; in unsettling ways, they have mirrored our own historic ambivalence regarding our situation in America. Was it our intention here to make the fact of our Jewishness entirely irrelevant, or was it to gain acceptance *as Jews?* There were enthusiastic advocates of each alternative, but most Jews supported both, their apparent incompatibility notwithstanding. As I indicated earlier, we wanted "them" to accept us in their clubs—and we wanted not to join those clubs. When they said we were "clannish," we accused them of anti-Semitism—and then we invested heavily in promoting our sense of clannish apartness. (In the early 1960s, in their *Christian Beliefs and Anti-Semitism,* Charles

Glock and Rodney Stark used, as one measure of anti-Semitism, Christian responses to the statement, "Jews want to remain different from other people, and yet they are touchy if people notice those differences." While it may well be that those Christians who think this true also think it bad, it is surely the case that those who think it false are simply mistaken.)

We wanted, in short, to make Jewishness publicly irrelevant and privately significant. And if, today, many of us are finally more comfortable with the public relevance of Jewishness, at least some part of the change may be attributed to the example blacks have offered us. The pushing and shoving of the 1960s, distressful though much of it was and though some of its aftereffects may be, helped extend America's understanding of itself and of the legitimacy of the group, the clan, the tribe, as the building block of American society. Until that time, whether or not it ever happened, the melting pot was the goal of liberal universalism; since that time, we have come to a more nuanced understanding of what pluralism means.

As a Jew, I rejoice in the development, yet I must add that as an advocate of pluralism and of civil rights, there is so far little cause for celebration. Pluralism, as I earlier proposed, requires that groups enjoy both coherence and interaction, that they have definable boundaries and that the boundaries be permeable. For far too many blacks, the boundary remains a doorless wall. The fact that the nation now has an enlarged appreciation (however grudging) of groupness, that the idea of the melting pot has been put to rest, has been of enormous benefit to the Jews; it has yet to be of comparable benefit to the blacks themselves, whose uprising was its proximate cause. We felt threatened by boundaries that had become, in fact, porous, and discovered in the new pluralism a way to balance our desire for acceptance and our concern for identity; the blacks were threatened by impenetrable boundaries, and threatened they largely remain, the new pride in black culture notwithstanding.

The mirror each of us provides the other is sometimes borrowed from the fun house. Jewish liberals used to be unadulterated universalists, preaching the virtues of integration (not less for themselves than for others). In the wake of the 1960s, many—most, I think— have rediscovered the merits of particularism, and now seek to live at what I have called "the intersection." Observing blacks these days, they are disturbed and offended by what appears to be an unmitigated particularism, even as they try to understand that it is a particularism born of imposition rather than of free choice. In the wake of that particularism, black students in the cafeterias of America's universities seat themselves at separate tables, and their Jewish peers, raised to liberality, become confused. In the name of that particularism, Louis Farrakhan fulminates, and black leaders who know better remain silent. "Jesse Jackson," an insightful black once told me, "is our Israel, the symbol of our strength. We don't agree with all he says or does, but just as you refrain from criticizing Israel in public, and just as you wonder whether such criticism isn't a cover for anti-Israelism or even anti-Semitism, we wonder whether the criticism of Jesse Jackson isn't a cover for racism." And those of us who have overcome our reluctance to voice our criticisms of Israel are distressed; we expect more, and better, from our black counterparts.

We look in the mirror, and the black looks back at us reproach- fully: we were the ones who were supposed to understand it all, and we understand only part of it. The black looks back at us, and he is wearing a yarmulke, he announces himself as the new Jew, and we, bare-headed, clean-shaven, we want to be the only Jew, we resent the fact that a generation is growing up knowing the ghetto as the place where blacks live and not as the place where Jews were once herded. The black asks by what right we present ourselves as brother victims, we who live so very well. The black wonders how we announce ourselves as both his brother and his benefactor, for if we are comfortable enough to be the latter, how can we pretend to be the former? Jews wonder why, "after all we've done for them," these are the thanks we get. Jews listen to the black indictment, and this, more or less, is what we hear: "You say you too were maligned, and worse, and we acknowledge that. But we have not experienced you as victims; we have experienced you as the successful, our landlords and our advisers, our shopkeepers and our social workers. We have cleaned your homes and worn your used clothing. And if, as you have told us, you were once despised, we are bound to ask ourselves—how did you break out of it, how did you come by those buildings and those stores and those college degrees and those houses?"

And the indictment moves to its climax: "We have heard you asking, 'Why can't they be like us?,' and that is our question, too: 'Why can't we be like them, like you?' You want to know about black anti-Semitism? It is an exercise in parsimony, for in one economical sentence, we can finally answer that painful and poignant question, explain both your success and our lack of it: You got it all by stepping on our backs. That is why we cannot be like you, or like you.

"You have Israel; we have bankrupt and incompetent black Africa. You, not three percent of this nation's population, have seven United States senators; we have none. And with all you have, you have the nerve and the insensitivity to keep babbling on about our kinship in suffering."

Or, as James Baldwin writes,

> One does not wish . . . to be told by an American Jew that his suffering is as great as the American Negro's suffering. It isn't, and one knows that it isn't from the very tone in which he assures you that it is. . . . The Jew does not realize that the credential he offers, the fact that he has been despised and slaughtered, does not increase the Negro's understanding. It increases the Negro's rage. For it is not here, and not now, that the Jew is being slaughtered, and he is never despised, here, as the Negro is, *because* he is an American. The Jewish travail occurred across the sea and America rescued him from the house of bondage. But America *is* the house of bondage for the Negro. . . .

He is right. But we would not and cannot give up on the alliance, for it has helped preserve our sense of ourselves as still, and in spite of all the successes we've known, among the oppressed, hence also among the decent, the just, the virtuous. The alliance was born not only out of our empathy for black misery, but also out of our continuing need to see ourselves among the miserable—or, at least, the still-threatened. And sometimes, not always but sometimes, we did the things that decent and just and virtuous people do on behalf of the oppressed.

What James Baldwin evidently does not understand is that yesterday is so very close that the hate and the slaughter are for us not just memories but also possibilities. True enough, neither memory nor possibility degrades us here and now, as here and now degrade the black. But for at least some of us, our slavery in Egypt is as real as Southern slavery is for the black. And that should be a place to start from. How shall we react when, instead, Baldwin tells us that our evocation of our past is an occasion for black rage, when, that is, he asks us to deny our past?

Is all this sufficiently intricate? No, because now we must factor in power and violence as well.

I have in an earlier chapter described the Jewish ambivalence toward power. Impotent for so long, we taught ourselves that impotence is a confirmation of virtue. We are and have been decidedly uncomfortable with power. Even when our own impotence finally culminated in the terrifying impotence of God, and we at last sought and won a measure of power, we remained queasy about it. And of all the forms that power takes, the kind of power we found most unsettling was the raw, physical stuff: violence.

Along come the blacks and announce, fists raised, "Black power!" Come the blacks and specialize in violence. And all our sympathetic sociology is not enough to withstand the fear we feel, and, yes, the antipathy. For it is one thing to sit in a sociology seminar and come to understand the sophisticated formulas, the culture of poverty, and whatever else, and it is quite another to be walking the street (or standing in a subway car) as three of "them" approach you, to be driving through "their" neighborhood and to know that here you must lock your car doors. You can get an "A" in the seminar, and even send an annual contribution to the NAACP or the United Negro College Fund, and still feel the fear. And once that fear takes hold, there's very little room to feel the other's desperation, the other's fear; there's very little room left for empathy.

Violence is a medium of exchange peculiarly alien to American Jews. We don't know about schools where kids carry knives or hit teachers. Such things make us afraid, and angry. And they cannot be omitted from an appraisal of the condition of the alliance.

Given all the abrasions and all the distortions, the reproach and the rejection, given Third World anti-Zionism and Jesse Jackson, too, given the fear, perhaps we should take Irving Kristol's advice when he tells us to turn from our anachronistic and obsessive preoccupation with the old alliance. Why take such thankless trouble to seek its resurrection? Is it really anything more than, as Kristol says, yet another example of cultural lag? Our memories, he tells us, obscure the new reality. Because of those "encrusted" memories, Jewish liberals "vigorously resist any suggestion that they rethink their social policy, and insist that, since we have obviously not done enough to help poor blacks, we must do more of the same"—the "same" that, in Kristol's view, not only failed the first time around but actually contributed to the worsening of the black condition. He does not tell us with what he would replace those programs. He tells us only that if we stand with the alliance during its new post–Jesse Jackson incarnation, we will "gag" on its terms, which come down to the pursuit of racial quotas.

Is Kristol right? Perhaps it is only nostalgia that informs our effort. Perhaps there are no fresher springs to nourish the dream that two such unlikely allies as the blacks and the Jews, with all their intimate and rocky and explosive history and with all the differences in their condition, may again work together in the labor of justice. Perhaps the fact that we both once knew Egypt is not enough to connect us now, so far away from the pyramids and the plantations. (And is it already not a symptom of Jewish arrogance that it is *our* metaphor we impose on our common slavery?) Why force today's tough choices into the metaphors of a distant yesterday?

Let us speak of affirmative action; that is what is happening today. And that, more than any other single issue, is why the neo-conservatives believe the time for alliance is over. They recoil at the prospect that a society that has heretofore counted us one by one now counts us group by group. They are appalled that Jews, so recently the victims of quotas, now endorse affirmative action programs that are, in the neo-conservative view, a reversion to quotas.

They are right about the endorsement. In spite of all the raw resentment, and in spite of all the claims to the contrary, America's

Jews continue to support affirmative action—a program from which they perceive themselves as deriving no direct benefit, a program most of them suppose will actually do them modest harm.

I do not enter here the debate over whether affirmative action is a good idea or a bad idea. Good or bad, it is an idea that black Americans have adopted and whose continuing implementation they urgently seek. Good or bad, it is an idea that many Jewish organizations, after extensive and careful and sometimes painful deliberation, have supported from the beginning and continue to support, as do most Jewish citizens. Survey after survey shows that a majority of American Jews endorses it, that a plurality even endorses "preferential treatment," which falls somewhere between affirmative action and quotas. In 1984, Steven M. Cohen found that 70 percent of American Jews favored affirmative action; only 20 percent opposed it. (In the same survey, he found that 22 percent favored job quotas on behalf of minorities; 64 percent were opposed.) The 1984 questions that elicited these responses were: "Do you favor job quotas to assure equal opportunity for minorities?" and: "Do you favor affirmative action without quotas to promote equal opportunity for minorities?" In 1985, Cohen framed his questions more sharply: "Even though many Jews think that some black leaders have been anti-Semitic or anti-Israel, American Jews should still support special efforts to recruit and hire black workers." (Followed by, "should still support efforts to recruit and admit black students into colleges and professional schools.") Even when so phrased, the "workers" question elicited a 49 percent agreement (with 33 percent opposed and 19 percent undecided), and the "students" question won an absolute majority, 55 percent agreeing to "special efforts," 28 percent opposed, 17 percent undecided.

No one can have remained unaware of the arguments the conservatives and the neo-conservatives have mounted against affirmative action programs. No one can pretend that affirmative action programs do not come very close to quotas. And no Jew can be indifferent to quotas. It is therefore unlikely that cultural lag accounts for the support Jews express for affirmative action. More likely, the rejection of the conservative argument is a considered rejection, based on a different way of calculating what is at stake for Jews. Perhaps we recall that we have not always been for the merit system. In the early decades of this century, during the pioneering resettlement of Palestine, the leaders of the *yishuv* (as the fledgling Jewish community was known) believed that the development of a healthy Jewish society required the creation of a Jewish working class. But employment opportunities for Jewish workers were few and far between; in the vineyards, for example, it was Arabs who traditionally did the work. Jewish workers were plainly less accomplished than the Arabs. Their hands were less callused, their wage demands were higher; they insisted on better working conditions even though their productivity was lower. And they won the fight.

Years later, Ben Gurion was to say that *kibbush avodah*—the "conquest of labor," as the endeavor was called—was the single most important ingredient in preparing for statehood. And still more years later, as Israel faced its own problem of ethnic equality, it accepted with scarcely a murmur of debate a program of radical preference for Sephardic Jews. To this day, in fact, Sephardim enjoy not only the benefits of wide-ranging compensatory programs, but also the advantages of legally prescribed preferences in education and employment.

Or perhaps it is that Jews have on the whole been more committed to equity than to excellence, and it is precisely that choice that is at stake in affirmative action programs. It is nowhere etched in stone that a society is bound to fill its empty slots "from the top down," taking merit alone into account. Values other than merit—say, for example, kinship—may well be, and have been, thought worth preserving. For many years, America chose to offer preferential treatment to its veterans. In dozens of municipalities today, there are stringent residence requirements for municipal employees. These kinds of compromises with merit may or may not be wise or appropriate; they are not irrational. The polity is not a merit-maximizing entity; it is "entitled" to defend such other values as it deems important. Pluralists understand that.

Whether it is these or other considerations that have led most Jews to resist the conservative assault on affirmative action, that resistance suggests to me that there is still the material out of which to rebuild the alliance.

Allies are allies, only that; they are not each other's clones. The immediate interests of Jews and blacks in America do not coincide, they merely overlap. These are not the 1960s, when together we could be outraged by the Bull Conners and the George Wallaces, together be inspired by Martin Luther King, Jr., and suppose that was enough. Our enemies today are more subtle and more sinister, the old problems remain, new problems are added. If the alliance is to be repaired, it cannot merely be resurrected. Too much has happened, too much has changed since the 1960s. But despite all that has happened and all that has changed, there are still numerous instances of cooperation. In dozens of cities, blacks and Jews meet regularly to work through issues of common concern; representatives of Jewish organizations are deeply engaged in the work of the Leadership Conference on Civil Rights; black leaders continue to participate in study missions to Israel, and to return from such missions with greater sensitivity to at least some aspects of the Jewish agenda. The Institute for American Pluralism of the American Jewish Committee sponsors and funds the National Coalition Building Institute, an effort to encourage black-Jewish dialogue on college campuses, and other organizations engage in similar efforts. More important, the Jewish community continues to be in the vanguard of support for full employment, progressive welfare reform, job training programs, and the rest of the wide range of programs and policies that most directly affect the black community, including, as we have seen, affirmative action. There is on both sides a recognition that the preservation of an alliance that was once so productive warrants continuing investment—not for old times' sake, but for the sake of us all, severally and together.

To Irving Kristol, Jewish support for affirmative action suggests something very different, and the difference frames my central point. Kristol tells us that "we must begin to see things as they are, not as [we] would like them to be." In the absence of any more substantive advice (save that we relocate from left to right), that is much the same as telling us to settle for things as they are, to stop trying to change them.

That is advice that Jews have not taken and are not likely to take. Were the Jews to take that advice, they would plainly be violating their own commitment—a commitment that sometimes leads to foolishness and sometimes even disaster, a commitment that sometimes involves an unacceptable hubris, but a commitment that is nonetheless critical to the Jewish understanding of who we are, and why. For the very last thing that Jews are or ever have been interested in doing is seeing things "as they are" rather than "as we would like them to be." More precisely, as we believe they were meant to be, are supposed to be.

And so we return to Jewish interests and to Jewish values. No, Egypt is not enough; it is only a starting place. But there is not only Egypt, there is also the River Jordan, not only where we've both been, but where at least some of us both still mean to go, the place where at last things will be as we would like them to be, as we believe they ought to be. Jewish self-interest? The overriding Jewish self-interest is for Jews to be Jews. Judaism is either an accident or it is a vocation. And if, as most Jews—though they may grumble about it—know, it is a vocation, it calls us not to make the world safe for Jews, nor even, for that matter, to make the world safe for blacks, but to make the world safe for God—which is to say, to help repair this fractured and despoiled planet, to hasten the day when each shall sit under his own fig tree and none shall make them afraid.

In order for Jews to be Jews, to be free to do God's work, they must first be free. Looking about at the current disrepair in the lives of America's blacks, what Jew can take freedom for granted? Will an America that permits an infant death rate among blacks twice as high and a maternal death rate more than three times as high as the white rates stay safe for and fair to its Jews? If the dream of decency is allowed to shrivel, will not the nightmare of hate one day replace it?

Jews need blacks to be reminded of that which we might otherwise seek to forget. We need blacks to remind us to be uncomfortable, to prevent us from being at ease, to insist that the battle's not over, that Jordan remains to be crossed. If the waters of our Jordan run dry, if the place we live and its today become our only home, our only time, we abandon and betray past and future alike. We betray our Jewish selves *and* our Jewish interests.

Jews need blacks. And blacks need Jews, or so I presume to insist. They need Jews not only to march with them and to vote with them but also to help them remember the most important lesson the Jews have to teach: the lesson of hope, and its utility. We are the world's leading exemplars of that lesson. History gave us a bum deal, but we refused to abide by it. We have known to spit in the face of despair.

All this is a very far cry from Louis Farrakhan, and even from Jesse Jackson, from the noisemakers and the troublemakers. But it is not so very far, at least for now, from the Jews and the blacks who serve together in Congress and work together elsewhere and who have, over the years, been each other's most dependable allies, not so far from the stepping stones to a refreshed alliance. Irving Kristol predicts that black nationalism "must and will lead, is already leading, to a new black political posture vis-à-vis American foreign policy in general, and American policy toward Israel in particular." We point to the continuing cooperation, and we ask whether if blacks and Jews turn their backs on one another, it will be because the blacks have listened to Jesse Jackson or because the Jews have listened to Irving Kristol.

And beyond our shared political agenda, there is the larger pragmatism, the defense of a tradition of hope and concern and finally of respect for the essential self that ought not lightly be abandoned. That tradition is not merely "good for the Jews"; it is essential for the Jews: "Where there is no vision, a people perishes." (Prov. 29:18)

It has become so very easy to dismiss such words as soft-minded mush, to demand that we be tough-minded, hard-nosed, unsentimental in our appraisal of interests. Indeed, Kristol himself anticipates some version of my argument: "[Liberals] wish to continue doing bad, while continuing to feel good—all in the name of compassion." He contends that liberal political discourse within the

Jewish community "is more likely to resemble a sermon in its rhetoric than a conventional political statement." He is, of course, correct. But why should it be otherwise? Jews are either informed by their tradition or they are not. If they are not, how can they be presumed to understand and interpret "Jewish interests"? But if they are informed by their tradition, which is a religious tradition, how can their rhetoric not have a sermonic tone? As well say of the prophets of old, who were (as we have seen) deeply engaged in the political struggles of their day, that their tone was inappropriately sermonic. One presumes that they chose to express themselves as they did for compelling rhetorical reasons—that is, because they knew that their rhetoric would move and would mobilize their audience. But by tapping into a familiar image, by using a familiar idiom, by appealing to a familiar doctrine, they sought not only to persuade; they sought as well to establish that their proposals arose from within a received tradition and were consonant with that tradition. And politicians and those who debate politics have been doing exactly the same ever since.

That does not mean that rhetoric alone is adequate. Uninformed by analysis, rhetoric becomes demagoguery. But unaccompanied by rhetoric, analysis is just another computer printout. It does not inspire us; it does not even tell us in what values our choices ought be grounded.

Jewish liberal rhetoric, Kristol has it, "tends to be abstractly universalistic and intensely moralistic, with a great stress on ideological motivation. To refer to specifically 'Jewish interests' is regarded as bad form, as are references to 'expediency' and 'realism.' In contrast, 'compassion' is a term that is much used, with a highly laudatory connotation. To be accused of being 'lacking in compassion' is to suffer a dismissal that is definitive."

This is bad political science, and worse Judaism. As I have argued, the Jews are a people particular in structure, universal in ideology. The survival of the Jews (as also, perhaps, the survival of universalism) requires defense of both the structure and the ideology. It is for that reason that one cannot and ought not ask the Jews to dispense with "ideological motivation"; we are not a neighborhood association, concerned exclusively with the defense of turf. And—

this seems to me the heart of the matter—it would be a betrayal of Jewish interests to say that we are, or to recommend that we should be. "Expediency" and "realism" do not satisfy the interests of a people that is enjoined to be holy. And if there is any merit to the argument I have been making throughout these pages, save as the Jews seek to be holy, they will be unable to sustain their morale, unable, that is, to survive. Which would hardly be in the Jewish interest, however defined.

Compassion? The Talmud teaches that "by ten things the world was created," and compassion is one of the ten. Was the Talmud overly sentimental? Here are the other nine: wisdom, understanding, reason, strength, rebuke, might, righteousness, judgment, and loving-kindness. (Moed: Hagigah, 12A, citing Rab) Not a bad mix. (In fairness, I am bound to add that at another point, the Talmud says, "Our Rabbis taught: There are three whose life is not life; the [over-] compassionate, the hot tempered, and the [too] fastidious.") Does it violate the Jewish interest to cite the Jewish sources?

We are not asked to choose between sentiment and self-interest. Conservatives are as wrong when they accuse liberals of fatuous disregard for self-interest as liberals are when they allege that conservatism necessarily implies an absence of compassion. The characteristic conservative formulation, as I observed in the last chapter, presumes a dichotomy between self-interest and utopianism. But self-interest is far more complex than conservatives commonly suppose; it is hardly sufficient to list the substantive differences between liberals and conservatives and then to claim that whoever takes the liberal side of the argument has betrayed the Jewish self-interest. One might, after all, argue that it is in our interest to feel right with ourselves. It is in our interest to feel at one with our gentler instincts. It is in our interest to draw on our tradition. It is in our interest to reach beyond the moment. And yes, it is in our interest to be analytic, too. (More precisely analytic, one hopes, than Kristol when he says, "It is nice to provide free lunches to poor schoolchildren, and it is unquestionably nice for the nutritionists, the food-service industry, and the farmers." In a nation where millions of schoolchildren are provided their only nourishing meal of the day through the school lunch program, "nice" doesn't quite make it as analysis.)

The Jewish tradition does not instruct us to endorse this welfare program or that, to enter into alliance with this group or that. The tradition is not a political tract. But the fact that it is not a political tract does not mean that it is politically irrelevant. The tradition tells us that in considering our policy choices, there are things we are *required* to take into account, things we ignore at our peril. We may debate the impact of a particular program on, say, the poor, and we may disagree; but we may not refrain from considering the impact of that program on the poor.

I have said before, and I must now say again: the irreducible self-interest of the Jews, that interest on which Jewish survival most immediately depends, is that the Jews behave as they have been taught Jews are supposed to behave. Just that.

13

Jews and the Liberal Tradition

I HAVE BEEN WRITING as if the world we inhabit were a tidy place, a place without real disagreement on how Jews are "supposed to" behave and without real barriers to such behavior. Alas, that is not the world we inhabit; it is only the world we seek. In the world we inhabit, there is much arguing over what we mean by Jewish interests, much dispute over the ordering of our values. Sometimes the problem is one of definition, amenable to resolution through reasoned discussion. But sometimes we come away from such discussion reminded that in this world there are competing interests and conflicting values, that our urgent interests often point us one way, our abiding values another.

I have been writing as if Jewish liberals, though tired, were still essentially untroubled, as certain of their convictions as the neoconservatives plainly are, as if the liberals need only out-argue the upstarts on the right for their joyful march to utopia to be resumed. But today we know some things that those who shaped modern liberalism did not know. We know something about the limits of rationalism; we know about the Holocaust; we know about the unintended and unanticipated and untoward side effects of programs for reform; we know that Israel is not the sunny *altneuland* that Herzl imagined—nor, for that matter, is America the New Zion its founders envisioned; we know a fair amount about disappointment. It is not the neo-conservatives who becloud our guiding star; it is these things we've learned and are still learning.

Take Israel, for example, and its effects on our understanding of Jewish interests and Jewish values, its bearing on our political perceptions and commitments.

On the evening of June 9, 1977, a small group of American Jews, lay and professional leaders of several of America's major Jewish organizations, met in a private home in New York City. Menachem Begin had just weeks earlier become Israel's prime minister; the meeting had convened in response to a letter outlining the dimensions of "the Begin problem." The discussion, which lasted for several hours, roamed through the several aspects of the "problem" as those present understood it: insofar as Begin was known to them at all, he was known as a right-wing demagogue; his election was as disconcerting as would have been, say, the election of George Wallace as president of the United States. Moreover, Begin's exposure both to America and to American Jewry had been quite limited, and it was feared he would be insensitive to both, disrupting Israel's delicate relationship with the first and its intimate relationship with the second; similarly, American Jewish access to Israel's key political leaders might now be limited.

The discussion ended inconclusively, as it was bound to. The citizens of Israel had made their choice, and it was not for a group of American Jews to rescind it, no matter how shocked they were by it. Instead, it was decided to encourage an early meeting between representatives of American Jewish leadership and the new prime minister, a meeting in which the urgent concerns of the Americans would be delicately put before Mr. Begin.

The storied figures of Israel's early years, the heroes and heroines of the Jewish national renaissance, had all been Labor Zionists. American Jews did not know, in any detail, what Labor Zionism was about, but there was a vague appreciation that the kibbutz movement, the Histadrut (Israel's giant trade union), and the government were all cut from the same pioneering cloth.

By 1977, twenty years after independence, the names of those heroes and heroines were widely known here. David Ben Gurion, Moshe Sharett, Levi Eshkol, Golda Meir, and Yitzhak Rabin had all served as prime minister; Moshe Dayan and Abba Eban and Yigal Allon were scarcely less well known. All were frequent visitors at major Jewish assemblies in America, and, with all their differences, represented a now familiar Israel.

Menachem Begin, by contrast, was hardly known here at all. Begin had come to Israel in 1942 and assumed command of the Irgun Tzva'i Leumi, an underground group whose purpose was to force the British out of Palestine. In 1948, when the British left, Begin assumed the leadership of a small opposition party called Herut (Freedom). In that capacity, he served in the Knesset for the next nineteen years. These were, in effect, years of political exile for him. The overwhelmingly dominant political fact in Israel during that period was Mapai, Israel's Labor Party. Herut had few seats and little influence, and Begin himself was widely regarded as a neo-Fascist outcast. Ben Gurion loathed him, most others simply ignored him. Together with the Communist Party, Herut was refused representation on the Knesset's Foreign Affairs and Security Committee; it was perceived to be outside the national consensus.

By 1967, on the eve of the Six Day War, Herut's political fortunes had improved. A 1965 coalition with the centrist Liberal Party had moderated its image, and in the elections of that year the combined parties won twenty-six Knesset seats (out of 120), up from Herut's low point of just eight in the 1951 elections. When, therefore, Prime Minister Eshkol sought to broaden the national consensus on the eve of the war, he invited Begin to join the cabinet as a minister without portfolio.

Thus began Begin's rehabilitation. By 1973, the newly named Likud, incorporating the old Herut along with several smaller right-of-center parties, won thirty-nine seats and was plainly a coherent opposition party, Israel's first. Still, no one imagined that the Likud might actually displace Labor as Israel's leading political party.

Likud's 1977 victory and Begin's accession to the prime ministership came to knowledgeable American Jews not merely as a surprise but as a shock. Begin's reputation had preceded him. The Irgun, which defined itself as an underground army of freedom fighters, was widely seen as a terrorist organization, its leader therefore hardly the person to reassure the international community of Israel's peaceful intentions. The symbol of the party Begin had led through all the lonely years of his political exile remained a silhouette map of the Land of Israel—of all the Land of Israel, including not only the state itself, but also the West Bank and Gaza—and the Kingdom of Jordan as well. The anthem of Begin's party included the words, "There are two banks to the Jordan; this one is ours, and that one is also ours." (The original mandate for Palestine awarded to Great Britain by the League of Nations in 1919 had, indeed, included both "banks" of the Jordan River; in 1922, Great Britain had severed all the land to the river's east and established there the Hashemite Kingdom.) And the platform on which Begin had been elected included a promise never to relinquish Israel's claim to sovereignty over the whole of the "historic Land of Israel," an area far larger than the State of Israel.

It was widely understood here that the victory of the Likud owed principally to economic considerations and to ethnic tensions, as well as to disenchantment with Labor in the aftermath of the Yom Kippur War, that it was not an electoral endorsement of Begin's foreign policy. But many people feared that the populist economic program that had helped bring Begin to power was only a cover for the prime minister's enduring commitment to what he called "the integrity of the Land of Israel." An American Jewish community used to the conciliatory (some would say vacillating) posture of the Labor Party with regard to Israel's international intentions was ill-prepared to make the radical adjustment that Begin's election implied.

Indeed, the principle that the way to peace with the Arabs depended on partition of the land between the Mediterranean Sea and the Jordan River had been at the center of the Jewish perspective ever since it was accepted by the World Zionist Congress in 1937. True, the Arabs had rejected that principle in 1937 when it was put to them by Great Britain's Peel Commission. And they had rejected it again when it was voted by the United Nations in 1947, preferring instead to make war against the fledgling Jewish state. When Israel's War of Independence was over, Israel had established its sovereignty not only over all the land that had been allocated it under the UN plan, but also over some one-third more, part of the land the UN had designated as an Arab state in Palestine. The Arabs might have chosen to establish a Palestinian state in the land that remained under their control; they did not, for to have done so would have been to accept the principle they had made war to defeat. The territories that remained under their control—those territories now known as the West Bank and the Gaza Strip, whose disposition is today the subject of such intense controversy—were instead absorbed by Jordan and Egypt. Jordan proclaimed its sovereignty over the West Bank, a sovereignty acknowledged only by Great Britain and Pakistan; for its part, Egypt merely governed, but did not annex, the Gaza Strip. Gaza residents were not permitted Egyptian citizenship.

(The obvious irony of the post-1967 period is that today the Arabs argue fiercely for precisely that which was in their complete power to accomplish in the period between 1948 and 1967—an independent Palestinian state in the West Bank and Gaza. Similarly, many Israelis have come to oppose just as fiercely a resolution they would have gladly settled for prior to the Six Day War—peace with their neighbors within Israel's prewar boundaries. But that, of course, is another story, for a different book.)

From 1937 until 1977, then, the Jewish people—America's Jews included—and the Jewish state understood and accepted that if peace were to be achieved, the land would have to be partitioned. Those who opposed partition were regarded as fringe factions, on a par, say, with those in the United States who continue to insist on "liberating" Cuba.

And then, in 1977, a militant anti-partitionist assumed the leadership of the Jewish state. How—and why—did American Jews learn to live with, and in many cases to love, so unlikely and unpalatable a leader as Menachem Begin? For the fact is that within two months of his election, Begin came to this country and was received with a welcome as genuinely warm as if he had all along been regarded with affection and respect.

A part of the answer, no doubt, derives from Begin's own personal demeanor and skills. For all his reputation as a hard-liner, he

can be remarkably ingratiating; his much-noted "Old World courtesy" is a powerful element in his way of presenting himself. But,
with all due credit to the man himself, the more important part of
the answer has to do with how American Jews relate to Israel.

I have described the motives and meanings of the relationship in
earlier chapters. Here we may observe how those motives are translated into the world of daily affairs. Most simply put, America's
Jews have characteristically sought ways not merely to accept Israel's policies and decisions but to endorse them. In the light of what
has been happening in Israel these last years—really, since the 1967
war, a full decade before Mr. Begin's accession—this means that
many of America's Jews have had to find ways to feel comfortable
with policies that—how shall I put it?—do not always conform to
liberal theory. The ways of accommodation have been, as we might
expect, diverse. Some Jews have preferred to focus on Israel's relative virtue, emphasizing, for example, the evidence that its administration of the occupied territories is, by historical standards, quite
benign, even humane. Others have regarded Israel's behavior as
irrelevant; in their view, the occupation was forced on Israel by
Arab obduracy, and ultimate responsibility for the entire matter
therefore rests with the Arabs. Still others have persuaded themselves to accept one or another of the doctrines that bar territorial
concession—either that the Land has been promised Israel, or that
security considerations require that Israel retain it.

Some Jews have been unable to make the accommodation, have
demurred in varying degree from Israel's policies. But the traditional
norm of the community is that our differences with regard to Israel
are to be kept private, a virtual iron curtain drawn around them; the
rest of America is meant to understand that there are no differences
at all, that we are at one with Israel and its leaders. The iron curtain
stays in place not because heavy-handed Israelis or their militant
American acolytes prevent its parting, as is sometimes claimed.
(Which is not to say they don't try.) In the first instance, it stays
there because when Israel engages in controversial actions—the
bombing of Iraq's nuclear reactor, or the closing of West Bank
universities, or the pursuit of relationships with retrograde, even
pariah, states such as South Africa—America's Jews energetically

search out ways to endorse, or failing that to accept, or failing that at least to understand Israel's actions. And when there is no explanation that will wash, there remains the stubborn resolve "not to wash Israel's dirty linen in public," not to "give aid to Israel's enemies," not, that is, "to break ranks."

All of which helps give rise to the impression that the Jews have moved rightward. So also does the emergence in recent years of a group of Jewish political activists who support politicians whose only merit is their fervent endorsement of Israel; on virtually every other issue of Jewish interest, these politicians are very far from where most Jews are.

Mark Siljander, for example, was from 1982 to 1986 the Republican Representative in Congress from the 4th District of Michigan. In 1984, the American Conservative Union gave him its highest rating—100. The Americans for Democratic Action gave him its lowest—zero. Siljander was a leader of anti-abortion and Christian fundamentalist forces in the House of Representatives. He opposed the Equal Rights Amendment; he introduced a bill providing for a series of postage stamps commemorating 1982 as "the Year of the Unborn Child," and for 1983 he had in mind another, "the Year of the Bible." He favored a constitutional amendment guaranteeing the right to prayer in the public schools, arguing that "humanists are shoving their narrow, distorted, perverted self-loving concept down our throats." List the domestic and foreign policy issues that elicit the broadest Jewish consensus, then list Siljander's votes, and step away. Oil and water.

More: In 1984, Siljander co-signed a letter to church officials in the neighboring Congressional District, represented by Howard Wolpe (a Jew), urging them to support Wolpe's opponent and "send another Christian to Congress."

But this same Siljander, with less than 1,200 Jews in his district, was also a prime mover of legislation that would have required the United States to move its embassy in Israel from Tel Aviv to Jerusalem. He co-authored an amendment forbidding the sale of advanced weaponry to Jordan until it negotiates with Israel. On virtually every issue affecting Israel, he was a zealous spokesman for the most ardent (and sometimes most extreme) pro-Israel position. And so it came to pass that in the election season of 1984, Mark Siljander received support from more Jewish political action committees (PACs) than any other Republican candidate for the House.

The Siljander story is interesting because it signifies the emergence of a new group of considerable energy whose political preferences are based on one issue, and one issue only. Be the candidate hemophiliac liberal or sclerotic conservative, so long as he is ardently pro-Israel he wins the support of this new group. If two equally pro-Israel candidates are competing, it prefers the incumbent, even if he or she is in all other respects far to the right of most Jews; the incumbent is, presumably, the better investment. So it was, for example, that incumbent Senator Robert Kasten of Wisconsin, a right-wing conservative, was the recipient in his victorious 1986 campaign for re-election of massive out-of-state support from Jewish political action committees.

Who are these new activists, and how do they rationalize their behavior? Some are authentic conservatives, for whom no rationalization is required. Others are closet conservatives, for whom the neo-conservative dispensation has meant that they can, at last, reveal themselves without embarrassment. But for others, perhaps even for most, the fact of a Senator Kasten's conservatism is irrelevant. They may be new recruits to the political arena, roused from their ideological indifference by the one issue that touches Jews most deeply. Or they may be erstwhile liberals who have either become genuine converts or who have responded to Israel's crisis by making a tactical sacrifice of their traditional political convictions.

Invariably, the rationale for their behavior is the same: "If we don't stand up for Israel, no one else will. And if we don't reward politicians who are pro-Israel with our support, that support will collapse." They make a good case. They ask how an incumbent conservative—say, for example, Senator Kasten, who until the Democrats regained control of the Senate in 1986 was chairman of the appropriations subcommittee on foreign aid—would behave if Jewish support were to flow exclusively to his liberal opponent. They point to their experience with Senators Jesse Helms and Steve Syms, both of whom had abominable records on every issue of Jewish concern, including Israel—until they were assiduously cultivated and, apparently, converted by the new single-issue activists. Now both are much more supportive of Israel's interests.

They also argue that PACs by their very nature must be single-issue-oriented. No legislator can respond to a PAC that importunes him with a laundry list of issues. If a Jew wants to be both pro-Israel and, say, pro-abortion, let him contribute to two PACs. Or let him reconsider his priorities and decide which issue matters most. That is what it means to defend the Jewish interest.

Finally, they argue, it is well for the Jews to be represented in all political camps. Whether or not they can successfully influence the outcome of the election, they must be sure that whoever wins, the Jews will have access to the victor. And many who are discomfited to find Jews in the camp of a Jesse Helms are at the same time relieved to find them there; it may not be good ideology, but it's smart politics.

All this is interesting and makes for good copy, but an interesting story is not yet an important story. Upon examination, it turns out that there's much less to the story of the single-issue PACs than meets the eye. The PACs have had only limited impact on the pattern of Jewish political contributions, still less on the pattern of Jewish voting, notwithstanding the fuss that's been made about them. In May of 1986, for example, *The New Republic* featured on its cover, in very large type, an article entitled "Unholy Alliance: The New Role of Jewish PACs and How They May Save the Republican Senate." The article, by Robert Kuttner, begins with the phrase from *Exodus*, "Now there arose a new king over Egypt, who knew not Joseph." The opening accurately suggests the tenor of the article. It reports that, "By 1985, in a general climate of pro-incumbent campaign-finance and single-issue politics, [Jewish PACs] were giving about 60 percent of their funds to Republicans and over 90 percent to incumbents."

But six months later, working with more detailed and timely data, Michael J. Malbin offered a rather different analysis. In "The Jerusalem Letter" (November 3, 1986), Malbin examined the fifteen largest PACs, which together accounted in 1986 for more than 75 percent of all contributions by Jewish PACs, and he found that 35 percent, not 60 percent, of their contributions went to Republicans. Recalling that roughly one third of Jewish voters are Republican, why be surprised that 35 percent of Jewish political contributions are to Republican candidates? Furthermore, Malbin showed that in the 1986 elections, Jewish PACs supported Republicans only where they were incumbents: in thirteen key Senate races, the single exception was in Louisiana, an open seat where PAC money went to both the Republican and the Democrat. In three of the races, the PACs supported Democratic challengers of Republican incumbents; in none did a Republican challenger of a Democratic incumbent receive support. In *every* case where the seat was open, PAC support went to the Democratic nominee; all Democratic incumbents were supported.

It may sound logical that the combination of liberal disarray and Jewish concern for Israel has rendered the liberal-conservative choice irrelevant to Jews, that they are distributed not on a left-right spectrum but on a "good for Israel versus bad for Israel" spectrum. But the facts apparently follow a different and older logic. That is why at the same time Robert Kasten was getting all those single-issue contributions, he was losing the Jewish vote in Wisconsin decisively, and that is why if Mark Siljander had been running from a district with a significant Jewish population, he would surely have failed to win more than a sprinkling of Jewish votes.

Happily, we can move beyond informed speculation here. In his 1986 survey, Steven Cohen asked respondents to rank four hypothetical candidates for the United States Senate: a liberal Democrat who is very pro-Israel; a liberal Democrat who is moderately pro-Israel; a conservative Republican who is very pro-Israel; and a conservative Republican who is moderately pro-Israel. In all, 72 percent preferred one of the two liberal Democrats, 80 percent favoring the one who is "very pro-Israel"; by contrast, the two conservative Republicans were the first choice of only 30 percent (again, 80 percent favoring the pro-Israel candidate). There is no surprise in the preference for Democrats, nor in the finding that within each party, it is the pro-Israel candidate who is favored. It is more interesting to see what happens when people are forced to choose between moderately pro-Israel candidates who share their party preference and very pro-Israel candidates who differ from that preference. Here we find that two thirds of the respondents choose loyalty to their party preference over an increase in "pro-Israelism." For most of the sample, the leap from liberal Democrat to conservative Republican (or vice versa) is harder to make than the move from "very" to "moderately" pro-Israel. In Cohen's words, "most American Jews choose to remain loyal to their larger political philosophy than to opt for marginally increased support for Israel."

In time, the single-issue PACs may lead to a change in Jewish attitudes and preferences; the active support of conservative candidates by prominent Jews does, after all, provide an acceptable rationale for the political reorientation of larger numbers. But for now, Jewish voters remain by and large liberal Democrats, and the number of Jewish political activists who play critical roles in promoting liberal candidates has almost surely not diminished over the years. Moreover, the single-issue debate has recently been explicitly joined by the founding of MIPAC (for multi-issues political action committee), which asserts that while a candidate's support for Israel is a necessary condition for MIPAC endorsement, it is not a sufficient condition: human rights, Church-State separation, civil rights, social justice, women's rights, and the nuclear threat must all be taken into account. Already, MIPAC has been joined by six more Jewish PACs—out of some seventy-five—that explicitly reject the single-issue strategy. Together, these have recruited a significant number of leaders of the Jewish liberal community, and have thereby begun to serve, albeit still modestly, as alternatives to the continuing ascendancy of the single-issue PACs.

I write these paragraphs, and they are a fair summary. But they are too easy, too pat. Squeezing the concern of American Jews for Israel's safety into the ongoing debate between liberals and neoconservatives illuminates only a small part of Israel's impact on how we perceive ourselves and the world "out there." Israel is such an overwhelming issue for us that it collapses the conventional categories of politics. And in a curious way, not at all related to the single-issue argument, our ties to Israel do put our traditional liberalism at risk.

Before the Lebanon War of 1982, there were pockets of people within American Jewry who disagreed with the policies of Israel's government. But because people were made to feel that to air their dissent vocally would be to commit a near-treasonous act, their criticisms were mostly whispered. One stood with Israel and its policies or one had the decency to be silent—or one stood outside the Jewish community.

But there were exceptions. In 1978, thirty-seven American Jews sent a cable of support to a rally of the Peace Now movement in Israel. In 1980, fifty-six American Jews, many of them pillars of the Jewish community, associated themselves with a declaration that had been signed by 240 prominent Israelis—including several former cabinet ministers, members of the Knesset, and military leaders. In both cases, all the American signers were people of impeccable pro-Israel credentials; the signers of the second, which kicked up much the greater storm, included three past chairmen of the Conference of Presidents of Major Jewish Organizations, five members of the World Zionist Executive, a dozen past or current officers of the United Jewish Appeal, another dozen rabbis. Both statements expressed opposition to Mr. Begin's West Bank peace policy in general and to his settlement policy in particular. Both were quite restrained, well within the range of accepted political debate in Israel. And both were widely covered in the American press.

I had signed both statements, and was identified in the press as one of those who had helped gather the other signatures. In the ensuing weeks, I received many letters. Some applauded my behavior; most did not, and it is illuminating to read what the critics had to say. Israel, they wrote, is a vulnerable place, and the Jews are a vulnerable people. Israel's enemies are legion, and those enemies will pounce gleefully on discord among its defenders and seek however they can to exploit it. The task of those who would defend Israel from afar is to defer to Israel's own choices and to defend those choices. Or to be silent. More specifically, as one of my correspondents reminded me, no one can be certain how much of the extraordinary level of support that Israel enjoys in the Congress depends on the perception that virtually all American Jews stand resolutely with it. And as many of my critics insisted, there is, too, the ethical problem: by what right do we here, from our safely distant perspective, presume to advise our brothers and sisters in Israel, whose choices may well determine whether their sons and daughters live or die?

This brief summary does not begin to capture the passionate feelings of my correspondents. Here are some representative excerpts from their letters:

> You seem to belong to the group of professors who really have not learned from our experience with Nazi Germany. . . . But truth will prevail, and in the end, after more murder and anguish, we shall survive in spite of good doers like you.

> It was bad enough that a large segment of the American intellectual left prevented us from winning the war in Vietnam. . . . We cannot let thinkers of this ilk prescribe for Israel. The results will be the same.

> You people who want to give in to the Arabs are only helping in the destruction of Israel. You have indeed gone over to the Arab side in this war. . . . Every person who signed that stupid statement condemning the West Bank settlements should hang his head in shame for the knife he has plunged into Israel's back. . . . May G-d forgive you for your crimes against Israel. I certainly won't.

> We have had enough talk about the pinpricks of [West Bank] settlements from the State Department Arabists. We don't need any more from Jewish American leaders.

> A husband-wife can tolerate private criticism of each other, but public airings are too damaging. We Jews are one big family, and we need to present a solid front to the world.

> You and others should not complain so publicly against Israel. You did not fight in its many wars in which so many thousands of Israelis gave up their lives or were badly wounded.

> G-d forbid that a Palestinian state should be established in Judea and Samaria because of the efforts of Uncle Toms such as you. . . . Israel at this time needs our wholehearted support, and not a stab in the back from timid and renegade Jews, those who are afraid of what their Christian neighbors may say, which is the old ghetto complex.

The seat of the government of Israel is Jerusalem, not Boston. The debate about Israeli government policy should be waged in the Knesset.

What right do you have to publicly speak out against your own flesh and blood? Would you publicly disgrace or shame your own family? What about your collective family?

There is an absolute, traceable relationship between the solidarity of the American Jewish community's support of Israel to the support that legislators feel compelled to give. If our legislators sense a fragmentation of that solid front they must question their own judgment in continuing to support Israel.

It is tempting to dismiss such arguments, even to view them with the contempt we reserve for know-nothing loyalists. But it is not their thumping anger nor even their insult that deserves our attention; it is the active distress they express. Simply put, my correspondents felt betrayed.

Betrayed? Ruth Wisse states the issue pointedly: "The cynical attack on Zionism, drawing no distinction between the politics of the state and its existence, put all Jews on the firing line. Those who donned 'I am a Zionist' buttons and those who did not, understand equally what the historian, J. L. Talmon, eloquently argued, that 'it has become impossible to maintain the distinction between anti-Zionism and anti-Semitism since Auschwitz and since 1948.'"

Here we arrive back where we started in the early chapters of this book. It is exceedingly difficult, perhaps not possible, to disentangle Israel's present from the Jewish past. Given that entanglement, how can we neatly separate anti-Zionism from anti-Israelism and both from anti-Semitism? We claim that our enemies cannot make the distinction; it is no more certain that we can. The memories of Auschwitz and of Hitler are too near. If Wisse's view is accepted, it follows that one may not criticize Israel, for to do so is not merely to give aid and comfort to Israel's enemies; it is to come dangerously close to anti-Semitism.

The same conclusion from a different point of departure: Practical Zionism came to repair the anomalies of the Jewish condition, and utopian Zionism came to create an ideal state. Neither has (yet) fulfilled its promise. Is it not more natural to cling to the older explanation—anti-Semitism is simply endemic to the human condition—than to examine the flaws in Zionist theory? With a sigh or a shudder, we confess that Israel has brought a change in our geography, not in our destiny, a destiny that still threatens, wherever we are, to overwhelm us. And so we conclude that the attack on Israel is to be seen as an attack on the Jews and that Jewish criticism of Israel, therefore, is yet another dreary example of Jewish self-hatred. And worse than dreary; Israel's situation renders such criticism a danger, a threat. A betrayal.

In yet another letter in my file, a man who was at the time the leading spokesman for the organized Jewish community writes that "although I am privately critical of some actions of the Begin government that I regard as short-sighted and counterproductive, I will not be diverted from the main issue by engaging in public debate about those actions." The main issue, in his view, is that the PLO is committed to Israel's extermination. From his letter, we learn that all the arguments for silence are not merely a convenient cover for those whose real agenda is to drum up support for Israel's policies; they inhibit even those who take issue with those policies. With the possible exception of interdenominational hostility, no issue in recent memory has so divided, aggravated, and perplexed the American Jewish community as this matter of dissent, but neither the efforts to squelch dissent nor its denunciation when such efforts fail are evidence of a turn to the right. They are evidence, instead, of the tragedy of Israel's history, of our own troubled memories, and of our intense desire to cling to the dream even as the gray light dawns. Interests and values and memories and this morning's headlines crowd in, confusion and pain in their wake. It is not cowardice that keeps us quiet; it is something else, much deeper, and it must be understood.

Jean Amery was a Jew who lived in France. In one sense, he was a strange sort of Jew: his mother was in fact a Catholic. In another sense, however, he was an entirely conventional Jew: in 1943, he was captured and tortured by the Gestapo and then sent to a series of concentration camps. Here is what he had to say about the difference between those Jews who survived and those who dwelt in safety from 1933 to 1945:

It is with a certain shame that I assert my sad privilege and suggest that while the Holocaust is truly the existential reference point for all Jews, only we, the sacrificed, are able spiritually to relive the catastrophic event as it was or fully picture it as it could be again. Let others not be prevented from empathizing. Let them contemplate a fate that yesterday could have been and tomorrow can be theirs. Their intellectual effort will meet with our respect, but it will be a skeptical one, and in conversation with them we will soon grow silent and say to ourselves: go ahead, good people, trouble your heads as much as you want; you still sound like a blind man talking about color.

Like blind men talking about color; that is how the survivor looks at the rest of us Jews. And that is how the rest of us look at *them*, at all those who so emphatically denounce fascism, cruelty, genocide, but who nonetheless find it possible to patronize Israel by presuming to know better than the Israelis how Jews in our time should behave. When we hear them, we become one with our right-wing brothers and sisters, Orthodox and Reform link arms, secular Jews discover God and soft-spoken Jews shout out.

Here is Amery again:

The existence or the disappearance of the Jewish people as an ethnic-religious community does not excite me. In my deliberations I am unable to consider Jews who are Jews because they are sheltered by tradition. I can speak solely for myself—and, even if with caution, for contemporaries, probably numbering in the millions, whose being Jewish burst upon them with elemental force, and who must stand this test without God, without history, without messianic-national hope. For them, for me, being a Jew means feeling the tragedy of yesterday as an inner oppression. On my left arm I bear the Auschwitz number; it reads more briefly than the Pentateuch or the Talmud and yet provides more thorough information. It is also more binding as a basic formula of Jewish existence.

The reader who recalls my own observations about these matters in Chapter 4 will know that I approach them quite differently. I do not accept, not at all, that Auschwitz provides more thorough information than Sinai. And yet I am bound to say that I am drawn to Amery's words, I understand them, I am, if he will allow me, his brother.

I am his brother even though he tells us that "with Jews as Jews

I share practically nothing: no language, no cultural tradition, no childhood memories," while I share with Jews as Jews all these things. "Before the Holocaust," he says, "my interest in Jewish things and Jews was so slight that with the best of intentions I could not say today which of my acquaintances at that time was a Jew and which was not." Entering a crowded room, I instinctively search out the Jews, as if I were preparing a route of escape should that prove necessary. But though our premises are so radically different, I know him, he is my brother. And here is what this brother writes:

> I read in the paper that in Moscow they discovered an illegally operating bakery for unleavened Jewish Passover bread and arrested the bakers. As a means of nourishment the ritual matzoth of the Jews interest me somewhat less than rye crisps. Nevertheless, the action of the Soviet authorities fills me with uneasiness, indeed with indignation. Some American country club, so I hear, does not accept Jews as members. Not for the world would I wish to belong to this obviously dismal middle-class association, but the cause of the Jews who demand permission to join becomes mine. That some Arab statesman calls for Israel to be wiped off the map cuts me to the quick, even though I have never visited the state of Israel and do not feel the slightest inclination to live there.
>
> . . . Solidarity in the face of threat is all that links me with my Jewish contemporaries, the believers as well as the nonbelievers, the national-minded as well as those ready to assimilate. For them that is perhaps little or nothing at all. For me and my continued existence it means much, more probably than my appreciation of Proust's books or my affection for the stories of Schnitzler or my joy in seeing the Flemish landscape. Without Proust and Schnitzler and the wind-bent poplars at the North Sea I would be poorer than I am, but I would still be human. Without the feeling of belonging to the threatened I would be a self-surrendering fugitive from reality.
>
> I say reality, with emphasis, because in the end that is what matters to me. Anti-Semitism, which made a Jew of me, may be a form of madness; that is not what is in question here. Whether it is a madness or not, it is in any event a historical and social fact. I was, after all, really in Auschwitz and not in Himmler's imagination.

It is frightfully easy to dismiss this way of looking at things as just another Jewish attempt to win sympathy through the baring of old wounds. "There they go again; when everything else fails, they dredge up the Holocaust." But that seems to me entirely too facile a conclusion. It is true that we do a poor job of disentangling past from present, and that can be and often is a very real liability. It is however also true that our past comes as an urgent warning. We do not ask for indulgence. And we are not trying to score points. We are merely insisting that a particular reality of this century, one of which we, as it happens, have special knowledge, be included in the assessment. It is not the only reality, but neither is it just yesterday's misfortune. When we call attention to it, we do not do so in order to say, "Please, we have just come from the madhouse and we must still be permitted our excuses." It is not *our* madness that is at issue here, but theirs. We call attention to it to say, "Be careful. There is a deadly bacillus out there. We know something of the places that bacillus feeds and of the people it infects. And we know a great deal about the damage it can do. It is a killer bacillus that dramatically lowers the life expectancy of the Jews, the same way that smoking or being born in Africa lowers other people's life expectancy. The Jews look perfectly healthy, we know, but this is a bacillus that can strike even the healthiest-looking people with great swiftness. Though its ultimate victims are the Jews, it is not the Jews who are its carriers, it is their neighbors. It is they who succumb to the mad disease called anti-Semitism the bacillus breeds.

"There are, fortunately, two ways which in combination offer considerable protection against it. The first, the more comprehensive, is called liberal, pluralist democracy. And the second is remembering. So we defend democracy and we remind our neighbors. It is up to them to remember, or to forget, for it is they who are threatened with becoming hosts to the bacillus. We are truly sorry to have to call all this to their attention, and we realize that some of them will resent us, so entirely immune do they suppose themselves to be. But please, please: it would be unrealistic for them to claim that they cannot and could not be its carriers. And we do, obviously, have a vested interest here, for once they succumb to anti-Semitism, our lives are in jeopardy."

Most days, we hold back on the warning. Truly, we don't want to spoil everyone's good time. But when it is the fate of Israel that is on the agenda, we are bound to become more vocal. So all of us, loyalists and dissenters alike, agree: We will not be lectured to about Israel's shortcomings, not until those who lecture to us have established their sound health beyond question. Does this sound like Menachem Begin speaking? It does, and I can think of no better illustration of the complexity of these matters than the fact that there are very, very few Jews anywhere, no matter how generous of spirit and liberal of thought, who have not felt these words. Perhaps we cannot distinguish as exactly as we should between neurotic obsession and sober caution. Then again, perhaps our neighbors are too blithe; perhaps it is their capacity for distinction that is wanting. So we say that to err on the side of obsession is not so serious an error.

Saul Bellow wrote that "There is one fact of Jewish life unchanged by the creation of a Jewish state: you [the Jews] cannot take your life for granted. Others can; you cannot." Those words are the conviction—not the sentiment, not the neurosis, but the conviction—of very nearly every Jew.

On the morning the Six Day War began, when the first reports were of Israel being bombed, my liberal friend who had time and again sought to impress upon me the plight of the Palestinian refugees and Israel's responsibility for their plight called to say that his heart was one with mine, that he would pray for the peace of Jerusalem and the safety of the Jews. His words meant much to me during the anxious hours that followed. But his words of the following week, after Israel's victory, meant more: "Haven't you people gone a little too far? I mean, Jerusalem, too?"

Leave to the side the nasty anti-Israelism that so often masks a malignant anti-Semitism; I am thinking of good people, who would be shocked and offended to be classed as enemies, of all those who, upon hearing a scathing attack against Israel, are inclined to say something like, "It went too far, of course, but on the other hand . . . " And that "all" includes many people of the left who are in all other respects my natural comrades.

It is very sad; it hurts, it disturbs. It is sad whether the wedge is driven between liberal Jews and Israel or, as is more often the case, the wedge is driven between the liberal Jew and the liberal non-Jew.

A wedge: There are nine of us at the dinner party, all vaguely part of an academic/literary community, all liberal. Six are Jews, three are not. The conversation is about wine and Kundera, and somewhere along the way it turns to the Jews, and the psychiatrist, known for his blustering confusion regarding his own Jewishness, allows as how "the thing that most Jews are afraid of these days is that they will come to behave like Nazis." And in an entirely conversational tone, as if he were simply stating a piece of conventional wisdom, the man across from him, not Jewish, replies, "Afraid? It's a little late to be afraid, isn't it, with Israel already a Nazi state?"

That scene ended with apology, whether in order to preserve the evening's conviviality or out of conviction I do not know. At how many other such dinner parties are such comments made with or without rebuttal? I do not know that, either. But there is surely the gathering sense that the number grows, that among the very people of the left who yesterday were rooting for Israel there is now impatience, anger, even resentment, that we are therefore talking about something more than conventional sensitivity to criticism from outside the family.

I think that is why so many Jews whose politics are light-years distant from those of Jack Kemp—let alone from those of Jerry Falwell—are cheered by the endorsement such otherwise unfamiliar bedfellows offer Israel. We take reassurance and support from wherever they are offered. The day may come when, listening to and applauding what conservatives and neo-conservatives have to say about Israel, we will begin, without even knowing we have begun, to listen and then to applaud the other things they say. If we turn to a politics of resentment, a choleric and illiberal politics, it will not be because the right has seduced us, but because the left is no longer the home it once was.

Israel, they tell us, trades with South Africa; Israel traffics with the contras; Israel closes universities on the West Bank; Israel is Sparta. And the queasy feeling that it is becoming Sparta by choice, not merely out of necessity, spreads. Israel is adored by Jeane Kirkpatrick and Jack Kemp and liked by the CIA and the Pentagon; all that makes it suspect. Israel is criticized by its own best-known writers;

that makes it suspect. Israel is criticized by liberal American Jews; that makes it suspect. And if those same liberal Jews and Israeli writers try to suggest that there is still much of Athens in Israel, and not only of Sparta, their words are ignored as special pleading.

The better-informed critics speak of the economic gap between Ashkenazim and Sephardim in Israel; we observe that the gap is narrowing, that *that* problem, at least, is on the way to being solved. They speak of Meir Kahane; we remind them of the vigor with which Israeli institutions have responded to Kahane. They speak of Ariel Sharon and his influence; we point out that all nations have their share of brutes, often in high places. They speak of Israel's lack of initiative in the pursuit of peace; we recall to them Hussein's timidity and Assad's bellicosity and Arafat's travesties.

We speak of the kibbutz; they note its embourgeoisement. We speak of the rally of the 400,000 after Sabra and Shatilla; they talk about the Arab students who were killed at Bir Zeit University. We speak of open democracy; they refer to censorship of the Arab press. We speak of a vigorous and independent Supreme Court; they remind us of the murder in cold blood of two captured terrorists, and of the attempted cover-up of those murders by Israel's Security Service. We speak of social democracy, and they remember corruption. The non sequiturs are endless.

No matter that in the privacy of our own conversations we—some of us, at any rate—are troubled by all the things that trouble them. They think, of course, that we are either dissembling or, worse yet, that our zeal has caused us to filter the information we absorb, that we, normally so intricately informed, have with regard to Israel opted to be simpletons. But when we find ourselves defending Israel against their criticisms, we are not dissembling, nor are we unaware of the ways in which Israel falls short of our hopes, and theirs. Our defense is about other things: it is they, we fear, not we, who have permitted preconception to determine conclusion, they who have chosen the data that will confirm their distaste for the Jewish state.

Is it, we wonder, that they simply cannot abide the image of the Jew as muscular? Is it really as simple as that, that the Western imagination can comprehend the Jew only in his historic role as victim, that it can manage the existential Jew but not the actual Jew, that Israel's sin is that it insists on defending itself not merely with words but also with swords?

Perhaps. In the end, we do not understand what it is that causes people with whom we have so much shared history and shared vision to reject, to shun, even to despise that complex place that is so infinitely dear to us. Or we do understand, and do not want to.

I have said that Jews are prisoners of hope. There are Jews who have broken out of that prison, and have joined the cynics or become, as they like to put it, realists. I prefer a more rebellious realism, the hope of the wakeful dream. But the truth is that our dream of a mended world has been choked by disappointments and sorrows beyond counting. To breathe, it needs—we need—reassurance. Until now, we've found that in the house of the left, which has meant much more to us than temporary shelter; it's not been just a house for us, but our home, the place we've found the strength that comes from living with people who share the dream. And it is a bitter hurt that some of these now say that we can't live there any more, not unless we renounce that part of the hope and the dream we call Jerusalem. We don't need the left to say, "Thank you," but we cannot handle its saying, "You're not welcome."

So we may, after all, be on the verge of a new turn in the politics of the Jews. While there is no evidence that traditional Jewish suspicion of the right has softened, it is entirely possible that traditional Jewish at-homeness on the left has been shaken. It has been assaulted ever since the New Left chose to dissociate itself from Israel; it has suffered from the perceptible rise in anti-Semitism among educated blacks, by the evident anti-Zionism of some leading mainstream Protestants, by the assault on Jewish women at the UN women's conferences in Mexico City, Copenhagen, and Nairobi, by insufferable remarks at congenial dinner parties.

Of course, one might argue that insofar as old allies have turned against the Jews and/or Israel, they have themselves abandoned liberalism. But that only compounds the problem of Jewish political homelessness. For if that be the case, it simply feeds the traditional Jewish sense of abandonment. We have stayed pure; it is the others who have betrayed us. It is for this reason that the effects of the assault may not show up (immediately) in increased Jewish support of the right. Instead, we may observe a two-stage process: disenchantment with the left unaccompanied by any new dispensation, only then leading to some new and still unpredictable realignment in the politics of America's Jews.

The signers of the two statements *did* go public, all these vexing matters notwithstanding. What was it that finally led them to do that? With what arguments did they stand against the weight of Jewish sentiment, both organizational and popular, and against the logic that underlay the sentiment?

A general appreciation of free speech is not enough. Although a community that declares its most passionate concerns to be beyond debate may soon lose the capacity for civil disagreement, prudential wisdom may well lead people to conclude that in any specific instance, their own freedom to speak is best not exercised. If you believe that Israel is reluctant to tackle the problem of peace with the needed sense of urgency, do you propose to the American government that it press Israel harder? How hard? Do you propose that the sale of American arms to Israel be made contingent on a change in Israel's policies? Are you that sure of your position, and of Israel's capacity to defend itself without those arms?

I cannot speak for all the other signers. I assume, though, that their reasons were not so very distant from my own. Here is one: Why should the leaders of Israel's government be able to make the unrebutted claim that American Jews are united behind their policies when that is not, in fact, the case? When they make that claim, they inject American Jewry into Israel's ongoing political debate. If our alleged support is a relevant datum in that debate, is not the fact that some of us, at least, side with their domestic critics also relevant?

And another: What are we to do, those of us who deeply believe that a particular course that Israel has chosen is profoundly mistaken, endangers the nation? Are we to be silent, or is it our duty to speak out? We are advised to speak our views in private; what is the use of political pillow-talk?

And again, do we not, as a community, lose our credibility if we rubber-stamp every action the Israelis take? Following the telegram of 1978, its signers were asked to oppose, as a group, the proposed sale of F-15 fighter aircraft to Saudi Arabia. (They agreed, and did.) Why were they asked? Because, it was explained to them, their earlier dissent had established that they were not merely—as Jewish organizations were—an echo of Israel's government. (And again, in 1980, the fifty-six signers were asked to issue a statement endorsing the status of Jerusalem as Israel's undivided capital. And again, they did.)

And more: Is it wise to imply to the Jewish public that there is no room in the organized Jewish community for those lovers of Zion whose views do not accord with its government's? Must one either stand in locked embrace with, say, Ariel Sharon—or, for that matter, with Yitzhak Rabin—or else be thought a traitor?

And what if everything you know and believe tells you that when one people rules another, hostile people, no matter the power of the justification, no matter the elegance of the rationale, the result is inevitably a corruption of the soul?

And finally, if, in your judgment, this or that course of Israeli action is likely to lead to blood and to death, must you not—even from your own safe home—speak words of warning? From the Talmud: "Whoever can remonstrate against the sins of his household and does not, is seized [held responsible and punished] for the sins of his household; whoever can remonstrate against the sins of his fellow townsmen and does not, is seized for the sins of his fellow townsmen; and of the whole world, he is seized for the sins of the whole world." (Shab., 54b; Ab. Zar., 18a) Where does responsibility lie?

Before Lebanon, invited to lecture to a Jewish audience, I'd often be asked to talk about something other than the Middle East. Since Lebanon, that hasn't happened. Nor do people any longer come up to me after a lecture on these matters and say, "Thank you so much for saying out loud what we've been whispering to each other." The war itself, and the events at Sabra and Shatilla in particular, mark the beginning of the change, and it has accelerated since, pushed by a series of Israeli behaviors that have confused, outraged, and even alienated significant numbers of America's Jews. The key events include, but are not limited to, the Pollard affair and the evident inability of the Israelis to come to grips with their Jewish fundamentalists.

More generally, it is now clear that Israel is a nation that makes its fair share of mistakes, that has its fair share of rogues. America's Jews are just now beginning to adjust to this new understanding, and it is not an easy adjustment. We have to learn how to defend Israel without apology—without apologizing for Israel's blunders, without apologizing for the fact of our defense. We have to learn how to sustain our attachment despite our disappointments. We have to learn how to prevent the disappointments from unbalancing our appraisal of the earthly Jerusalem, where flowers still bloom, where good men and women daily do battle for justice and sometimes win. We have to learn how to regather our energies lest our dream be reduced to yet another page in the book of Jewish nostalgia. The voices that now cry, "Woe unto us, what happened to the dream?" must learn again to cry out, "Clear in the desert a road for the Lord!" Most of all, we have to learn, together with the Israelis, how to understand Israel as the joint endeavor of the Jewish people. There is a place to stand between the impossible dream and the rude awakening, and we—and the Israelis—have to find that place, and stand there.

I cannot gainsay the disappointments we feel, and not just in Israel. It is tempting to give up, to accept that Irving Kristol is right when, as I have already noted, he says, "Evils exist, we don't know why they exist, and we have to have faith that, in some larger sense, they contribute to the glory of the world," as also when he asserts that "Human nature and human reality are never transformed." In our fatigue and disappointment, we may be inclined to agree.

But to agree, to allow the disappointment to defeat the commitment—the commitment to tomorrow, the commitment to *tikun olam*—would be a tragic error. It would be to join in what might be called a "self-fulfilling rabbinism," to prescribe an attitude that would aggravate rather than cure the evil. It would, I think, subvert our survival, for it would deprive us of our reason to survive. And surely it would betray the particular wisdom that comes of our being that new thing in history, the American Jew.

Faith helps, but not a faith that counsels resignation. We are not, after all, "gardeners without flowers." We have flowers in profusion, and even though we must live with the ugly prospect that the flowers we plant in the morning will be trampled before night, we come back to plant again the next morning. We do that because we recall and have faith in the promise: They who plant in sorrow will reap in joy. We do it because we have faith that in this, a world that once knew Eden, the weeds will not defeat the flowers. We do it because of our experience: We have seen not only death and misery, but life and kindness. We do it because of our character: We are a stiff-necked people. We do it out of self-interest: To refrain from doing it, to close our eyes and mind our tongues, to withhold our hands and seal our hearts, would be to choose less than life. And we do it because it is the work of the Jews; save as we do it, we will be idle. Hence we do it in the Jewish interest, as well as in God's.

But even faith is not enough.

14

The Vocational Education of America's Jews

BEYOND FAITH, there are the ways and the works of a community. If our concern is with the particular question of how Jewish survival may best be assured, then look to the vigor with which the community seeks to translate its announced commitments into its behavior. If our concern is with the universal question of how the world may best be mended, then look to the tenacity with which the community seeks to preserve and transmit its definition of the good life. The ways and the works of the community are our curriculum.

Our curriculum had its origins at the base of a desert mountain some 3,200 years ago; it has since been amended, expanded, contracted, by the choices of every generation of Jews. Now it is ours. Some Jews are satisfied to pay vague homage to the tradition of compassion that seems somehow to come with being Jewish, but that is dishonest; compassion does not just "come," it is not in our genes. Compassion and all those other things we value are transmitted from generation to generation through the living community, through what it chooses to remember and how it chooses to live. Other Jews try to "renew our days as of old," whether old be the times of the shtetl or of Birmingham, Selma, and the March on Washington. Imitation of days gone by flatters those who came before, but it, too, is dishonest; these are neither the 1860s nor the 1960s. Whichever the yesterday we try to copy, we will fail, for yesterday was not an abstraction. It was a specific point in space and time and a specific community living and responding there and then. Here and now, it is our own story we must write, and live. That is the starting place for authenticity.

At the same time, we want our story to belong in the chronicle of our people. It is no more authentic to pretend that we are not who we are than it is to pretend that we are not where and when we are. We are American Jews, heirs to a hundred generations of interpretation, now charged and challenged to add our own.

I have quite pointedly avoided writing that we are in any sense required to advocate this social policy or that. The policy choices that confront us are matters of prudential judgment, and reasonable people, equally learned and devoted Jews, men and women of goodwill all, will inevitably differ in such judgments. The tradition does not provide a detailed political program for our time. But it does provide a framework. That is what I have been arguing, and the argument rests, finally, on my view of Jewish and of human authenticity.

The Jewish commitment to pluralism, a commitment that reflects both our interests and our values, carries with it certain implications. It implies, for example, a bias in favor of civil liberties and civil rights, and shifts the burden of proof onto those who would in any way restrict or impede them. The Jewish commitment to social justice, a commitment that grows out of both our texts and our experiences, implies a bias in favor of programs and policies that express our responsibility one for the other. As Michael Walzer wisely observes, the radicalism of the Bible in this regard is reinforced by the history of the "internal life, the social and moral character of the [pre-modern] diaspora communities"; they were, he says, "participatory welfare states." Isadore Twersky, arguing from a very different point of view but coming to very much the same conclusion, tells us that the medieval community that was governed by Talmudic law was, in effect, "a modified welfare city-state, with its special functionaries who collect the compulsory levy and act as trustees for the poor and the needy."

Of course the analogies are imperfect; of course there are other roads from then to now. Still, I think it no accident that this generation of American Jews has seen fit to travel the road that leads from Isaiah's clothing the naked and feeding the hungry through the medieval communities Walzer and Twersky describe to the modern welfare state. At our best, we have found on that road a future for our past, an authentic meaning.

No, we are not paragons of virtue. Just as some Jews are mesmerized by religious ritual, never moving beyond rhythm to melody, so are some entranced by the beauty of prophetic rhetoric, never moving beyond words to works. I have listened to Jews praise their own concern for the black Jews of Ethiopia and have heard those same Jews contemptuously say "shvartzeh" when talking about American blacks. I have known Jews who readily sign generous checks for all manner of worthy philanthropy but who scorn the street people. We cheat on our taxes, we speak with malice, we trade on insider information, we neglect our parents, we own slum buildings and do nothing to repair them, *ashamnu, bagadnu,* we have sinned, we have transgressed, we have been inauthentic. And we settle too soon for some sweet words and noble sentiments that will make us feel good.

But the words alone will not do. Words alone cannot make us whole. A vocabulary list is not yet a language; it lacks a grammar to bring it to life. One can easily point to the shortcomings of this generation and conclude that it has no grammar, hence no living Jewish language. One can dismiss this generation with contempt, so often does it seem that all it knows of language is S.O.S., the language of distress. But it seems to me that though we are not fluent, though many of us have had to learn to do Jewish as a second language, though some of us can only follow others' conversation and some of us not even that, most Jews remain at least accessible. We are not, save as we choose to be, reduced to the telling of how it used to be; there is that road, and most of us still know where it is and where it leads.

I believe that not as an act of faith, but on the evidence. One exhibit: All the data of the last several chapters, showing how we remain committed to a progressive politics. I know, of course I know, how far the programs and policies we support are from a politics of righteousness. They are, however, still farther from a politics of selfishness. What they lack in indignation they make up in compassion. Sometimes they tilt too far in the direction of stability, but never so far that the claims of justice are forgotten. Assert those claims, and they are a homing call to Jews; that is what being accessible to the language means.

Another exhibit: In the late 1960s, the tenants of several slum buildings owned by an Orthodox Jew in Boston's South End neighborhood decided to picket their landlord. Afraid that they would be accused of anti-Semitism, they invited a prominent local rabbi, known for his civil rights activism, to join with them on the picket line. He agreed, and, while marching, had a flash of inspiration: Since the landlord was Orthodox, and since he was plainly not only in violation of the city's housing code but also of Jewish law, why not ask the local Beth Din—the Jewish religious court—to become involved? The court, administered at the time by an uncommonly innovative and energetic rabbi, agreed to hear the tenants' complaint, and the landlord accepted its jurisdiction. For some weeks, it took evidence, and then, for the better part of a year, sought to arrive at a constructive solution of the dispute. Finally, an agreement was reached whereby the tenants would be enabled to buy the buildings from the landlord and, with government help, to repair them. The price the landlord was to be paid was considerably less than his profits as an owner, and the agreement also forbade him ever again to purchase property in a slum or a marginal neighborhood anywhere in the United States. Because the circumstances were so unusual, and the agreement so novel, the formal signing of the agreement was a much-publicized event, well covered by all the local media.

Shortly before the event was to begin, three of us who had been involved in one way or another with the case were standing in a corner of the room with the landlord. He was fully aware that the agreement he was about to sign was, from a business standpoint, unwise. Plaintively, he turned to us and asked, "What was it I did that was so wrong? All I wanted was to put away a few pennies for my old age, to have something to leave my children. Is that so bad?"

Whereupon one of our group responded, "Which is more important, money or a good name?"

At that question, no minimally literate Jew can hesitate. The answer, of course, is, "A good name."

To offer that answer, one need not recall the original form of the question: *Tov shem mishemen tov*—literally, "A good name is better than fragrant oil"—nor know that its origin is in the Book of Ecclesiastes. Functional literacy is all that is required.

The landlord, having attained that level, gave the appropriate response and, minutes later, found himself signing the documents in the glare of the television cameras. (It makes a nice ending to the story to add that when it came time for the administrator of the Beth Din to make a speech—the cameras still going—he proceeded to thank the various people who'd been involved, from Boston's mayor on down, and came, finally, to the landlord, whom he described as "a prince of a man, a uniquely caring and responsible human being, a model for us all." It took a few minutes for those of us who listened to the praise with disbelief to understand that what the good rabbi had done was to keep his end of the bargain. He'd given the landlord a good name.)

Anecdotes are not evidence; they are merely suggestive. In this case, the anecdote of a particular man in a particular place suggests that perhaps others, elsewhere, can still be called home. I think, for example, of the story of Mazon, an organization that was founded in 1985 to help in the fight against hunger, in America and around the world. The Mazon idea is disarmingly simple: Whenever Jews celebrate a bar or bat mitzvah, a wedding, non-ritual occasions as well, let them add 3 percent to the cost of their celebration and forward it to Mazon for distribution to soup kitchens and food pantries and agencies that work to put an end to hunger. On Yom Kippur, hundreds of rabbis take the time to talk about Mazon, to call attention to the fact that ours is a voluntary fast, that around the world there are a billion people whose fast will not end at sundown. At Passover, Mazon takes the traditional words, "Let all who are hungry enter and eat," and proposes a more modest and more achievable goal, "Let *one* who is hungry enter and eat." Add the cost of one more guest at the seder table, one who was too weak or too distant to hear the invitation, and let Mazon give meaning to our words.

I tell of Mazon here not to explain the idea but to describe the response. Within months of its founding, it had received thousands of contributions, and with as many as half those contributions there came notes and letters of thanks. Its growth has been far more rapid than its founders had anticipated, and the reason, I think, goes back to the matter of a living language. Jews remember, however vaguely, that we used to leave the corners of our fields ungathered so the poor could come and take. Perhaps they even remember that in East Europe, the beggars of the town were routinely invited to attend the wedding celebrations. Surely they know the words of the Passover Haggadah. And the letters of thanks suggest that they are grateful to be afforded the opportunity to breathe life into those words.

Viewed differently, Mazon can be dismissed as an exercise in cheap grace; it's all too easy, too tepid, too removed from the hard work of real repair, of *tikun olam*. It is, at best, about social kindness; it is not about social justice. Where are the barricades, where is the banner?

No barricades, not this time, not here. That is the point of America. Here the challenge is to retain the sense of urgency, the passion, absent the thrill of the ramparts. And the point of Judaism, and its challenge, is not to stop with kindness, to remember always that praiseworthy though kindness be, it is no substitute for justice. Mazon refreshes a language and thereby helps renew a commitment. Where public policy is indifferent to that commitment or inadequate to meet it, alms are a practical and moral necessity, a stopgap way of living our language. But the commitment is not about making ourselves feel good; it is about healing the sick and clothing the naked and feeding the hungry, it is about building a society in which the downtrodden are not dependent on individual largess, are instead our collective responsibility.

It would be much easier to regard the synagogue as a sanctuary from such challenge, a place to retreat from the political debate. In its nurturing rituals, it does offer such refuge. But there is an intrinsic connection between the pulpit and the public square. While there are many ways to help mend the world, it is through public policy that we define what we mean by freedom and by justice. Ours is a communal commitment, and I know of no serious argument that permits an apolitical Judaism.

Our problem may well be with the words we use. "Public policy" has a nice, clean, non-partisan sound, one can study it at Harvard or Berkeley; "politics," on the other hand, sounds—and is—messy, vaguely disreputable. Well, the world is messy. That is why it needs mending. It will not lie down quietly on the orthopedic surgeon's table and let its fractures be set. It is difficult to see how it can be redeemed without entering the frayed debate, called by whatever name it is. So for all that we might prefer a religion of customs and ceremonies, or even of acts of loving-kindness, that is not how ours was intended.

We are not unique in that. American Catholics vehemently debate the social mission of the Church, the wisdom, for example, of the United States' Bishops Pastoral Letter on the Economy. There are those who hold that as the Church can claim no special competence in economic matters, it should keep its distance from them. But since Leo XIII's encyclical *Rerum novarum* in 1891, there has come into existence a body of official Catholic Church teachings on social and economic issues. And since the Second Vatican Council in 1965, the basis for such teachings has been dramatically extended. In 1971, the Synod of Bishops asserted that "Action on behalf of justice and participation in the transformation of the world fully appear to us as a constitutive dimension of the preaching of the gospel, or, in other words, of the church's mission for the redemption of the human race and its liberation from every oppressive situation."

Charles E. Curran (the Catholic theologian who, in 1987, was relieved of his teaching duties at the Catholic University of America by the Vatican) details the unfolding view of the Church in his book *Toward an American Catholic Theology,* and goes on to observe that "One can have magnificent liturgy, great preaching, and a marvelous internal community life, but without a social mission one does not have church or the gospel. . . . If the church does not become involved in social transformation, it has betrayed the gospel and its own redemptive mission."

Does that not hold as well for the Jews? We have no Synod of Rabbis who can authoritatively proclaim it, but the People Israel knows it. What else is there for us? Except as we are sustained and connected by our wakeful dream of a tomorrow more whole, what difference can it make whether we continue to cling together? For a touch of human warmth? For safety's sake? Is that what remembering tomorrow comes down to?

We grumbled when we left Egypt; better, we thought, the visible taskmaster than an uncharted desert, an unknowable god, an uncertain promise of a better place: "If only we had died by the hand of the Lord in the land of Egypt, where we sat by the fleshpots, where we ate our fill of bread." (Ex.16:3) We mutter and grumble still: fleshpots still, and still a tomorrow uncharted. But between then and now, our people has written itself into history. We have believed some things about who we are and what we stand for, about what we are capable of and what our vocation is. All that, which is what has sustained us through all our travails, cannot be reduced to a few code words, whether the words are drawn from the vocabulary of fear or from the vocabulary of hope. No list of words can take on the burden that rightfully belongs to a community; there is no substitute for the language of life. We need better schools and we need better teachers, that we may lay competent claim to the received experience of our people. It is folly to imagine that without knowing whence we have come, we can know where we must go. But above all, we need a living community that nourishes our vision, that lives our language and thereby helps make us fluent once again, a community that reminds us not only of the yesterdays we've shared but also of the tomorrow we anticipate.

So on to the work of translation, the translation of the language of a silent God into the voice of a human community, into the ways of an ancient people. In the mending, that translation happens and our hope is fulfilled. Our hope: That despite the evidence of absurdity, meaning is possible. I call it a hope and not a prayer because if there is meaning to be found, it must be searched out, we must be alive to it. It is not God who gives us meaning, but our own quest for godliness, there where we reconnect with the broken world. And so with each other.

Many pages ago, I began this book with a question, and then a *midrash* on the question. It is the first question, and, as I said then, the most important question we are asked: Where are you?

But it is, in truth, only half a question. Its corollary happens just twenty-three verses later in the Biblical narrative: Where is your brother?

The one question implies the other, for in order to know the answer to the one, we must know the answer to the other. To say, "I do not know where my brother is," is to confess that I do not know where I am, for in the family of humankind, I can have no independent location.

And then, of course, there is a third question, to save us from smugness: *Who* is our brother?

And then come all the other questions, the flood of questions, signposts for a life whose paths are paths of pleasantness, whose ways are ways of peace. And of outrage, and of hope. Signposts for life as an answer, as a vocation.

Where are we? *Hineinu;* here, if we so will it, we are.

Source Notes

Introduction

Hentoff's quote is in Hentoff, ix. For a general background to contemporary American Jewry, including demographic information, see especially Cohen, *American Modernity and Jewish Identity* and Silberman, *A Certain People.* All biblical quotations are from the Jewish Publication Society translation.

Chapter 1: Starting Over

The gloomy prognoses were legion. See, for example, Thomas B. Morgan, "The Vanishing American Jew," in *Look,* May 5, 1964 or Eric Rosenthal, "Jewish Fertility in the United States," in *American Jewish Yearbook,* 1... ..., 1961. On "a resurgence of interest," see especially Silberman. Data on Jewish population growth in both the United States and in European cities are from Mendes-Flohr and Reinharz. On "psychic mobility," see both Becker and Lerner. On the "transformation" of the Jews in the wake of the Enlightenment, see Hertzberg, both *The French Enlightenment* and *The Zionist Idea,* as well as Katz, *Out of the Ghetto.* There is a fascinating discussion of Zangwill and *The Melting Pot* in Sollors. On "keeping your god," see

Bellah's "Civil Religion," as well as the discussion of Bellah in Cutler. The Wolfson quote is from "Pomegranates" in *Menorah Journal,* February 1918. The Jefferson, Adams, and Wilson quotes are cited in Gordon at pp. 91, 94, and 101. The Deutscher quote is from a companion essay, "Who Is A Jew?," in Deutscher at p. 51.

Chapter 2: Jews, God, and Judaisms

"Predicate theology" is described in Schulweis, *Evil and the Morality of God.* Anski is at pp. 51–52. The literature on *midrash* is vast; for a brief introduction, see Stern. My discussion of the relationship between the Jewish text and the Jewish reader draws on Edmond Jabes' essay, "The Question of Displacement into the Lawfulness of the Book," in Jabes, pp. 227–44. On interpretation, see especially Walzer, *Interpretation and Social Criticism.* Shazar is at pp. 189–90. Schulweis on "absence of structured ethical theory" is in "The Single Mirror" at p. 5. Bleich's quote is at p. 32.

Chapter 3: Competence and Meaning

The Klass quote is from *The Jewish Press* of August 14, 1987. Soloveitchick is quoted in the *Long Island Jewish World* of May 29–June 4, 1987, at p. 20. Biale is at p. 108. The 1981 survey of the religious beliefs of Americans is in Martire and Clark at p. 99. Lenn provides the data on Reform rabbis; the 1986 survey is Cohen's *Ties and Tensions.* The responses to "Without Jewish religion . . ." and "To be a good Jew . . ." are from Woocher at pp. 110 and 113. Data on religious practice are from the several Cohen surveys, as also from Silberman and Woocher. Christian perceptions of Jews are described in Martire and Clark as also in Tarrance et al. I am indebted to Dr. Alvin Schiff for making the data from the Board of Jewish Education study available to me even as it was being readied for publication. The Buber quote is from *Israel and The World* at p. 95.

Chapter 4: Mourning as Meaning

The Roth quote is at pp. 41–42. The Cardinal O'Connor episode was reported by Joseph Berger in *The* .... january 3,

1987. Fackenheim's "614th commandment" recurs throughout his writings; a detailed exposition is in *God's Presence in History*, at p. 84 ff. Kovner is at p. 93. The Levi quote is at pp. 35–36. Nelly Sachs poem is at p. 59. The Pagis poem is in Carmi at p. 575.

Chapter 5: Israel as Meaning: The Faith, The Place

The Gilboa poem is in Carmi at p. 562. Hertzberg is in his *Being Jewish in America* at p. 223. The Agnon poem appears in *Moment*, October 1977. The measure of New York Jewish student attitudes toward Israel is from *Inventory of Jewish Knowledge, Jewish Involvement and Jewish Attitudes*, a study by the Board of Jewish Education of New York. (Prime Minister Begin, annoyed during the 1982 Lebanon War that he was charged with having initiated Israel's first optional war, countered by claiming that earlier wars had also been fought at Israel's option. The debate over his claim was vigorously pursued, over a period of several months, in the Israeli press. There is by now a very substantial literature, both scholarly and polemical, on Israel's wars; with the exception of the Sinai Campaign of 1956, there is no clear consensus on their genesis. Lately, even Israel's War of Independence, in 1948, which had generally been assumed to be beyond debate, has been subjected to revisionist scrutiny; see, in particular, Flapan.) The exchange between the soldier and Prime Minister Shamir was reported in *The New York Times* of November 9, 1983. The quotes from *The Seventh Day* are at p. 22 and pp. 253–54. For an account of the Lebanon War of 1982, see esp. Shiff and Ya'ari. The Kahan Commission citations are from *The Beirut Massacre*, passim. The "two kinds of Jews" article is from my "Days of Awe," *Moment*, September 1982. The data on American Jewish attitudes toward Israel are from Cohen, 1983 and 1986.

Chapter 6: Israel as Meaning: Where Is Jerusalem?

For an enlightening discussion of the Jewish attachment to the land, see Davies. The description of Herzl is from Elon. The Halpern citation is at p. 100. Rotenstreich is from *Essays* at pp. 90–91. Among the most useful general histories of Zionism are Hertzberg's *The Zionist Idea*, Avineri, Avishai's *The Tragedy of Zionism*, Vital, and Halpern's *The Idea of a Jewish State.* The Sartre quote is at p. 57. Halkin is at p. 24. The Memmi citations are at pp. 284–85, 294, 290, and 293. The Yehuda Halevi quote is from the second volume of *The Kuzari* at p. 24. Drumont is cited by Bredin. Sartre is at pp. 80–82. On the Jonathan Pollard affair, see the forthcoming books by Wolf Blitzer and by this author. The Harman and Shapira quotes are at p. 40 and p. 37 of *Zionism Today: A Symposium,* a 1986 publication of the Institute on Jewish-Israeli Relations of the American Jewish Committee. (Larry Cohler reports in the *Washington Jewish Week* of October 8, 1987, that at a breakfast meeting with Jewish leaders in Washington, Israel's minister of education and former president, Yitzhak Navon, observed that, "Many Jews are alienated from themselves. By the year 2000 there won't be 11 million Jews outside Israel anymore. There will be only 8 million. And later, that will go down to 5 million.") The Eban quote on American Jewry is from an interview in *Moment,* July/August 1987, pp. 11–16. Halpern is at p. 100 and p. 101. Neusner is from *Stranger,* p. 104. Oz is at pp. 240–41.

Chapter 7: Survival as Vocation

The discussion of descent and consent derives from Sollors. Rawidowicz is at p. 221–22. The story of the Ba'al Shem Tov and his successors appears in a number of places; this is my own rendering. Woocher is at p. 76, and Marmour at p. 28. Hertzberg's discussion of Pollard is in *Hadassah* magazine of May 1987, at p. 9. The Wiesenthal book was published in 1987 by Henry Holt & Co. in New York. The Silberman quote on Bergman is at p. 161. See also Lieberman and Weinfeld, as well as Massarik. The Yankelovitch data are from Martire and Clark at p. 108 and p. 110.

Chapter 8: The American Jewish Synthesis

The Marty quote is at p. 34. Beverly is from his letter to William Fitzhugh on July 20, 1775, quoted in Kammen at pp. 83–84. The first West India letter is from Kammen at p. 64; the second is in Mendes-Flohr and Reinharz at p. 358. (But see also the subsequent letter from the directors of the West India Company, less than a year later, in which they explain their unwillingness to grant the Jews the right to the free and public exercise of their abominable religion," quoted in Mendes-Flohr and Reinharz at pp. 358–59.) The Ciardi is from his poem "Most Like an Arch This Marriage," in *I Marry You*, New Brunswick, 1958. The Pittsburgh Platform, along with a transcript of the proceedings out of which it arose and a discussion of its consequences, may be found in Jacob. The Sklare and Greenblum data are at pp. 240–41. The 1986 data are from Cohen, 1986. Woocher is at p. 83. Eisen is at p. 177. Hertzberg is at p. 98 of his *Zionist Idea*. Prager is at p. 5. The Einstein and Peretz quotes are from Goodman, at pp. 113 and 131. D'Allonnes is at pp. 50–51. Samuel is from "The Ethos and Techniques of Survival" in Hindus, at p. 266. The Goldscheider and Zuckerman quotes are from pp. xi, 241, 225. "A detailed examination" is from Goldscheider, p. 171.

Chapter 9: Particularism and Universalism

Feldman is in *Jewish Action*, Vol.46, No.4 (1986) at p. 23. Roth is in "Symposium: Jewishness and the Younger Intellectuals," *Commentary*, April 1961, at p. 351. Howe is in Bloom at p. 386. Kazin is cited by Podhoretz in the *Commentary* 1961 symposium at p. 307. The Abelson, Epstein, Gold, Polsky, Roth, and Podhoretz quotes are at pp. 312, 323, 346, 351, and 309–10 of the symposium. The letter of response appeared in the June 1961 *Commentary* at p. 530.

Chapter 10: Intersections

The Ahad Ha'Am quotes are from "The Transvaluation of Values," in Simon, at p. 228 and p. 231. Rosselli is in Zucotti at p. 246. Scholem is from "Judaism" in Cohen and Mendes-Flohr at p. 506. Ahad Ha'Am is in Simon at pp. 229–31. Friedman is at p. 89. The Kristol quotes are from *Confessions* at pp. 317, 318, and 316. Biale is at pp. 32–33. Walzer is from *Interpretation* at p. 75. (Walzer's detailed comparison of Jonah and Amos (pp. 76–92) brilliantly extends the point.) Kafka is from "The Coming of the Messiah," in Kafka at p. 81. Ignatieff is at p. 141.

Chapter 11: Politics as Vocation

The Lasswell definition, which became a catechism for a generation of political scientists, first appeared in his *Psychopathology*. Himmelfarb is in Isaacs at p. 7. Cohen is in his *American Modernity* at p. 35. The data on Jews and Communism in America are from Klehr, passim. Glazer is from his "The Jewish Role in Student Activism," at p. 20. Perlmutter is from "Jews and American Politics, 1984 and After," in *This World,* Winter 1985, at p. 16. Alan Fisher is at p. 25. Lipstadt, Pruitt, and Woocher are at p. 16. Himmelfarb is from his "Are Jews Becoming Republican?" at p. 31. Glazer is from "Jews and American Politics," in *This World,* Winter 1985, at p. 18. Dawidowicz is from "Politics" at p. 29. Richler is at pp. 76–77. The NJCRAC quotes are at p. 56. Dawidowicz and Goldstein are in "The American Jewish Liberal Tradition" at p. 300. The Podhoretz quotes are from the 1961 *Commentary* symposium; "My Negro Problem," February 1963; "The Tribe," February 1971. Avishai is from "Breaking Faith" at p. 71. Whitfield is from his "Persistence of Liberalism" and his "The Legacy of Radicalism," both in *Voices of Jacob.* Dawidowicz and Goldstein are at p. 300. Kristol is from "The Political Dilemma" at pp. 28, 29, and 23.

Chapter 12: Is It Good for the Jews?

Kristol is from "The Political Dilemma" at p. 25. Wieseltier is in *"This World" Symposium,* "Jews & American Politics: 1984 and After," Winter 85. The ADL study is by Tarrance, Hill, Newport, and Ryan. Baldwin is from "Negroes Are Anti-Semitic Because They're Anti-White," and is included in Hentoff; the quote is from pp. 8 and 9. Kristol's "we must do more of the same" is from "Jewish Voters" at p. 15, and his "We must begin to see things as they are" is from "The Political Dilemma" at p. 28. His "new black political posture" is from "Jewish Voters" at p. 15. (On Jesse Jackson, see the interview with Jackson and the responses in *Tikkun,* November/December 1987, as well as Landess and Quinn.) Kristol on "wish to continue feeling good" is from "Jewish Voter" at p. 15, and on "sermons" and "Jewish interests" from the same article, at p. 14. Kristol on "free lunches" is from "The Political Dilemma" at p. 24.

Chapter 13: Jews and the Liberal Tradition

(There is a growing revisionist literature on Israel's early years, as on the Arab-Israel conflict in general. It is, in my view, too early to assess the importance of the new data and arguments that have been put forward; accordingly, I have presented here, more or less, the conventional understanding.) The material on Begin is drawn from my own experience. Kuttner on PACs is on pp. 19–25. Malbin presents his data in *Jerusalem Letter* of November 3, 1986. Wisse is from "The Anxious American Jew," at p. 48. The Amery quotes are from pp. 93, 94, 97, and 98. Bellow is at p. 26. Kristol on "evil" and on "human nature" is from his *Confessions* at pp. 317 and 318.

Chapter 14: The Vocational Education of America's Jews

Walzer is from "Is Liberalism (Still) Good For the Jews?," in *Moment,* March 1986, at p. 15. Twersky is at p. 146. Curran is at p. 176.

Bibliography

Ahad Ha'Am. *Selected Essays.* Edited by Leon Simon. Philadelphia, 1912.

Amery, Jean. *At the Mind's Limits: Contemplations by a Survivor of Auschwitz and Its Realities.* Translated by Sidney Rosenfeld and Stella P. Rosenfeld. New York, 1986.

Anski, S. *The Dybbuk,* in Joseph C. Landis, *The Great Jewish Plays,* New York, [illegible]

Arendt, Hannah. *The Jew As Pariah: Jewish Identity and Politics in the Modern Age.* New York, 1978.

Avineri, Shlomo. *The Making of Modern Zionism: The Intellectual Origins of the Jewish State.* New York, 1981.

Avishai, Bernard. "Breaking Faith: *Commentary* and America's Jews." *Moment,* March/April 1981.

————. *The Tragedy of Zionism.* New York, 1985.

Baeck, Leo. *This People Israel: The Meaning of Jewish Existence.* Translated by Albert H. Friedlander. New York, 1964.

Bauer, Yehuda, and Rotenstreich, Natan. *The Holocaust as Historical Experience.* New York and London, 1981.

Becker, Howard, and Barnes, Harry Elmer. *Social Thought From Lore to Science,* Vol. 2. 3d ed. New York, 1961.

Bell, Daniel. "Where Are We?" *Moment,* May 1986.

Bellah, Robert N. "Civil Religion in America." *Daedalus,* Winter 1967.

————, and Greenspahn, Frederick E., eds. *Uncivil Religion: Interreligious Hostility in America.* New York, 1987.

Bellow, Saul. *To Jerusalem and Back: A Personal Account.* New York, 1976.

Bendix, Reinhard. *Max Weber: An Intellectual Portrait.* New York, 1960.

⸺, Peter L. *The Sacred Canopy: Elements of a Sociological Theory of Religion.* Garden City, 1969.

Bergman, Elihu. "The American Jewish Population Erosion." *Midstream,* October 1977.

Biale, David. *Power and Powerlessness in Jewish History.* New York, 1986.

Bleich, J. David. "Parameters and Limits of Communal Unity from the Perspective of Jewish Law." *L'Eylah,* No. 21, 1986.

Bloom, Alexander. *Prodigal Sons: The New York Intellectuals and Their World.* New York, 1986.

Borden, Morton. *Jews, Turks, and Infidels.* Chapel Hill, 1984.

Bredin, Jean Denis. *The Affair: The Case of Albert Dreyfus.* New York, 1986.

Buber, Martin. *Israel and the World: Essays in a Time of Crisis.* New York, 1963.

⸺. *On Zion: The History of an Idea.* Translated by Stanley Godman. New York, 1973.

⸺. *The Eclipse of God.* New York, 1957.

⸺. *The Prophetic Faith.* New York, 1949.

Bulka, Reuven P. *The Coming Cataclysm: The Orthodox-Reform Rift and the Future of the Jewish People.* Oakville, Ontario, 1984.

Carmi, T., ed. and trans. *The Penguin Book of Hebrew Verse.* New York, 1981.

Cohen, Arthur A., and Mendes-Flohr, Paul, eds. *Contemporary Jewish Religious Thought.* New York, 1987.

Cohen, Steven M. *American Modernity and Jewish Identity.* New York and London, 1983.

⸺. "Attitudes of American Jews Toward Israel and Israelis." New York, 1983.

⸺. "The 1981–82 National Survey of American Jews." *American Jewish Yearbook,* 1983, pp. 89–110.

⸺. "The 1986 Survey of American Jewish Attitudes Towards Israel and Israelis." New York, 1987.

⸺. "The Political Attitudes of American Jews." New York, 1984.

Curran, Charles E. *Toward An American Catholic Moral Theology.* Notre Dame, 1987.

Cutler, Donald R., ed. *The Religious Situation, 1968.* Boston, 1968.

D'Allonnes, Olivier Revault. *Musical Variations on Jewish Thought.* Translated by Judith Greenberg. New York, 1984.

Davies, W. D. *The Territorial Dimension of Judaism.* Berkeley, 1982.

Dawidowicz, Lucy S. *On Equal Terms: Jews in America, 1881–1981.* New York, 1982.

———. "Politics, the Jews, and the '84 Election." *Commentary,* February 1985.

———, and Goldstein, Leon S. "The American Jewish Liberal Tradition," in Sklare, *The Jewish Community in America.*

Deutscher, Isaac. *The Non-Jewish Jew and Other Essays.* Edited by Tamara Deutscher. London, 1968.

Diner, Hasia R. *In the Almost Promised Land: American Jews and Blacks, 1915–1935.* Westport, Conn., 1975.

Eisen, Arnold M. *The Chosen People in America.* Bloomington, 1983.

———. *Galut: Modern Jewish Reflections on Homelessness and Homecoming.* Bloomington, 1986.

Elazar, Daniel J. *Community and Polity: The Organizational Dynamics of American Jewry.* Philadelphia, 1976.

———, and Cohen, Stuart A. *The Jewish Polity: Jewish Political Organization From Bibilical Times to the Present.* Bloomington, 1985.

Eliade, Mircea. *Myth and Reality.* New York, 1963.

Elon, Amos. ....

Fackenheim, Emil. *Encounters Between Judaism and Modern Philosophy.* New York, 1973.

———. *God's Presence in History: Jewish Affirmations and Philosophical Reflections.* New York, 1970.

———. *The Jewish Return into History.* New York, 1978.

———. *To Mend the World.* New York, 1982.

Fein, Leonard. *The Ecology of the Public Schools: An Inquiry Into Community Control.* New York, 1970.

Feingold, Henry. *A Midrash on American Jewish History.* Albany, 1982.

Fisher, Alan. "The Myth of the Rightward Turn." *Moment,* November 1983.

Flapan, Simha. *The Birth of Israel: Myths and Realities.* New York, 1987.

Freeman, Gordon M. *The Heavenly Kingdom: Aspects of Political Thought in the Talmud and Midrash.* Lanham, Md., 1986.

Friedman, Murray. *The Utopian Dilemma: American Judaism and Public Policy.* Washington, 1985.

Fuchs, Lawrence. *The Political Behavior of American Jews.* Glencoe, 1956.

Gates of Prayer: The New Union Prayerbook. New York, 1975.

Gerth, H. H., and Mills, C. Wright, eds. *From Max Weber: Essays in Sociology.* New York, 19858.

Glazer, Nathan, *American Judaism.* 2d ed., rev. Chicago, 1972.

———. "The Jewish Role in Student Activism." *Fortune,* January 1969.

Glock, Charles Y., and Bellah, Robert N. *The New Religious Consciousness.* Berkeley, 1976.

Glock, Charles Y., and Stark, Rodney. *Christian Beliefs and Anti-Semitism.* New York, 1966.

Goldberg, Harvey E., ed. *Judaism Viewed From Within and Without.* Albany, 1987.

Goldscheider, Calvin. *Jewish Continuity and Change: Emerging Patterns in America.* Bloomington, 1986.

———, and Zuckerman, Alan S. *The Transformation of the Jews.* Chicago, 1984.

Goldsmith, Emanuel S., and Scult, Mel, eds. *Dynamic Judaism: The Essential Writings of Mordecai M. Kaplan.* New York, 1985.

Goodman, Saul L., ed. *The Faith of Secular Jews.* New York, 1976.

Gordon, Milton M. *Assimilation in American Life: The Role of Race, Religion, and National Origins.* New York, 1964.

Halkin, Hillel. *Letters to an American Jewish Friend.* Philadelphia, 1977.

Halpern, Ben. *Jews and Blacks: The Classic American Minorities.* New York, 1971.

———. *The American Jew: A Zionist Analysis.* New York, 1956.

———. *The Idea of a Jewish State.* 2d ed. Cambridge, Mass., 1969.

Handlin, Oscar. *The American People in the Twentieth Century.* Cambridge, Mass., 1954.

Harris, Louis, and Swanson, Bert E. *Black-Jewish Relations in New York City.* New York, 1970.

Hartman, David. *A Living Covenant: The Innovative Spirit in Traditional Judaism.* New York, 1985.

Hartman, Geoffrey H., and Budick, Stanford. *Midrash and Literature.* New Haven, 1986.

Hentoff, Nat. *Black Anti-Semitism and Jewish Racism.* New York, 1970.

Hertzberg, Arthur. *Being Jewish in America: The Modern Experience.* New York, 1979.

———. *The French Enlightenment and the Jews.* New York, 1968.

———, ed. *The Zionist Idea: A Historical Analysis and Reader.* Garden City, 1959.

Heschel, Abraham Joshua. *The Prophets: An Introduction.* 2 vols. New York, 1969.

Himmelfarb, Milton. "Are Jews Becoming Republican?" *Commentary,* August 1981.

———. *The Jews of Modernity.* New York, 1973.

Hindus, Milton, ed. *The Worlds of Maurice Samuel: Selected Writings.* Philadelphia, 1977.

Ignatieff, Michael. *The Needs of Strangers.* New York, 1984.

Isaacs, Harold R. *Idols of the Tribe: Group Identity and Political Change.* New York, 1975.

Isaacs, Stephen D. *Jews and American Politics.* Garden City, 1974.

Jabes, Edmond. *The Sin of the Book.* Edited by Eric Gould. Lincoln, Nebraska, 1985.

Jacob, Walter, ed. *The Pittsburgh Platform in Retrospect.* Pittsburgh, 1985.

Jacobson, Dan. *The Story of Stories: The Chosen People and its God.* New York, 1982.

Kafka, Franz. *Parables and Paradoxes.* New York, 1961.

Kallen, Horace M. *Culture and Democracy in the United States: Studies in the Group Psychology of the American Peoples.* New York, 1924.

Kammen, Michael. *People of Paradox: An Inquiry Concerning the Origins of American Civilization.* New York, 1975.

Kaplan, Mordecai M. *Judaism as a Civilization.* New York, 1934.

Karp, Abraham J. *Haven and Home: A History of the Jews in America.* New York, 1984.

Katz, Jacob. *Exclusiveness and Tolerance: Jewish-Gentile Relations in Modern Times.* New York, 1961.

———. *Out of the Ghetto.* New York, 1978.

Katz, Steven T. *Post-Holocaust Dialogues: Critical Studies in Modern Jewish Thought.* New York, 1983.

Kazin, Alfred. *A Walker in the City.* New York, 1951.

Klehr, Harvey. *The Heyday of American Communism: The Depression Decade.* New York, 1984.

Kovner, Abba. "A First Attempt to Tell," in Bauer and Rotenstreich.

Kristol, Irving. "Jewish Voters and the 'Politics of Compassion.'" *Commentary,* October 1984.

———. *Reflections of a Neoconservative.* New York, 1983.

———. "The Political Dilemma of American Jews." *Commentary,* July 1984.

Kurzweil, Zvi. *The Modern Impulse of Traditional Judaism.* Hoboken, 1985.

Kuttner, Robert. "Unholy Alliance." *The New Republic,* May 26, 1986.

Landess, Thomas, and Quinn, Richard. *Jesse Jackson and the Politics of Race.* Ottawa, Ill., 1985.

Lasswell, Harold. *Psychopathology and Politics.* Chicago, 1977.

Lenn, Theodore I., and Associates. *Rabbi and Synagogue in Reform Judaism.* New York, 1972.

Lerner, Daniel. *The Passing of Traditional Society.* Glencoe, 1958.

Levi, Primo. *Survival in Auschwitz.* New York, 1986.

Levine, Etan, ed. *Diaspora: Exile and the Contemporary Jewish Condition.* New York, 1986.

Levy, Mark R., and Kramer, Michael S. *The Ethnic Factor: How America's Minorities Decide Elections.* New York, 1972.

Lieberman, Samuel S., and Weinfeld, Morton. "Demographic Trends and Jewish Survival." *Midstream,* November 1978.

Liebman, Charles S. *The Ambivalent American Jew: Politics, Religion and Family in American Jewish Life.* Philadelphia, 1973.

Lipstadt, Deborah; Pruitt, Charles; and Woocher, Jonathan. "What They Think: The 1984 American Jewish Young Leadership Survey." *Moment,* June 1984, pp. 13–17.

Mannheim, Karl. *Ideology and Utopia.* New York, 1936.

Marmour, Dow. *Beyond Survival: Reflections on the Future of Judaism.* London, 1982.

Martire, Gregory, and Clark, Ruth. *Anti-Semitism in the United States: A Study of Prejudice in the 1980s.* New York, 1982.

Marty, Martin E. *Religion and Republic: The American Circumstance.* Boston, 1987.

Massarik, Fred. "Rethinking the Intermarriage Crisis." *Moment,* June 1978.

Mayer, Egon. *Love and Tradition: Marriage Between Jews and Christians.* New York, 1985.

Memmi, Albert. *The Liberation of the Jew.* New York, 1966.

Mendes-Flohr, Paul R., and Reinharz, Jehuda. *The Jew in the Modern World.* New York and Oxford, 1980.

Merkle, John C. *The Genesis of Faith: The Depth Theology of Abraham Joshua Heschel.* New York, 1985.

Miller, Alan W. *God of Daniel S.: In Search of the American Jew.* New York, 1969.

Morse, Arthur D. *While Six Million Died.* New York, 1968.

Mosse, George L. *German Jews Beyond Judaism.* Bloomington and Cincinnati, 1985.

Murray, Charles. *Losing Ground: American Social Policy 1950–80.* New York, 1984.

"Negro-Jewish Relations in America: A Symposium." *Midstream,* December 1966.

Neusner, Jacob, ed. *Contemporary Jewish Fellowship in Theory and in Practice.* New York, 1972.

———. *Judaism in the Secular Age.* London, 1970.

————. *Self-Fulfilling Prophecy: Exile and Return in the History of Judaism.* Boston, 1987.

————. *Stranger at Home: "The Holocaust," Zionism, and American Judaism.* Chicago, 1981.

Oz, Amos. *In the Land of Israel.* Translated by Maurice Goldberg-Bartura. San Diego, 1983.

Padover, Saul K., ed. *Thomas Jefferson on Democracy.* New York, 1946.

Parsons, Talcott. *Essays* _____ _____ _____ New York, 1954.

————, and Shils, Edward A., eds. *Toward A General Theory of Action.* New York, 1951.

Podhoretz, Norman. "My Negro Problem and Ours." *Commentary.* February 1963.

————. "The Tribe of the Wicked Son." *Commentary,* February 1971.

Prager, Janice, and Lepoff, Arlene. *Why Be Different? A Look Into Judaism.* West Orange, 1986.

Rawidowicz, Simon. *Studies in Jewish Thought.* Edited by Nahum N. Glatzer. Philadelphia, 1974.

Richler, Mordecai. *St. Urbain's Horseman.* London, 1971.

Rieder, Jonathan. *Canarsie: The Jews and Italians of Brooklyn Against Liberalism.* Cambridge, Mass., 1985.

Rosenberg, Bernard, and Goldstein, Ernest. *Creators and Disturbers: Reminiscences of Jewish Intellectuals of New York.* New York, 1982.

Rosenberg, Harold. *Discovering the Present: Three Decades in Art, Culture, and Politics.* Chicago, 1973.

Rotenstreich, Nathan. *Essays on Zionism and the Contemporary Jewish Condition.* New York, 1980.

————. "Religion, Modernity, and Post-Modernity." *International Journal for Philosophy of Religion* 18:33–49, 1985.

————. *Tradition and Reality.* New York, 1972.

Roth, Philip. *The Anatomy Lesson.* New York, 1983.

Rothman, Stanley, and Licher, Robert S. *Roots of Radicalism: Jews, Christians, and the New Left.* New York, 1982.

Rubinstein, W. D. *The Left, the Right, and the Jews.* New York, 1982.

Sachar, Howard M. *A History of Israel: From the Aftermath of the Yom Kippur War.* New York, 1987.

Sachs, Nelly. *The Seekers and Other Poems.* New York, 1970.

Samuel, Maurice. *The Worlds of Maurice Samuel.* Edited by Milton Hindus. Philadelphia, 1977.

Sarna, Jonathan D., ed. *The American Jewish Experience.* New York, 1986.

Sartre, Jean Paul. *Anti-Semite and Jew.* New York, 1965.

Schiff, Ze'ev, and Ya'ari, Ehud. *Israel's Lebanon War.* New York, 1984.

Scholem, Gershom. *The Messianic Idea in Judaism and Other Essays on Jewish Spirituality.* New York, 1971.

Schulweis, Harold. *Evil and the Morality of God.* Cincinnati, 1984.

———. "The Single Mirror of Jewish Images: The Pluralistic Character of Jewish Ethics." *University Papers.* Los Angeles, 1982.

Segre, Dan V. *A Crisis of Identity: Israel and Zionism.* Oxford, 1980.

Sennett, Richard. *The Fall of Public Man: On the Social Psychology of Capitalism.* New York, 1974.

Shafran, Avi. "The Perils of Pluralism." *Baltimore Jewish Times.* July 4, 1986.

Shazar, Zalman. *Morning Stars.* Philadelphia, 1967.

Shils, Edward. "The Theory of Mass Society." *Diogenes,* Fall 1962.

Sidorsky, David, ed. *The Jewish Community in America.* New York, 1973.

Siegel, Seymour, and Gertel, Eliot, eds. *God in the Teachings of Conservative Judaism.* New York, 1985.

Silberman, Charles E. *A Certain People: American Jews and Their Lives Today.* New York, 1985.

Sklare, Marshall. *America's Jews.* New York, 1971.

———, ed. *The Jewish Community in America.* New York, 1974.

Sollors, Werner. *Beyond Ethnicity: Consent and Descent in American Culture.* New York, 1986.

Soloveitchik, Joseph B. *Halakhic Man.* Translated by Lawrence Kaplan. Philadelphia, 1984.

Solveitchik, Joseph B. "The Lonely Man of Faith." *Tradition,* Summer 1965.

Sorin, Gerald. *The Prophetic Minority: American Jewish Immigrant Radicals, 1880–1920.* Bloomington, 1985.

Stark, Rodney, and Bainbridge, William Sims. *The Future of Religion: Secularization, Revival, and Cult Formation.* Berkeley, 1985.

Steinberg, Stephen. *The Ethnic Myth: Race, Ethnicity, and Class in America.* New York, 1981.

Stern, David. "Midrash," in Cohen and Mendes-Flohr, pp. 613–20.

Tarrance, Hill, Newport, and Ryan. *Nationwide Attitudes Survey.* September 1986. Houston, 1986.

The Beirut Massacre: The Complete Kahan Commission Report. Princeton, 1983.

The Torah: A New Translation. Philadelphia, 1962.

The Prophets, A New Translation. Philadelphia, 1978.

The Writings: A New Translation, Philadelphia, 1982.

Timerman, Jacobo. *The Longest War.* New York, 1982.

Tonnies, Ferdinand. *Community and Society* Translated and edited by Charles P. Loomis. New York, 1957.

Twersky, Isadore. "Some Aspects of Jewish Attitudes Toward the Welfare State." *Tradition,* Spring 1963.

Urofsky, Melvin. *American Zionism from Herzl to the Holocaust.* Garden City, 1975.

Vital, David. *The Origins of Zionism.* Oxford, 1975.

Walzer, Michael. *Exodus and Revolution.* New York, 1984.

———. *Interpretation and Social Criticism.* Cambridge, Mass., 1987.

Weber, Max. "Science as a Vocation." In *From Max Weber: Essays in Sociology.* Edited by Hans Gerth and C. Wright Mills. New York, 1969. 129–56.

Weisbord, Robert G., and Kazarian, Richard, Jr. *Israel in the Black American Perspective.* Westport, Conn., 1985.

Whitfield, Stephen J. *Voices of Jacob, Hands of Easua: Jews in American Life and Thought.* Hamden, Conn., 1984.

Wiesenthal, Simon. *Every Day Remembrance Day: A Chronicle of Jewish Martyrdom.* New York, 1987.

Wisse, Ruth. "The Anxious American Jew." *Commentary,* September 1978.

Woocher, Jonathan S. *Sacred Survival: The Civil Religion of American Jews.* Bloomington, 1986.

Yehoshua, A. B. *Between Right and Right.* Translated by Arnold Schwartz. Garden City, 1981.

Yerushalmi, Yosef H. *Zakhor: Jewish History and Jewish Memory.* Seattle, 1982.

Zangwill, Israel. *The Melting-Pot.* New York, 1910.

Zucotti, Susan. *The Italians and the Holocaust. Persecution, Rescue, and Survival.* New York, 1987.

INDEX